CONCISE
DICTIONARY OF LITERARY TERMS

Harry Shaw

McGRAW-HILL BOOK COMPANY

New York   St. Louis   San Francisco
Düsseldorf / Johannesburg / Kuala Lumpur / London
Mexico / Montreal / New Delhi / Panama
Rio de Janeiro / Singapore / Sydney / Toronto

First McGraw-Hill Paperback edition 1976

56789   FGRFGR   8321

Library of Congress Cataloging in Publication Data
Shaw, Harry

  Concise dictionary of literary terms.
  A condensation of the author's Dictionary of literary terms.
    1. Literature—Terminology.   I. Title.
[PN44.5.S46   1976]   803   76-15974
ISBN 0-07-056483-3

CONCISE
DICTIONARY
OF LITERARY
TERMS

abecedarius

A composition in verse in which the *stanzas or *lines begin with the letters of the alphabet in regular order. The first stanza of Chaucer's *A B C* begins with the word *Almighty,* the second with *Bountee,* the third with *Comfort,* etc. A more rigid kind of abecedarius is that in which every word in a line begins with the same letter, progressing through the alphabet from line to line:

An Austrian army, awfully array'd,
Boldly by battery besieged Belgrade.

abridged

Abridged means "shortened by condensation or omission." *Unabridged* means "complete," "not cut down." Many works of literature have been abridged with the aim of making them more easily and quickly read. Publishers of books in paperback form usually announce that their versions are "complete and unabridged," that is, copies of the original works.

abridgment

The noun form of *abridged* is *abridgment* (from Latin *ad,* meaning "toward," and *breviare,* meaning "to shorten"), a condensed version intended to retain the principal ideas and basic form of the original. Terms related to *abridgment* are *abstract, *aperçu, *brief, *condensation, *conspectus, *epitome, *précis, *redaction, *résumé, *summary, and *synopsis.

abstract

This term, derived from a Latin word meaning "to pull or draw away," is applied to a *summary of a document, speech, or statement. *Abstract* is usually applied to nonfictional types of writing; it presents the main points of the original in the order of their first appearance; it neither possesses nor claims independent literary worth of its own.

abstract diction

A word or phrase is abstract when it is not specific and definite in meaning.

Abstract words vary in their degree of indefiniteness. Such words as *nation, crime,* and *taxation* are not really specific, but they have more tangible meanings than *beauty, culture,* and *honor.* The word *housing* is somewhat abstract, but the idea can be made less so by substituting terms like *apartment house, mansion, bungalow, cabin, shanty,* and *lean-to.*

Abstract nouns, especially prevalent in philosophical essays, are less exact and less forceful (because less understood) than concrete words. Consequently, a writer may use an abstract term but immediately make it more communicative by providing concrete examples of what is meant or by translating its meaning into other terms. In Robert Louis Stevenson's *An Apology for Idlers* appears this sentence: " . . . The services of no single individual are indispensable." Despite the partial abstraction of "services," "individual," and "indispensable," the statement is seemingly clear. Yet Stevenson follows it with a concrete *figure of speech which reinforces his idea: "Atlas was just a gentleman with a protracted nightmare." The concept is now unmistakable.

An effective writer, Stuart Chase, once used the abstract term *laissez faire* and several allied ones but made his meanings clear by equating governmental "laissez faire" with a city that had "no traffic system"; by referring to "enforced competition" as a system in which "traffic cops protect little cars"; by referring to "government regulation" as being similar to "traffic cops advising how to drive"; and by referring to "government ownership" as a procedure according to which "a traffic officer throws the driver out and gets behind the wheel himself."

Abstract diction appears often in literature and cannot be avoided. But many writers unfailingly remember the

2

adage that "all we know gets into our heads as itemized bits of experience" and thus employ concrete diction or else attempt to make abstract diction more specific and meaningful.

For instance, in *The Eve of St. Agnes,* John Keats wished in the first stanza to make as concrete and specific as possible the somewhat abstract idea of "coldness." Not a single word in the stanza is abstract:

St. Agnes' Eve—Ah, bitter chill it was!
The owl, for all his feathers, was a-cold;
The hare limped trembling through the frozen
    grass,
And silent was the flock in woolly fold:
Numb were the Beadsman's fingers, while he told
His rosary, and while his frosted breath,
Like pious incense from a censer old,
Seemed taking flight for heaven, without a death,
Past the sweet Virgin's picture, while his prayer
    he saith.

abstraction

The act of considering or evaluating something in terms of general characteristics or qualities apart from specific objects and concrete realities. For example, Robert Burns stated that his love was like "a red, red rose." From the actual qualities of a rose he abstracted the ideas of beauty, freshness, and fragrance and omitted the realities of thorns and decay.

This process of thought has led to the further meaning of *abstraction* as something considered visionary and unrealistic.

Absurd, Theater of the

See THEATER OF THE ABSURD.

academic

This term is derived from the name of the olive grove where Plato had his "classroom" in fourth-century-B.C. Athens. *Academic* is now applied to the nature and functions of schools and colleges, particularly to studies that are not directly vocational or applied. Hence come the meanings of *academic* as "theoretical," "unrealistic," "not useful," and "impractical."

Academic drama is a name given to plays written, studied, and produced by students in continental Europe and in

3

Great Britain during the *Renaissance. *Academy* is a name for a body of established opinion, such as the French Academy established in the seventeenth century to compile a dictionary and to set authoritative standards for the French language.

acatalectic

This is a term applied to a line of poetry that carries out the full basic metrical pattern of the poem in which it appears; a verse complete in the number of syllables called for by a metrical scheme. A *catalectic line is one that is incomplete at the end, that is, not containing the full number of syllables called for by a set metrical pattern. Of these lines from a poem by John Keats, the first is acatalectic (full), whereas the second line is catalectic (lacking the final syllable):

> And this / is why / I so/journ here
> Alone / and pale/ly loit/ering.

accent

Several meanings of *accent* apply particularly to writing and speech.

1. Accent is the *emphasis or *stress placed on a certain *syllable in a foot of poetry. Three types of accent appear in English: *word* accent, *rhetorical* accent (in which the placement of stress determines meaning), and *metrical* accent. English verse consists of a series of stressed and unstressed syllables. For details on this meaning of accent, see FOOT, METRICS, SCANSION.

2. When some person or some character in a literary selection has an accent, he reveals his distinguishing regional or national manner of pronouncing or the tone of his voice ("a Boston accent," "a Southern accent," "a hillbilly accent," "a Scottish accent"). In literature, such accents are indicated largely or entirely by the dialogue of the various characters.

3. *Accent* may refer to emphasis placed upon some part of an entire artistic design or composition. In most of Thomas Hardy's novels, the role of Egdon Heath is accented (played up, made dominant); the accent in Poe's *The Fall of the House of Usher* is on foreboding, decay, and impending doom; in *Othello,* the theme and role of jealousy are accented.

4

accismus

From a Greek word meaning "demure" or "coy," accismus is an insincere refusal of something offered with the hope that the offer will be renewed forcefully. In Shakespeare's *Richard III*, the title character, desperately plotting to be crowned, protests that he is "unfit for state and majesty."

acronym

A coined word, a *neologism, formed with the initial letters or syllables of successive words in a phrase: *loran* ("long-range navigation"), *radar* ("radio detecting and ranging"), *pluto* ("pipeline under the ocean").

acrostic

A composition of some sort (puzzle, poem, series of lines) in which the first, last, or other particular letters form a word, phrase, or sentence. If written on successive lines, the words *heart, ember, abuse, resin,* and *trend* read the same from left to right and top to bottom. The first letters of the surnames of five ministers of Charles II of England (Clifford, Arlington, Buckingham, Ashley, and Lauderdale) formed an *acronym reputed to have given added meaning to the word *cabal* (clique, coterie). See ABECEDARIUS, ACRONYM.

act

One of the principal divisions of a play or opera. In classical drama, such major divisions were indicated by appearances of a *chorus, thus usually resulting in plays of five acts. Many Roman tragedies, following this division observed by Aristotle, also appeared in five acts. These divisions in tragic drama generally indicated action as follows: (1) preliminary and background information, details about characters and prior situations; (2) *complication, *rising action, increasing *conflict; (3) the *climax, or *crisis, a turning point in action involving the highest emotional response from spectator or reader; (4) *falling action; (5) final *catastrophe.

Elizabethan and other "modern" playwrights likewise tended to present tragic drama in five acts, but in the nineteenth century, certain dramatists, including Ibsen, began to write in four acts. Most modern full-length plays appear in three acts, although some have only two, like most comic *operas and *musical comedies. Some modern plays eliminate act structure entirely and appear as scenes or episodes. See ONE-ACTER.

action

Action means an event or series of real or imagined happenings forming the subject of a novel, story, play, or narrative poem. Such an unfolding of events in drama or a work of fiction supplies an answer to the question "What happens?" What characters say, do, and think and what results from their saying, doing, and thinking constitute the action of all narrative literature. A *planned* series of related and interrelated actions, which may be physical or mental or both, is said to make up the *plot of a work of fiction or drama.

adage

A traditional saying expressing a universal observation or experience, such as "It never rains but it pours" and "It is always darkest before the dawn." *Adage,* a statement given credit by general acceptance and long usage, is related to other terms that denote expressions of general truth: *aphorism, *apothegm, *axiom, *gnomic, *maxim, *motto, *proverb, *saw, and *saying.

adaptation

The recasting of a work to fit another medium while retaining the *action, *characters, and as much as possible of the language and *tone of the original. *Novels are frequently adapted for films, the stage, or television; a play may reappear as an adaptation in novel form or as a radio presentation, etc. Stephen Vincent Benét's short story *The Devil and Daniel Webster* was adapted for films and radio.

adventure story

In the sense that all *fiction and much *nonfiction deal with events and with undertakings of man's mind and body, nearly every work of literature can be called an adventure story. The term is usually applied to literary material in which the reader's primary attention is focused upon "What happens next?" to the exclusion of such questions as "Why?" and "How?" Well-known types of adventure stories are *science fiction, *Western stories, *mystery stories, and all writing in which *action seems more important than *characterization, *theme, or *setting. However, a reader might consider *Hamlet, War and Peace,* and *Moby Dick* as adventure stories (which they are); more skilled readers understand them to be adventure stories plus.

6

Aeolic

Also spelled *Eolic, Aeolic* refers to the Greek *dialect of ancient Aeolis and Thessaly, coastal regions of Greece. The term is applied also to a style of architecture used in Greek territories of the Aegean Sea in the seventh and sixth centuries B.C. Specifically, *Aeolic* is applied to the dialect in which certain ancient Greek poets, including Alcaeus and Sappho, wrote their lyric poems. See ALCAICS, SAPPHIC.

A related but different term, *Aeolian,* refers to Aeolus, who in classical mythology was the ruler of the winds and the legendary founder of the Aeolian (Greek) nation.

aesthetic distance

This term from criticism, and especially *New Criticism, means detachment from, and nonidentification with, the circumstances or characters of a work of art. It involves a kind of *objectivity which permits an author to present imagined characters or events without expressing his own views or revealing his own judgments and personality. Aesthetic distance also represents the degree of detachment and objectivity that a critical reader maintains if he wishes fully to understand and evaluate what he is reading. In short, aesthetic distance rules out personal involvement with subject matter on the part of both writer and reader, lest art become confused with reality. According to the theory of aesthetic distance, Hawthorne, for example, was not personally involved with the characters and episodes in *The Scarlet Letter;* a reader of this novel should form his opinions of it without regard to his own feelings about Puritanism, adultery, or hypocrisy. See CRITICISM, OBJECTIVE CORRELATIVE.

aesthetics

A study of the emotions and the mind in relation to their sense of beauty in literature (and all the fine arts) as distinguished from moral, social, political, practical, or economic considerations. Aesthetics is concerned with concepts of what is beautiful or ugly, sublime or comic, and has no direct concern for usefulness or morality. Aestheticism, a movement that followed "art for art's sake" (*ars gratia artis), has been influential in French, English, and American literature for the past century. The supreme statement on the subject is John Keats's lines in his *Ode on a Grecian Urn:*

"Beauty is truth, truth beauty,"—that is all
Ye know on earth, and all ye need to know.

affectation
Artificial behavior or manners intended to impress others, mannerisms for effect involving some kind of show or pretense. Characters in novels or plays who exhibit qualities or provide appearances not really possessed are usually considered by both author and readers to be artificial, pompous, and pitiable.

affective fallacy
The "error" of judging a literary work by its emotional effects upon readers; a confusion between the work itself and its results ("what it *is* and what it *does*"). This term is related to *intentional fallacy, the error (if such it be) of analyzing a literary work in terms of its author's expressed aim and biographical background. (See EXPLICATION, NEW CRITICISM.) Those critics who claim that these attitudes toward a work are genuine fallacies insist that Mark Twain's *Huckleberry Finn,* for example, should be judged for what it is and not for its effects upon readers' opinion of slavery or Twain's disclaimer of motives and plot. Perhaps most readers would agree with Alexander Pope:

In every work regard the writer's End,
Since none can compass more than they intend.

It should be noted that Aristotle's theory of *catharsis is a notable example of the affective fallacy.

afflatus
An impelling force acting from within a person. *Afflatus* is synonymous with *inspiration*. Many writers have claimed that they received *divine afflatus in the conception and execution of a given work, meaning that they experienced communication to their inner beings of knowledge and insight from some outside source. See DIVINE AFFLATUS.

Age of Reason
Any period in history noted for its critical approach to social, religious, and philosophical concerns; an age which tends to deny beliefs or systems not based upon, or justified by, reason. It is especially a term applied to the seventeenth- and eighteenth-century philosophical trend in

Europe and Great Britain that emphasized the importance of scientific methods and discoveries and that tried to overthrow entrenched superstitions and tyrannies of all kinds, social, religious, and political. A French writer, Diderot, summed up the extreme aims of "enlightened" thought when he wrote, "Man will never be free until the last king is strangled with the entrails of the last priest." Less radical advocates of the philosophy of the *Enlightenment were Benjamin Franklin and Thomas Jefferson. See DEISM.

agon

A Greek term meaning "a contest." In ancient Greek drama, *agon* was the name of a debate or argument between two characters, each of whom was supported by a *chorus. In every kind of literature, *agon* refers to *conflict and is a root appearing in such words as *antagonist, *deuteragonist, *protagonist, and *tritagonist.

alazon

A stock character, the braggart of Greek comedy. Under one name or another, such a type appears as the *miles gloriosus of Plautus, in Shakespeare's *The Comedy of Errors,* and in Molière's *Tartuffe.*

alcaics

Verses written in the manner of Alcaeus, a sixth-century-B.C. Greek poet. Alcaics are poems of four stanzas of four lines each, each line having four stresses (accents). No true alcaics exist in the English language; the closest approximation is Tennyson's *Milton,* which begins:

O mighty-mouthéd inventor of harmonies,
O skilléd to sing of Time or Eternity,
God-gifted organ-voice of England,
Milton, a name to resound for ages.

alexandrine

A verse line with six *iambic *feet (iambic *hexameter) that derives its name from French romances about Alexander the Great. It was used in the early English sonnets of Wyatt and Surrey and appears in all *Spenserian stanzas. An *alex-*

andrine and its effect are illustrated in Alexander Pope's *Essay on Criticism:*

Ă needˊ/lĕss Álˊ/exănˊ/drĭne endsˊ / tȟe sóng
That, líke / ă woúnd/ĕd snáke, / drăgs itsˊ /
slŏw léngth / ălongˊ.

allegory

A method of representation in which a person, abstract idea, or event stands for itself *and* for something else. *Allegory* may be defined as extended *metaphor: the term is often applied to a work of fiction in which the author intends characters and their actions to be understood in terms other than their surface appearances and meanings. These subsurface or extended meanings involve moral or spiritual concepts more significant than the actual narrative itself.

The most famous and most obvious of such two-level narratives in English is Bunyan's *Pilgrim's Progress;* in this religious allegory, Christian, Faithful, Mr. Worldly Wiseman, and Despair are real people who are also symbols of mankind, personifications of abstract ideas applicable to everyone. In Spenser's *Faerie Queene,* figures are actual characters and also abstract qualities. Parts of Dante's *Divine Comedy* and Tennyson's *Idylls of the King* are allegorical in that action is revealed not so much for the story as for the purpose of presenting moral or spiritual truth.

Forms of allegory are the *parable, in which a story is told primarily to express a religious truth, and the *fable, in which animals by their speech and actions reveal supposed truths about mankind. *Satire can be a form of allegory, as in Swift's *Gulliver's Travels,* where the adventures of Lemuel Gulliver, surgeon, sea captain, and traveler, are intended as satiric comment on man's foibles and weaknesses. Aside from literature, a great painting or statue also suggests or implies far more than meets the eye.

alliteration

A device commonly used in poetry and occasionally in prose: the repetition of an initial sound in two or more words of a phrase, line of poetry, or sentence ("Cupid and my Campaspe played / At cards for kisses"). Alliteration is considered ornament or decoration to appeal to the ear, a device to create an effect such as *onomatopoeia. Shakespeare clearly made fun of alliteration in *A Midsummer Night's Dream:* "Whereat, with blade, with bloody blameful blade, / He bravely broach'd his boiling bloody breast." An American poet, Vachel Lindsay, created a similar effect in "Booth led boldly with his big bass drum," but his intent was not to mock the device. Coleridge's line "The fair breeze blew, the white foam flew" and Tennyson's "The moan of doves in immemorial elms / And murmuring of innumerable bees" illustrate the appealing effects of alliteration and closely related methods of ornamentation.

allonym

The name of another person assumed by an author as a pen name; also, a work published under a name that is not that of the author. The signature "Publius" masked the collaboration of Alexander Hamilton, John Jay, and James Madison in *The Federalist,* a series of papers influential in the ratification of the United States Constitution. *Allonym* is closely related to the general term *pseudonym,* a fictitious name used by an author to conceal his identity. Synonyms for *pseudonym* are nom de plume and alias.

allophone

A speech sound constituting one of the variants of a *phoneme (a basic unit of sound in any language). The short *a* in *bat* and the long *a* in *rate* are allophones.

allusion

A reference, usually brief, often casual, occasionally indirect, to a person, event, or condition presumably familiar but sometimes obscure or unknown to the reader. In *The Merchant of Venice,* Shakespeare used a Biblical allusion when he referred to a "Daniel come to judgment." Complex allusions abound in the work of such modern writers as T. S. Eliot; one cannot understand *The Love Song of J. Alfred Prufrock* without digging into its classical and Shakespearean allusions. The purpose of allusion is to bring in a wealth of experience and knowledge beyond the limits of plain statement.

almanac

In current use, an almanac is an annual publication containing a calendar, tables of phenomena, and much other statistical and general information on a variety of topics of widespread interest. This name for a compendium of useful and interesting facts appears in Spenser's *Shepheardes Calender* (1579), a series of twelve poems under the subtitles of the twelve months. During the eighteenth century, almanacs began to contain humor and bits of homely wisdom, as in Franklin's *Poor Richard's Almanac* (1732–1758). The *Almanacs* of Davy Crockett in the middle of the nineteenth century contained *tall tales and other revelations and aspects of American frontier culture.

ambience

The *mood, quality, *tone, character, or *atmosphere of an environment or *milieu. For example, it has been said that the company of actors to which Shakespeare belonged had a hard-working, professional ambience and that the ambience surrounding Hawthorne was one of guilt, gloom, and foreboding.

ambiguity

Doubtfulness or uncertainty of intention or meaning. Derived from a Latin word meaning "to wander about," "to waver," *ambiguity* refers to a statement that is subject to more than one interpretation. Some ambiguity is due to carelessness, but the term is applied in genuine literature to words that suggest two or more appropriate meanings or that convey both a basic meaning and overtones that are rich and complex. The difficulty in understanding some literature stems from a deliberate choice of words that simultaneously causes several different streams of thought in the reader's mind. See PLURISIGNATION.

ambivalence

Uncertainty; having opposed attitudes toward the same person or object; a capacity to see two or more sides of an issue or a personality. For example, some historians have claimed that Lincoln was ambivalent in his attitude toward the Civil War because his hatred of slavery conflicted with his overriding desire to save the Union.

American Dream

This often-used term can have no clear and fixed definition because it means whatever its user has in mind at a particular time and has whatever interpretation the reader chooses to give it. Perhaps to most authors and readers, the phrase has *connotations of "life, liberty, and the pursuit of happiness." The American Dream, like all dreams, is a succession of images, emotions, and thoughts passing through the mind when one is either asleep or awake.

amphibrach
A metrical *foot consisting of three *syllables, the second accented, the first and third unaccented:

The ŏld oăk/ĕn búckĕt, / thĕ íron-/bŏund búckĕt.

amphigory
Nonsense verse; lines that sound all right but contain little sense or meaning. Swinburne mocked himself in a poem that begins with amphigory: "From the depth of the dreamy decline of the dawn through a notable nimbus of nebulous moonshine." See DOUBLE TALK.

amphimacer
A metrical *foot consisting of three *syllables, the first and last accented, the second unaccented: man-at-arms, three fifteen. Tennyson's poem *The Oak* contains these lines: "Live thy life, / Young and old, / Like yon oak, / Bright in spring, / Living gold."

anachronism
From a Greek word meaning "to be late," an anachronism is an error in chronology: placing an event, person, item, or language expression in the wrong period. For example, an absolute monarchy is an anachronism in the twentieth century. It is apparently difficult to avoid anachronisms when writing about an earlier time: Shakespeare referred to cannon in *King John,* a play set in time long before cannon were used in England; Shakespeare also placed a clock in *Julius Caesar.*

In a serious or realistic work of literature, an anachronism can destroy an effect and damage a reader's confidence in the author. Realizing this, motion-picture and television producers maintain staffs to avoid such mistakes as having Cleopatra wear a wristwatch. In romantic writing, not always to be taken seriously, an anachronism may seem amusing to an alert and knowing reader. Mark Twain deliberately used a series of anachronisms to achieve his satirically humorous purposes in *A Connecticut Yankee in King Arthur's Court.* And Edwin Arlington Robinson's Miniver Cheevy was a human anachronism ("born too late") who longed for earlier times in which he thought he might have been happier.

anacoluthon

Failure to complete a sentence according to the structural plan on which it was begun. From the Greek term meaning "out of sequence," anacoluthon may result from ignorance or carelessness, but it is also a recognized figure of speech used for emotional and rhetorical effects. The term is applied to units of writing greater than sentences, especially in talks where the speaker judges that a sudden shift in subject matter will regain the interest of his audience. See APOSIOPESIS.

anacrusis

An unstressed syllable or group of syllables that begins a line of verse but is not considered a part of the first foot. The word *anacrusis* literally means an upward or back beat; in music, *anacrusis* refers to the note or notes preceding a downbeat. The word *from* in this line from Shelley's *To a Skylark* is an anacrusis: "From / rainbow / clouds there / flow not."

anagnorisis

A term applied to ancient Greek tragedy signifying the critical moment of recognition or discovery preceding the reversal of fortune for the *protagonist. In comedy, anagnorisis leads to his success; in tragedy, it leads to his fall. See CLIMAX, CRISIS.

anagoge

A spiritual or mystical interpretation or application of words, especially of words considered to be of divine origin, such as those of the Bible. For example, Jerusalem is actually a city in ancient Palestine (Israel), but it is also an anagoge for "the heavenly city of God."

anagram

A word or phrase formed by the transposition of letters in another word. Samuel Butler's novel *Erewhon* derives its title from the word *nowhere*. A tribe in *Erewhon* is called the Sumarongi, which is *ignoramus* spelled backward. See ACRONYM, PALINDROME.

analogue

Something having analogy (similarity) to something else; for example, Racine has been called a French analogue of Shakespeare. In word study, related words from different languages are called analogues (*father, pater, padre,* etc.). In literature, two versions of the same story are called analogues; for example, many *Western stories are analogues of the *Robin Hood theme, in that the poor are defended against the rich and justice triumphs over might. *Romeo and Juliet* and *West Side Story* are analogues.

analogy

A partial similarity of features on which a comparison may be based: an analogy between the heart and a pump. In *argumentation and *persuasion, analogy is often employed as a form of reasoning in which one thing is compared to or contrasted with another in a certain respect on the basis of known similarity or dissimilarity in other respects. *Metaphors, *similes, and *antonomasia are forms of analogy. This simile from Pope's *An Essay on Criticism* is a kind of analogy:

'Tis with our judgments as our watches, none
Go just alike, yet each believes his own.

The implied comparison is always an analogy buried in a literary work, awaiting discovery by a reader. Much of *Gulliver's Travels* implies lessons the reader should draw (infer) from Swift's comparison of human life and a society of pygmies. Again, an entire literary selection may be based upon an extended analogy as, for example, Thomas Huxley's *A Liberal Education,* in which life is explained as analogous to a game of chess, or another essay by the same author in which the method of scientific investigation is compared with the customary workings of the human mind.

anapest

A trisyllabic metrical foot consisting of two unstressed syllables followed by a stressed syllable: *condescend.*

Oh he flies / through the air / with the great/est
of ease.

anaphora

Also called *epanaphora,* anaphora is the repetition of a word or words at the beginning of two or more successive lines of verse, sentences, etc. A well-known example is the Beatitudes in the Bible, nine successive statements that begin with "Blessed are." ("Blessed are the poor in spirit, for theirs is the kingdom of heaven. Blessed are they that mourn, for they shall be comforted," etc.)

anastrophe
Reversal of the usual, logical, or normal order of the parts of a sentence. The second and third lines of this *quatrain from Lewis Carroll's *Jabberwocky* exhibit anastrophe; the first and fourth lines are in normal word order:
> He took his vorpal sword in hand;
> Long time the manxome foe he sought.
> So rested he by the Tumtum tree,
> And stood awhile in thought.

anecdote
A short narrative account of an amusing, curious, revealing, or otherwise interesting event. Anecdotes present individuals in actions that illustrate or reinforce specific ideas and illuminate certain aspects of character or personality. Every effective anecdote has a single, definite point; in each, *dialogue, *setting, and *characters are subordinate to the main point. Except in poolrooms or behind closed doors, the anecdote never stands alone. But such short narratives abound in *exposition because of their effectiveness in making instantly clear otherwise possibly difficult ideas. Anecdotes "humanize" individuals and turn abstract concepts into concrete ones. The effectiveness of anecdotes is obvious: probably most of what is remembered about Washington or Lincoln or Churchill, for example, is recalled as stories (anecdotes) about them and their characteristics.

Anglo-Saxon
The name of a Teutonic tribal group which invaded what is now England in the fifth and sixth centuries. Comprised in the group were Angles, Saxons, and Jutes, who came from the northern shores of the Continent. The Angles gave their name (Angle-land) to England. The term *Anglo-Saxon* is now used to distinguish "English" peoples resident in Great Britain, the United States, Canada, and certain other dominions and territories. *Anglo-Saxon* is also a name given to the language known as *Old English. See SASSENACH.

angst
A feeling of anxiety, dread, or anguish. Angst is especially nota-

ble in the work of such writers as Jean-Paul Sartre and Albert Camus. See EXISTENTIALISM, THEATER OF THE ABSURD.

annals
Historical records, especially those of yearly events arranged in chronological order. *Annals* is also applied to periodical publications containing formal reports of scientific, political, literary, and other organizations.

annotation
A note, or notes, supplied to explain, comment upon, or criticize literary or other written material. An annotated edition is one printed with comments by the author or by someone else. An outstanding example of annotation is the *variorum editions of the plays of Shakespeare.

annuals
Books or reports issued annually. Annuals usually review the events of the year just passed within specified fields of interest, such as college annuals. In the nineteenth century, the term was used for compilations of poems, essays, and stories issued in time for Christmas sale. Annuals are important in American literary history because in them first appeared the work of such writers as Poe, Hawthorne, and Emerson.

antagonist
One who contends with, or opposes, another in a fight, conflict, or battle of wills. In literature, such an adversary is the principal opponent, or *foil, of the main character and is thus often called, sometimes loosely and incorrectly, the *villain. If the dominant plot centers in the career or exploits of a *hero who overcomes an opponent trying to thwart him, the latter is the antagonist, the hero a *protagonist. If main interest centers upon the career of a villain whose plans are overcome by a hero, the latter is the antagonist, the former a protagonist.

In *Hamlet,* Laertes and the King (Claudius) are among the antagonists; Hamlet is himself the protagonist. In Melville's *Billy Budd,* the young British sailor is the protagonist opposed by the master-at-arms of the *Indomitable,* the antagonist Claggart. See AGON, DEUTERAGONIST, PROTAGONIST, TRITAGONIST.

antecedent action

Events that took place before the beginning of action in a novel, play, story, or narrative poem. When it is necessary for the viewer or reader to understand what has happened in the past, this antecedent action is revealed in *dialogue or by direct *exposition. See FLASHBACK, IN MEDIAS RES.

anthem

A *hymn of praise, patriotism, or devotion. In literature, *anthem* is sometimes used to refer to a *psalm or hymn chanted responsively (that is, in alternate parts).

anthology

A book or other collection of selected writings by various authors; sometimes, a gathering of works by one author. (The origin of *anthology* is revealing: it comes from two Greek words meaning "flower" and "to gather." *The Greek Anthology,* a grouping of early poems, was "a collection of flowers.") See CHRESTOMATHY.

anthropomorphism

Ascribing human form or characteristics to animals or inanimate objects. The mythological concept that the gods have human form and attributes is a form of anthropomorphism. Most *fables illustrate this belief. See BESTIARY.

antibacchius

A rare trisyllabic foot in which the accent falls on the first two syllables: *five dozen.*

anticlimax

A drop, often sudden and unexpected, from a dignified or important idea or situation to a trivial one, a descent from something sublime to something ridiculous. In fiction and drama, anticlimax involves action which is in disappointing contrast to a previous moment of intense interest; in a story or play anything which follows the *climax (the decisive, culminating struggle and resolution of *conflict) is called an anticlimax. Some popular novels devote a final chapter to comment on the futures of prominent characters whose actual story has already ended. Such an anticlimax satisfies the interest and curiosity of readers but frequently weakens narrative effect as a whole.

George Bernard Shaw had afterthoughts about his play

Pygmalion. But even this talkative playwright ended his play at its climax, or nearly so, and added anticlimactic comments in a *sequel, a separate essay which begins, "The rest of the story need not be shown in action, and indeed, would hardly need telling if our imaginations were not so enfeebled by their lazy dependence on the ready-mades and reach-me-downs of the ragshop in which Romance keeps its stock of 'happy endings' to misfit all stories."

Pope effectively used anticlimax for humorous purposes in his line "Men, monkeys, lap-dogs, parrots, perish all," and so did E. E. Cummings in " 'Then shall the voices of liberty be mute?' / He spoke. And drank rapidly a glass of water."

antihero
A character who lacks the qualities needed for heroism; an antihero does not possess nobility of life or mind and does not have an attitude marked by high purpose and lofty aim. King Claudius in *Hamlet* is an antihero.

antimasque
A grotesque or comic performance, such as a dance or *mummery, presented before or between acts of a *masque (a pageant of music, drama, and dance). The purpose of an antimasque (or comic mask, as it is sometimes called) is to prevent the masque itself from becoming overly serious, meaningful, or disturbing. See COMIC RELIEF.

antiphon
Like an *anthem, an antiphon is a verse or song rendered responsively (in separate parts). The term is usually applied to church music; see LITURGY.

antiphrasis
The use of a word which conveys a sense opposite to its usual meaning. Antiphrasis can be a form of *irony, *sarcasm, or *satire. For instance, Shakespeare's Othello refers to "honest" Iago, when of course he is characterizing Iago as anything but honest.

antistrophe
One of the three *stanzaic forms of the Greek choral *ode, the other two forms being *strophe and the *epode. In early Greek plays the chorus sang (chanted) an antistrophe while returning

from left to right of the stage as an answer to a previous strophe (stanza).

antithesis

A *figure of speech in which contrary ideas are expressed in a *balanced sentence. The second part of "Man proposes, God disposes" is antithetically parallel to the first part. When asked where Polonius's corpse is secreted, Hamlet responds "At supper . . . not where he eats, but where he is eaten." Later in the same reply, Hamlet remarks, "We fat all creatures else to fat us, and we fat ourselves for maggots." See OXYMORON.

Outright assertion and flat denial are the clearest forms of antithesis, but a part of the word is *thesis, meaning a statement or proposal itself positive and thus more than merely "against" (*anti-*). Consequently, in a larger structural concept, the term *antithesis* may apply to a writer's entire contribution, an evaluation of what he was for and what he opposed. For example, with Shakespeare or Faulkner, formal religion may be a minor consideration, but it is a major one in the works of Dante and Milton. Whitman's insistence upon the brotherhood of man may or may not imply his opposition to an antithetical force or opinion. Discovering the pro and con of a writer's work is a valuable part of literary study.

antonomasia

The identification of a person by an *epithet or other term that is not his name; the use of a proper name for a common noun. Thus a great lover may be termed a Don Juan or an evil woman may be called a Jezebel. The device of antonomasia is shown in these lines from Gray's *Elegy:*

Some mute inglorious Milton here may rest,
Some Cromwell guiltless of his country's blood.

aperçu

A French word literally meaning "perceived" and used in English to mean "a hasty glance," "a glimpse." In criticism, *aperçu* means an *outline or brief *summary.

aphorism

A brief, pithy, unusually concise statement of a principle, truth, or sentiment. Notable more for its thought and wisdom than its wit, an aphorism is closely related in meaning to such terms as *maxim, *saw, *adage, *proverb, and *epigram, all of which agree in denoting a sententious expres-

sion of a general truth or belief. Examples [
Mark Twain, in commenting on his own prefer[
afterlife, wrote, "Heaven for climate, hell for soc[
Pope wrote, "The proper study of mankind is mar[

apocalyptic

Characteristic of literature that provides a prophecy or revelation. The term is derived from the Apocalypse, or Revelation of Saint John the Divine, the last book in the Bible. *Apocalyptic* is now used to refer to any literary selection that reveals and predicts the future.

apocope

Loss or omission of the last letter or syllable of a word. *Curio,* from *curiosity,* is an example of apocope.

apocryphal

This adjective means "of doubtful authenticity," "spurious," "mythical," or "untrustworthy." The term implies a mysterious or dubious source of origin and consequently suggests sham or fakery. It is derived from the noun *apocrypha,* a general term first and most prominently applied to writings not admitted by Protestants into the *canons of the Old and New Testaments (the Bible). In literary study, *apocryphal* refers to any piece of writing of unknown or uncertain authorship. For example, a few Elizabethan plays of doubtful origin, attributed to Shakespeare, are considered apocryphal and not in the Shakespearean canon. *Apocryphal* has been further extended in meaning so that it is now used to refer to a story *about* an individual which may or may not be authentic. Many *anecdotes about Shakespeare, Washington, Jefferson, Winston Churchill, and Joseph Stalin are considered apocryphal.

Apollonian

An adjective referring to Apollo, the ancient Greek and Roman god of light, music, healing, prophecy, and poetry. *Apollonian* is used to describe writing and authors who are serene, calm, poised, disciplined, and well balanced. The cult of Apollo is often contrasted with that of Dionysus (which represented the frenzied and undisciplined in life and literature). See DIONYSIA.

apologue

A moral *fable or didactic narrative. As a form of *allegory, an

21

apologue is represented by most of the *parables in the Bible, by some of Aesop's fables, and by James Thurber's collection of pithy tales entitled *Fables for Our Time.*

apology

An expression of regret, sorrow, or remorse; a defense and justification for some doctrine, piece of writing, cause, or action. The most famous apology of all time is Plato's dialogue in defense of Socrates before the tribunal that sentenced Socrates to death. At the end of *The Canterbury Tales,* Chaucer wrote what he called a "retractation," an apology for his work which is both an explanation and an expression of regret. One of Cardinal Newman's most famous writings is entitled *Apologia pro Vita Sua,* a spiritual autobiography. One of the most charming essays in English is Stevenson's *An Apology for Idlers.*

apophasis

Denial of one's intention to speak or write of a subject which is simultaneously named or suggested. Marcus Antonius (Mark Antony) illustrates apophasis in Shakespeare's *Julius Caesar:*

I come not, friends, to steal away your hearts.
I am no orator, as Brutus is;
But, as you know me all, a plain blunt man . . .
For I have neither wit, nor words, nor worth,
Action, nor utterance, nor the power of speech
To stir men's blood; I only speak right on.

aposiopesis

A sudden breaking off in the middle of a sentence, resulting from unwillingness or inability to proceed. In discussing his mother's hasty remarriage, Hamlet says:

Like Niobe, all tears—why, she, even she—
O God! a beast that wants discourse of reason
Would have mourned longer.

apostrophe

A figure of speech in which a person not present or a *personified nonhuman object is addressed (spoken to). Characteristic instances of apostrophe in poetry are *invocations to the *Muses and in oratory to the shades of men such as Julius Caesar, Oliver Cromwell, and Thomas Jefferson. Wordsworth's *London, 1802* begins "Milton! Thou shouldst be living at this hour." (Milton died in 1674.) Writers of *whimsy and *humor occasionally employ the device: in 1942, E. B. White wrote an essay in letter form addressed to a man who had been dead for eighty years. The essay begins: "Miss Nims, take a letter to Henry David Thoreau. Dear Henry...." Inspired by Lord Byron's "Roll on, thou deep and dark blue ocean, roll," W. S. Gilbert wrote *To the Terrestrial Globe,* beginning "Roll on, thou ball, roll on!"

apothegm
A terse remark, pithy comment, instructive saying. An apothegm is a pointed, often startling *aphorism, such as Dr. Johnson's remark "Patriotism is the last refuge of a scoundrel."

appendix
Material added at the end of a book or *article. An appendix is not part of the text but illustrates, expands, or illuminates it. An appendix provides useful information but is not essential to the work it follows. A *bibliography is an example of appendix material.

Arcadia
A mountainous region of ancient Greece, famed for the pastoral and contented innocence of its inhabitants, an ideal rustic paradise. *Arcadian* is applied to any region and period where life is considered idyllic, such as the imagined golden age described by Virgil or Shakespeare's Forest of Arden. See PASTORAL.

archaism
A word or phrase no longer in actual use, such as *enow* for *enough* and *gramercy* for *thank you.* Two archaic words appear in these lines from Coleridge's *The Rime of the Ancient Mariner:*

"Hold off! unhand me, grey-beard loon!"
Eftsoons his hand *dropt* he.

Archaism is also applied to the use of that which is archaic in literature and art and to the survival of a custom or attitude from the past.

archetype
The primary meaning of *archetype* is "the original model, form, or pattern from which something is made or from which something develops." Thus, one may say that the

...ment of Adam, as related in the first book of the ... ("In the sweat of thy face shalt thou eat bread, till ... return unto the ground ... "), is an archetype of all mankind's struggle and sorrow. Coleridge's *The Rime of the Ancient Mariner* is based on the archetype of Adam's fall. Another example: Thomas Babington Macaulay referred to the British House of Commons as "the archetype of all the representative assemblies which now meet." A well-defined example of a particular type of person may be referred to as an archetype: "The archetype of a stevedore: thick-chested, bull-necked, sweaty, and profane."

In the psychology of *Jung, the word is applied to inherited ideas or modes of thought derived from the experiences of a race and present in the subconscious of an individual—the *collective unconscious of mankind. Archetype is associated with *imagery and *myth and has indeed been defined as "a *symbol, usually an *image, which recurs often enough in literature to be recognizable as an element of one's literary experience as a whole." Sophocles used the deep-seated concerns of blindness, patricide, incest, and fratricide as a grouping of archetypes in several of his plays; Milton and Dante have treated Man, an archetypal human being, in their greatest works; much of Hawthorne's and Melville's fiction derives from archetypes which represent primordial images of sin, retribution, and death.

arena theater
An auditorium with seats arranged on at least three sides of a central stage. Such an arrangement is also known as *theater-in-the-round.

argument
In a specialized sense, the argument of a poem, play, or portion of a literary work is an *abstract or *summary of its content. The subject matter, central idea, or even *plot of a novel or narrative poem may also be called its argument. Milton prepared an argument for each book of *Paradise Lost,* and Coleridge used one at the beginning of *The Rime of the Ancient Mariner.* Some critics call the argument of a poem that part of its idea or *thesis which can be *paraphrased.

argumentation
All writing can be classified as argumentation, *narration, *description, or *exposition. These classifications, called *forms of

discourse, are arbitrary; further, none appears in pure (unmixed) form. The purpose of argumentation is to convince a reader (or hearer) by proving the truth or establishing the falsity of an idea or *proposition. (See PERSUASION.) Formal argumentation uses these special steps: (1) establishing the proposition, (2) analyzing the proposition, (3) formulating the argument, (4) preparing the *brief (a form of outline). .

Aristotelian

Based on, pertaining to, or derived from Aristotle, a Greek philosopher, pupil of Plato, and tutor of Alexander the Great. This fourth-century-B.C. writer has had a profound effect upon all subsequent logic, literary theories, criticism, and poetry. Aristotelianism, placing emphasis upon *deduction and upon the investigation of concrete situations and objects, has obviously influenced all contemporary science. Aristotelian criticism (as contrasted with *Platonic criticism) implies a logical and objective approach that centers upon the work under consideration rather than upon its moral or social *contexts. See NEW CRITICISM.

ars gratia artis

This Latin term ("art for art's sake") was the *credo of certain writers and other artists in England during the latter half of the nineteenth century. This concept of *aesthetics was that all art is independent of *morality, a view derided by many of their contemporaries but one still held firmly by several contemporary writers, especially those who work in the fields of *existentialism and *realism.

arsis

The part of a metrical *foot that bears the stress: *AR·ti·cle, con·VEX.* See ACCENT, ICTUS.

art ballad

A *ballad of known authorship which has some claims to literary distinction, as contrasted with the *popular ballad, which is notable for its simple narrative form and primitive emotional content. A well-known poem imitating ballad technique is Coleridge's *The Rime of the Ancient Mariner;* other successful art ballads are Keats's *La Belle Dame sans Merci* and Longfellow's *The Wreck of the Hesperus.*

art epic

A term applied to such works as Virgil's *Aeneid* and Milton's *Paradise Lost,* long narrative poems somewhat more sophisticated, idealized, and consciously artistic than such popular (or folk) epics as the *Iliad,* the *Odyssey,* and *Beowulf.* The distinction between the folk epic and the art epic has broken down somewhat because many scholars now tend to believe that the former also was the work of a single poet who wrote in accordance with traditional artistic techniques. See LITERARY EPIC.

Arthurian

Connected with, or related to, a legendary king in ancient Britain, the reputed leader of the *Knights of the Round Table. King Arthur and his knights provided subject matter for a large part of medieval *romance. Scholars now believe that the legend of Arthur grew from the deeds of an actual person who was probably not a king and may not have been named Arthur. The prevailing theory is that this figure was a Welsh (or possibly Roman) leader of the Celts in Wales who led his warriors against Germanic invaders in the fifth century. The popularity of Arthurian legend and tradition reached its height in Malory's *Morte d'Arthur* (1485). Later treatment of Arthur and his followers appears in such works as Tennyson's *Idylls of the King,* Edwin Arlington Robinson's *Tristram,* and T. H. White's *trilogy *The Once and Future King.* Mark Twain wrote a *burlesque treatment of Arthurian chivalry in *A Connecticut Yankee in King Arthur's Court* (1889).

article

A written *prose *composition, usually entirely *nonfiction, dealing with a specific topic. An article customarily appears as a self-contained, independent work in a *magazine but may also be a chapter of a book or other publication.

artificiality

A term used to characterize a literary work that is considered overly elaborate, deliberately mannered, and rigidly conventional. *Artificial* means self-conscious, studied, lacking in naturalness and spontaneity. The *Euphuism of Lyly is considered the height of artificiality. See CONCEIT, PRECIOSITY.

art lyric

A delicate, highly polished short poem usually noteworthy for triviality, conventional structure and theme, and mannered *artificiality. *Cavalier poets wrote many art lyrics; belonging to this *genre are such forms as the *rondel and the *triolet.

aside

A stage *convention used by a playwright to indicate words spoken by a character heard by the audience but not by other characters onstage. A novelist, short-story writer, or poet also may employ this somewhat artificial device to reveal words which are spoken aside or in a low tone so as to be inaudible to some person or persons actually present. Eugene O'Neill and a few other prominent modern playwrights resorted to asides, but the convention of the *stage whisper is somewhat rare in twentieth-century plays and fiction.

assonance

A resemblance of sound in words or syllables. *Assonance* applies especially to closely recurring vowel sounds in stressed syllables: "Twinkle, twinkle, little star, / How I wonder what you are." Assonance is a common device in poetry, particularly in the hands of a writer like Dylan Thomas or Marianne Moore. In prose and even in normal speech it is frequent but usually is accidental and not long continued.

asyndeton

A condensed expression in which words or phrases are presented in series, separated by commas only (that is, with conjunctions omitted). The best-known of all asyndetons is *Veni, vidi, vici* ("I came, I saw, I conquered"). In library science, *asyndeton* refers to the omission of cross references, as in a catalog or *index.

atmosphere

This term, borrowed from meteorology, is used to describe the overall effect of a creative work of literature or other example of art. It involves the dominant *mood of a selection as created by *setting, *description, and *dialogue. Thus, the setting of Thomas Hardy's novels (Egdon Heath), the description in the first paragraph of Poe's *The Fall of the House of Usher* and in the first chapter of Hawthorne's *The Scarlet Letter,* and the dialogue at the opening of Shakespeare's *Hamlet* and *Macbeth* each create the atmosphere (feeling and mood) of the entire work. Atmosphere embraces both physical and psychological details of the selection itself and the impression intended for the reader as well as his expected emotional response. See also DOMINANT IMPRESSION, TONE.

aubade

A poem about dawn; a piece of music sung or played outdoors at dawn. (See ALBA.) Shakespeare's "Hark! hark! the lark" and Browning's "The year's at the spring / And day's at the morn" from *Pippa Passes* are aubades. An *aube* is a song sung by a friend watching over lovers until dawn.

Aufklärung

A German word meaning "enlightenment," usually applied to the philosophical movement of the seventeenth and eighteenth centuries, called the Enlightenment, that stressed the power of human reason. Among major figures of this revival of arts and letters were Immanuel Kant and Gotthold Lessing. See AGE OF REASON.

Augustan

An adjective originally applying to the age of Augustus Caesar, emperor of Rome just before and after the beginning of the Christian era. His reign marked "the golden age of Latin literature." *Augustan* is now applied to any epoch in world history during which literary culture has been great. The Augustan age of English literary history refers to the period during which Addison, Steele, and Swift flourished—largely because those writers were fully conscious of the parallels in their work to Latin literature.

authorized

Given authority or endowed with sanction. The authorized body of a writer's work is his *canon, the selections that were unmistakably written by him and published with his approval and corrections. The term appears most often in connection with the Authorized Version of the Bible, an English translation that appeared in 1611 and is known also as the King James Bible. By extension, *unauthorized* refers to literary works that do not have the sanction of their reputed authors or the guarantee and approval of literary scholars.

autobiography

This type of writing is an account of oneself written by oneself. The author of an autobiography presents (or tries to present) a continuous narrative of what he considers the major (or most interesting) events of his life. Usually, an autobiographer reveals about himself only what he is willing to have known and remembered.

Autobiography resembles several other literary forms: *biography, *diaries, *letters, *journals, and *memoirs. A biography is the written history of a person's life composed by someone else; the other four related forms are recollections set down by the subject himself. An autobiography and a memoir are usually lengthy, organized narratives prepared for others to read, but the latter is more likely to focus on one phase of a person's life than on the whole of it. A typical memoir also emphasizes the subject's relations with notable persons or events more than most autobiographies, which are likely to be self-centered and introspective. A diary is a day-to-day or week-to-week chronicle of events and is thus closely related to a journal; the diary is usually more intimate than a journal and more deliberately chronological than autobiography. Letters are epistles, notes, and memoranda exchanged among friends and acquaintances; they afford an insight the intimacy of which varies with the personality of the writer, the identity of his correspondent, and the possibility of publication.

Of these allied types, autobiography is the most notable. Among great autobiographies are Saint Augustine's *Confessions,* Cellini's *Autobiography,* Pepys's *Diary,* Franklin's *Autobiography,* and *The Education of Henry Adams.* Also noteworthy are the strong autobiographical elements, personal and actual or imagined, in other types of fiction, notably in Defoe's *Moll Flanders* and *Robinson Crusoe,* Thackeray's *Henry Esmond,* Dickens's *David Copperfield,* Hardy's *Jude the Obscure,* James Joyce's *A Portrait of the Artist as a Young Man,* Maugham's *Of Human Bondage,* and all the work of Thomas Wolfe. Many essays, poems, and short stories are also based on autobiographical materials, a fully understandable situation since literature derives from the thought, imagination, and experience of its creators.

autotelic

Adjective describing a work not dependent upon attainment of outside objectives. An autotelic selection speaks its own message in its own terms without reference to any external truth. Its intention and purpose have nothing to do with *didacticism or the teaching or preaching of moral, social, or political values.

avant-garde

A French term literally meaning "fore-guard," *avant-garde* is applied to writing that reveals innovations in its subject matter or style, particularly experimental treatments. As a noun, *avant-garde* refers to the advance group in any field (especially in the literary, visual, and musical arts) the productions of which are characterized by unorthodox methods.

axiom

A self-evident truth, a universally accepted rule or principle. In logic and mathematics, an axiom is a *proposition that is assumed without proof, such as that there can be only one straight line between two points. One of the primary purposes of the *fable, the *parable, and the *proverb is to state axiomatic principles in narrative form.

B

babel

A confused mixture of sounds or voices. As recorded in the Book of Genesis, inhabitants of the ancient city of Babel began to erect a tower designed to reach heaven but were thwarted when confusion broke out in their language. *Babel,* usually spelled with a small letter, refers to any scene or situation that is noisy, turbulent, or confused.

Bacchic

An adjective referring to Bacchus, in classical mythology the god of wine and the Roman counterpart of Dionysus. (See DIONYSIA.) A bacchic *foot (sometimes called a bacchius) consists of one short syllable followed by two long ones or of one unstressed syllable followed by two stressed ones. See ANTIBACCHIUS.

Baconian

An adjective referring to the life, work, and times of the Elizabethan essayist and philosopher Francis Bacon (1561–1626). The Baconian theory attributes the plays of Shakespeare to Bacon, largely on the assumption that an unschooled countryman such as Shakespeare lacked the education, wit, and cosmopolitan knowledge necessary to create them. The theory is generally discredited; all available evidence is fragmentary and inconclusive.

balanced sentence

A *structure in which the parts of a sentence (clauses, phrases, words) are set off in parallel position so as to emphasize contrast or similarity in meaning. Bacon's best-known remark about studies appears in a balanced sentence: "Some books are to be tasted, others to be swallowed, and some few to be chewed and digested."

ballad

A narrative poem composed in short *stanzas and designed for singing or oral recitation. A ballad usually deals with an exciting or dramatic episode. Somewhat loosely, song hits, folk music, and *folktales set to music are called ballads. The standard collection of "true" ballads is *The English and Scottish Popular Ballads,* edited by F. J. Child. See ART BALLAD, BALLAD STANZA, LITERARY BALLAD, POPULAR BALLAD.

ballade

A French verse form usually consisting of three *stanzas having the same *rhyme scheme, followed by an *envoi (postscript, conclusion). In a typical ballade, the last lines of each stanza and of the envoi are identical. Among the best-known poems in this form are Chaucer's *Ballade of Good Advice* and Rossetti's adaptation of François Villon's *Ballade of Dead Ladies,* which contains as the last line of each stanza an envoi, "But where are the snows of yester-year?"

ballad stanza

The stanzaic form of the *popular ballad consists of four lines rhyming *abcb.* Usually, the first and third lines contain four accented syllables; the second and fourth contain three. With its strong, clear beat, the ballad stanza easily and fluently adapts itself to the singing of narratives:

> There lived a wife at Usher's Well
> And a wealthy wife was she;
> She had three stout and stalwart sons,
> And sent them o'er the sea.

barbarism

A word or phrase used only in coarse or uneducated speech, such as *keeped* for *kept* and *hisn* for *his.* A term originally applied only to expressions felt to be alien to established customs or modes, *barbarism* is also used to refer to any uncivilized and untamed state or condition existing in life or literature. See PHILISTINE, SOLECISM, VULGARISM.

bard

Loosely a "poet," but specifically one of an ancient *Celtic order of versifiers, especially one who composed and recited heroic and adventurous poems while accompanying himself on the harp or lyre. See SKALD, TROUBADOUR.

baroque

From a Portuguese word meaning "rough pearl," *baroque* is an adjective and noun referring or applying to literature that is extravagantly ornamented, elaborately ornate, exaggerated, and high-flown. Much *metaphysical poetry is baroque, as all conceits are. The early American poet Edward Taylor wrote in a baroque style, illustrated by a poem called *Huswifery,* in which he used the *metaphor of spiritual life as a spinning wheel, God's word as man's distaff, etc.

bathos

Applied to literature, *bathos* has two meanings: (1) *sentimentalism, mawkishness, insincere *pathos, and (2) *anticlimax, a descent from the lofty and exalted to the commonplace. The first meaning is illustrated in attempts by insipid writers to make readers sorry for public figures who have thrown away their opportunities for continuing popularity and esteem. The second meaning, "descent from the sublime to the ridiculous," a kind of anticlimax, is illustrated in Pope's witty lines from *The Rape of the Lock:*

> Not louder shrieks to pitying heaven are cast,
> When husbands, or when lapdogs, breathe their
> last.

beast epic

A narrative in which the adventures and misadventures of animals satirize human follies and foibles. A beast epic usually consists of a lengthy series of linked stories about contemporary life (politics, religion, social customs, etc.) that provide satirical comment on the depravity or stupidity of mankind. (A beast *fable is a short *tale in which the principal characters are animals.) The best-known beast epic is *Roman de Renart,* a poem of 30,000 lines consisting of twenty-seven sets of stories about Reynard the Fox. Chaucer's *The Nun's Priest's Tale* is perhaps the greatest of all beast epics.

beat generation, beatnik

The term *beat generation* is applied to persons coming of age after World War II who appear in rebellion against the culture and value systems they observe (or claim to observe) about them. American, English, French, and German writers of the beat generation tend to express revolt in works of loose structure and colloquial diction that assert the empty qualities of existence. For instance, the works of such American writers as Allen Ginsberg and Jack Kerouac place them in the *coterie of *existentialism and its offshoots. A beatnik is a member of the beat generation, not necessarily a writer, who rejects or avoids conventional dress, behavior, etc., as a form of social protest. The word *beatnik* was coined from *beat* (frustrated, defeated) and *nik,* a Russian suffix designating an "agent" or "concerned person."

belief

Acceptance of, or assent to, that which is offered as true; a state of mind in which confidence, trust, and reliance are placed in some idea, person, or thing. Readers are usually most strongly affected by literature which seems "true" and "believable," by authors who seem to merit trust, by ideas which seem "possible" and even "sensible" and "right." Except for so-called escape literature, which entertains by removing readers temporarily into a world of *fantasy or adventure, all that one reads succeeds to the degree that an author is able to secure and nail down belief, faith, and acceptance of his *assumptions and *thesis. See VERISIMILITUDE.

Wordsworth referred to "the willing suspension of *disbelief" to suggest what should occur when a reader is absorbed in a work of literature. Many stories and novels illustrate what Wordsworth meant: a reader, caught up in a story, forgets that it is not "true" and never really happened. Willingly, one suspends his ability to judge and evaluate and allows himself to accept ideas which, under some circumstances, he would reject. When a novel—or any type of literature—captures its reader's imagination, the author can and does use this resulting receptive frame of mind to present his philosophy, his set of ideas, his *point of view, through special techniques of literary composition. The belief inspired by all great literature is foundation for the saying that "the pen is mightier than the sword."

belles lettres

A French term literally meaning "fine letters," *belles lettres* is often used interchangeably with *literature. Usage sometimes restricts the meaning of *belles lettres* to light or even frivolous writing and to appreciative essays about literature rather than literature itself. This distinction is not entirely valid, however, because much of the work of Lewis Carroll and Mark Twain, for example, may be considered "light" and "frivolous" but definitely belongs in the category of literature.

bestiary

A type of literature in which beasts, birds, reptiles, and even fish are used to impart moral lessons, foster church doctrines, and provide lessons in natural history. A typical bestiary deals with the habits and reactions of such a fabulous creature as the unicorn, the phoenix, or the siren. Presumably the phrase *crocodile tears* (a hypocritical indication of sorrow) derived from the circumstance that in an ancient bestiary a crocodile was represented as weeping while consuming his victims.

bias

A feeling, tendency, or inclination that prevents objective and unprejudiced consideration of a question, topic, or person. For example, Dr. Johnson's attitude toward Scotland and Scots caused him to have a bias. Fairly or unfairly, such novelists as Thomas Hardy and Ernest Hemingway have been attacked for their alleged bias against women. A bias may also be favorable. Hardy, for example, is said to have had a bias in favor of rustic life and country people; Hemingway has been acclaimed (and attacked) for his bias favoring courage and strenuous physical activity.

Bible

Loosely called a book, the Bible actually is a collection, or library, of books containing history, *poetry, *biography, *stories, *letters, and divine revelations. The word *Bible* comes from a Greek term meaning "little books" and may refer to the sacred "book" of any religion; for instance, the Bible of Muhammadans is the Koran. In Christian countries, *Bible* refers to the sacred books of the Old Testament (written at various times in the pre-Christian era in ancient Hebrew) and the New

35

Testament (written in the Greek dialect of Mediterranean countries at the time of Christ and in the century following). Numerous translations of the Bible exist, the most famous of which is the so-called King James Bible. See AUTHORIZED.

The Bible is the best-selling book in all literature, the most quoted, the most influential and powerful. The themes and plots of works from Milton's *Paradise Lost* and Bunyan's *Pilgrim's Progress* to Faulkner's *Light in August* and Steinbeck's *The Grapes of Wrath* have been directly and subtly shaped by the unparalleled influence of the Bible upon the hearts and minds of men.

biblioclasm

The practice of mutilating or destroying books. Adolf Hitler was the most famous of all recent biblioclasts, but the fear and hatred of books, which have existed for centuries in many lands, have caused wholesale destruction of many libraries. The great library at Alexandria, Egypt, was burned in the seventh century by Muhammadan destroyers who felt that books were unnecessary, since all worthwhile knowledge was contained in the Koran.

bibliography

A list of readings on a particular subject. A bibliography of Thomas Jefferson, for instance, would consist of listings of all *secondary sources such as *biographies, books of *criticism, and magazine *articles and of *primary sources such as original *letters and contemporary *documents. In library work, *bibliography* refers to study of the history, physical description, and classification of books, graphic materials, etc.

bibliolatry

Extravagant devotion to books and excessive dependence upon them. A "bookworm" is a bibliolater or bibliolatrist. Persons who acknowledged their bibliolatry at some point in their lives include Charles Lamb and Benjamin Franklin. The term is occasionally used to refer to idolatrous reverence for the *Bible in a *literal interpretation of its meanings.

bibliomancy
The practice of opening a book, especially the *Bible or any collection of *aphorisms, to discover a verse or passage which is considered to be especially meaningful at the moment. The discovered item is then interpreted and applied to the finder's immediate situation.

bibliomania
Extreme fondness for acquiring and possessing books. A bibliomaniac collects and retains books, whereas a bibliolater reveres and reads books but may not actually acquire and keep them.

bibliophile, bibliophobe
The former term means one who loves books and possibly collects them (see BIBLIOMANIA). A bibliophobe hates, fears, and distrusts books (see BIBLIOCLASM).

Bildungsroman
A novel concerning the youthful life and development of a major *character. *Bildungsroman* is a combination of German *Bildung* ("formation," "development") and French *roman* ("novel"). Examples of Bildungsromane are Samuel Butler's *The Way of All Flesh,* Dickens's *David Copperfield,* and Somerset Maugham's *Of Human Bondage.* See ERZIEHUNGSROMAN.

billingsgate
Coarse and abusive language. The term was derived from the vulgar speech often heard at Billingsgate, a fish market in London located near a gate named after a man called Billing. Shakespeare's Falstaff occasionally indulged in billingsgate when he was being especially argumentative and scornfully abusive.

biography
A written account of a person's life or an account of the lives of any small and closely knit group, such as a family. Biography is thus a subtype of history, "a continuous, systematic narrative of past events as relating to a particular people, country, period, or person"; a subdivision of biography itself is autobiography. Thomas Carlyle once defined history as "the essence of innumerable biographies," and Emerson wrote, "There is properly no history, only biography."

Biography has long been a popular form of reading. Sketches of kings and members of the ruling class thrilled readers some two thousand years ago with their emphasis upon martial and other adventurous deeds. Readers vicariously experienced activity, securing release and a form of escape no less popular then than they are today. Curiosity about others is as old as the human race, and its potency and prevalence apparently have increased through the centuries. Within the past century, curiosity about others, great and small, has resulted in both a major industry and a recognized literary *genre.

Eagerness to know the intimate details of others' lives, curiosity about people's attainments, about their strengths and weaknesses, their ways of speaking and thinking and acting, their human and their inhuman qualities seem as dominant as man's urge to escape or live vicariously through *fiction. This fascination with the lives of others has been cultivated as biography has become a more settled type, as it has come to be more appealingly written, as it has dealt more and more with "ordinary" people and less and less with kings and princes.

The present-day popularity of biographical writing also traces to the fact that readers have come to realize that truth is actually "stranger than fiction." It would be more correct to say that "truth is stranger than fiction *dares* to be," for some of the *complications, *ironies, and *coincidences in almost everyone's life would have to be discarded by a competent narrative writer. Put into fiction, they would seem either impossible or improbable. The biographer is restrained by no such consideration. His whole work, if properly handled, seems authentic and credible, and its reader will willingly accept more hair-raising and heart-stopping *episodes than any novelist or story writer could hope to employ. See AUTOBIOGRAPHY.

black comedy

The so-called *humor of the absurd, perverted, and morbid. Since World War II, black comedy and black humor have developed into a literary *genre. (See EXISTENTIALISM, THEATER OF THE ABSURD.) Black comedy (humor) is sometimes called "sick" because of its generally alien attitude toward contemporary *society.

blank verse

Unrhymed lines of ten syllables each, the even-numbered syllables bearing the accents, is called blank verse, or unrhymed iambic pentameter. (See IAMBUS, PENTAMETER, METRICS.) An example of blank verse is this line by Wordsworth:

Sŏ throúgh / thĕ dárk/nĕss ánd / thĕ cóld / wĕ fléw.

This form of poetry is generally considered best adapted to dramatic verse in English; it was chosen by Milton for *Paradise Lost* and ever since has been used more than any other form for serious poetry in English. Shakespeare's plays contain many lengthy passages in blank verse. (Blank verse, which is "blank" only in rhyme, is sometimes confused with *free verse.) Ordinarily, the meter of blank verse is definite and regular but does permit variations as in these lines from Shakespeare's *A Midsummer Night's Dream:*

The poet's eye, in a fine frenzy rolling,
Doth glance from heaven to earth,
    from earth to heaven;
And, as imagination bodies forth
The forms of things unknown, the poet's pen
Turns them to shapes and gives to airy nothing
A local habitation and a name.

bombast

Pretentious, ranting, insincere, and extravagant language. An example of bombast from Shakespeare's *Hamlet* (act 2, scene 2):

With blood of fathers, mothers, daughters, sons,
Baked and impasted with the parching streets
That lend a tyrannous and damned light
To their vile murders. Roasted in wrath and fire,
And thus o'er-sized with coagulate gore,
With eyes like carbuncles, the hellish Pyrrhus
Old grandsire Priam seeks.

book review

A descriptive, evaluative account and discussion of a book. A book review is a form of *criticism, which is (or is generally thought should be) a process that weighs, judges, and evaluates. The primary purpose of a book review is to consider faults and excellencies and then to render careful judgment. Among types of reviews are (1) a reportorial method in which a book is presented as an item of news; (2) reportorial and critical commentary that explains, interprets, and judges a book in terms of its purpose, scope, and style; (3) the "springboard review" in which a reviewer uses a given book as a convenient starting point (or excuse) from which he launches into a critical essay that covers much more (and much less) than the specific book being considered. A springboard review of a war novel, for example, might become an analysis of the causes of international friction without comment on the particular narrative itself.

bourgeois

A term from French, *bourgeois* refers to a member of the so-called middle class: a businessman, shopkeeper, merchant, etc. In literature, the term is often applied to characters whose political, social, and economic attitudes are largely shaped by their concern for property values. Occasionally, *bourgeois* is applied to someone who is rigidly conventional or who lacks elegance and refinement. (See PHILISTINE.) "Bourgeois literature" is said to appeal to "middle-class" readers, a rather meaningless statement. *Bourgeois drama* is a phrase characterizing the social sphere of the *action and *setting of a play, not a class of audience (or readers).

bowdlerize

To amend by removing or modifying objectionable passages of a novel, play, or any piece of writing. The term is derived from the name of Thomas Bowdler, an English editor and physician who expurgated from an edition of Shakespeare's works all "indecent" and "indecorous" passages considered "unfit to be read by a gentleman in the presence of ladies." See CENSORSHIP.

braggadocio

Empty boasting and bragging, or a braggart. *Braggadocio* is derived from a character of that name in Spenser's *The Faerie Queene* who has a boastful tongue but a cowardly heart. See MILES GLORIOSUS.

Brahmin

A person of culture, refinement, and intellect, especially a member of a New England family that is (or was) considered aristocratic. The term *Brahmin,* derived from Hinduism, in which it applied to members of the highest, or priestly, caste among Hindus, is sometimes used disparagingly for persons thought to be socially or intellectually aloof. Oliver Wendell Holmes said of an acquaintance: "He comes of the Brahmin caste of New England. This is the harmless, inoffensive, untitled aristocracy."

breviary

A book of daily prayers and readings. The word, derived from a Latin term meaning "short" or "brief," applies to a collection of lessons, calendars, and outlines for services designed to help a cleric recite the Divine Office for each day and otherwise fulfill his churchly assignments.

brief

This term has several meanings, the most common of which in literature is that of an *outline (the form of which is determined by set rules) of all the *arguments and data on one side of a controversial question. *Brief* may also be defined as any concise statement in written form. (See PRÉCIS.) In legal circles, a brief is (1) a memorandum of points of law or fact for use in conducting a case, (2) a written summons calling for an answer to legal action, and (3) a written argument submitted to a court of law.

broadside

A sheet of paper, usually large, with printed or pictorial material on only one side, designed for distribution or posting. Beginning in the sixteenth century, broadsides were used for some three hundred years to publish news. A broadside ballad is a song (chiefly appearing in sixteenth- and seventeenth-century England) written on a topical subject, printed on a broadside, and sold or sung in public. The subjects of these broadsides (or broadside ballads) were accounts of accidents, murders, and miraculous events, dying speeches of criminals, and political speeches. See BALLAD.

bucolic

An adjective meaning rustic, rural, or unsophisticated. *Bucolic* is derived from a Latin word meaning "herdsman" and is especially applied to pastoral writing concerned with shepherds and country life. *Bucolic* is a term referring to the pastoral literature of such a writer as Virgil. See PASTORAL.

bull

This term, derived from a Latin word meaning "seal" or "sealed paper," is applied in literature to a formal papal document with a seal of office attached. *Bull* is sometimes loosely applied to any statement of doctrine or belief, not necessarily ecclesiastical (churchly).

burlesque

A form of comic art, an imitation intended to ridicule by exaggeration. Burlesque is an attitude, style, or idea handled by distortion in which an important, imposing, or elevated subject is treated in a trivial way, a low or trifling subject with mock dignity. Discrepancy between style and subject matter is the essential quality of burlesque.

Chaucer's *Sir Thopas* and Cervantes' *Don Quixote* are burlesques of medieval *romance. Fielding's *Joseph Andrews* began as a burlesque of Richardson's *Pamela.* Gay's *The Beggar's Opera* and Gilbert and Sullivan's *Patience* are well-known burlesques in musical literature.

Commonly referred to as "burlesque" is theatrical entertainment, often broadly humorous and earthy, consisting of comic skits, songs, dances, and striptease acts. Such performances are usually grotesque imitations of such legitimate dramatic arts as dancing, singing, and acting. See CARICATURE, LAMPOON, PARODY, TRAVESTY.

burletta

A term derived from an Italian word meaning "jest." A burletta is a musical drama containing rhymed lyrics and resembling comic *opera. Gay's *Beggar's Opera* is a burletta as well as burlesque. Neither the term nor the form itself has been operative since the eighteenth century.

Burns stanza

A six-line *stanza usually rhyming *aaabab,* named after Robert Burns, who often used it. Here is the first stanza of Burns's *To a Mouse:*

> Wee, sleekit, cow'rin', tim'rous beastie,
> O what a panic's in thy breastie!
> Thou need na start awa sae hasty,
> Wi' bickering brattle!
> I wad be laith to rin an' chase thee,
> Wi' murd'ring pattle!

buskin

A thick-soled, laced boot or half boot. The high, heavy-soled shoe worn by ancient Greek and Roman actors, also called a cothurnus, was associated with *tragedy rather than *comedy because buskins were thought to increase stature symbolically as well as physically. Actors in Latin comedies wore a soft shoe called a "soccus," with the result that *sock* is used to apply to comedy and *buskin* to tragedy. In *L'Allegro,* John Milton refers to "the buskin'd stage" and to Ben "Jonson's learned sock"—tragedy and comedy.

C

cabal

A clique, *coterie, or small, tightly knit group of persons. (For comment on cabal in the sense of a small political group, see ACROSTIC.) In literary, theatrical, and artistic fields, persons have tended for centuries to form themselves into cabals.

cacophony

A discordant mixture of sounds or a harsh, unpleasant combination of sounds. (See EUPHONY.) In music, *cacophony* refers to the use of discords difficult to understand. Cacophony may be employed deliberately for artistic effect, as in Poe's poem *The Bells:*

> In the startled ear of night
> How they scream out their affright!
> Too much horrified to speak
> They can only shriek, shriek,
> Out of tune.

cadence

The rhythmic flow, or sequence, of sounds in writing and speaking. *Cadence* has been broadened in meaning to refer to the time, measure, sequence, or beat of any rhythmical activity (dancing, rowing, marching). Specifically, cadence suggests the particular *rhythm of *prose and *free verse and is a convenient overall term to designate the measured repetition of emphasis and accent in writing or speaking which is not altogether metrical (as in poetry). Used as a natural, inherent alternation of stressed and unstressed syllables in prose writing and in speaking, cadence is a pleasing stylistic quality; overused, it develops artificial and singsongy effects. See METRICS.

caesura

A pause, or break, in a line of verse that results from the meanings of words, the natural rhythm of language, or both. In *prosody, such a "sense pause" is marked by a double line:

A little learning // is a dangerous thing;
Drink deep, // or taste not the Pierian spring.

calligraphy

Excellent penmanship, beautiful handwriting. The significance of the term in literature derives from use of the art in medieval times, during which learned monks laboriously copied, and sometimes decorated, ancient *manuscripts.

calumny

Slander; false and malicious statements designed to injure the reputation and career of someone. Calumny has often played a part in the professional jealousy of authors. For example, Walt Whitman was dismissed from a government post because of the calumny directed at him by critics for his "formlessness," frank treatment of sex, and "indecency." See LIBEL, SLANDER.

Calvinism

The doctrines and teachings of John Calvin (1509–1564), a French theologian and reformer who lived in Switzerland. Calvinism is important because for some four hundred years it has deeply influenced the literature of England and the United States. In colonial days, Calvinism was influential in the development of New England culture and, through extension, American life and letters. Calvinism stresses the sovereignty of God, the supreme authority of the *Bible, and the irresistibility of God's will for man in every act of his life from cradle to grave.

canon

This term from a Greek word meaning "measuring rod" or "rule" has several meanings applicable in literature: (1) a standard of judgment, a criterion; (2) the approved list of books belonging in the Christian *Bible; (3) the accepted list of works of any given author. The *Shakespeare canon,* for example, is a term applied to the thirty-seven plays established as authentic. See APOCRYPHAL.

canto

One of the main, or larger, divisions of a long poem. Dante's *The Divine Comedy,* Spenser's *The Faerie Queene,* and Byron's *Childe Harold's Pilgrimage* are arranged in cantos.

caption

A heading, or title, of a chapter or article. As a printing term, *caption* refers to a legend (descriptive statement) for an illustration in a book or magazine. The purpose of a caption is to secure attention; the Latin word from which it is derived means "seizure."

caricature

This term suggests ludicrous distortion of a particular feature, or features, of the characteristics of a person or idea. The word is derived from Italian *caricare* ("to load") and may be called a "loaded" or "overloaded" representation. Caricature is more often associated with drawing, as in *cartoons, than with literature, but in each medium exaggeration is used for comic effect.

Sometimes the distortion is so gross that *irony, not *humor, is the result: "The kangaroo court is a caricature of real justice." Caricature is related to *burlesque (imitation of the dignified and grand or of the trivial by means of inverted style); to *parody (heightening of a particular feature by methods which are humorous but often less obvious, less pictorial, and less boisterous); and to *travesty (clearly and even outrageously extravagant imitation designed to mock and scorn). Notable caricaturists include Max Beerbohm, Bill Mauldin, and James Thurber.

carol

Any joyous song and hymn of religious joy, especially one dealing with the nativity of Jesus Christ (Christmas carols).

Caroline

A term applied to the literature and writers of the period of Charles I of England (1625–1649). Among poets referred to as Caroline were Herbert, Herrick, Vaughan, and the more strictly *Cavalier poets, Lovelace, Suckling, and Carew.

carpe diem

A Latin phrase meaning "seize the day." In literature,

carpe diem refers to a *theme or *motif, chiefly in lyric
*poetry, that presents youth as short-lived and urges the
pursuit of pleasure. This philosophy of "eat and drink, for
tomorrow we shall die" has been present in literature since
the days of the first-century-B.C. Roman poet Horace. The
English poet Robert Herrick stated the theory of carpe
diem as well as anyone ever has:
> Gather ye rosebuds while ye may,
> Old Time is still a-flying;
> And this same flower that smiles today,
> Tomorrow will be dying.

catalexis (catalectic)
An incompleteness in the last *foot at the end of a *verse is
known as catalexis. (See ACATALECTIC, a term applied to a line
that does not exhibit catalexis.) These lines by Shelley are catalectic:
> Músic, / whén sŏft / vóicĕs / die,
> Víbrates / ín thĕ / mémŏ/rý.

catastasis
That part of a *play preceding the *catastrophe in which
*action is at its height. *Catastasis* and *climax are usually
interchangeable terms.

catastrophe
From a Greek word meaning "overturning," *catastrophe*
means (1) a final event or conclusion, usually an unfortunate
one; (2) a sudden and widespread calamity and disaster; (3)
any misfortune, failure, or mishap. In literature, especially
in *drama, *catastrophe* refers to the point at which circumstances overcome central motives and introduce a conclusion. The *resolution of a plot in which various
complications are unraveled is a *denouement, a term now
used more often than *catastrophe* in dramatic and narrative
works.

catharsis
This term is from a Greek word, *kathairein,* meaning "to
clean," "to purify," and was used by Aristotle (384–322 B.C.)
in his description of the effect of *tragedy—the purgation
or purification of emotions. *Catharsis* refers to any emotion-

al discharge which brings about a moral or spiritual renewal or welcome relief from tension and anxiety. The primary idea is that an audience—any audience—filled with confusions and unhealthy emotions, such as pity and fear, comes to see a *play developing make-believe actions that would be harmful if occurring in real life. The audience participates emotionally in the dramatic action and goes away psychologically cleansed, purged of injurious feelings and sensations. Literary critics have never agreed whether *catharsis* means that members of an audience thus learn to avoid the evil and destructive emotions of a tragic hero or that their inner conflicts are quieted by an opportunity to expend pity and fear upon such a *protagonist.

cause and effect

Much of what one reads is the result of cause-and-effect relations. When we read an answer to the question "Why did this happen?" we are dealing in *causes*. When we read the question "What will this do?" the answers involved deal with *effects*. A cause, therefore, is that which produces an effect, the person, idea, or force from which something results. An effect is that which is produced by some agency or cause. "The cause of their quarrel was a misunderstanding over money." "The effect of morphine is to dull pain and induce sleep."

In such literature, especially *essays and other forms of *exposition, *paragraphs are developed by a plan of cause and effect. The topic sentence of a paragraph makes a generalized statement or draws a conclusion based on data (details, ideas, suggestions) that make up the supporting material of the paragraph. Conversely, supporting material may indicate what are the results (effects) of the generalized statement in the topic sentence. For example, here is the topic of a paragraph from *The Sea Around Us,* by Rachel Carson: "The birth of a volcanic island is an event marked by prolonged and violent travail: the forces of the earth striving to create and all the forces of the sea opposing." The remainder of the paragraph is a vivid recital of specific details of the violent struggle, the causes of the travail. Again, Will Durant, in *Why Men Fight,* opened a paragraph with this topic sentence: " . . . a modern war brings complex economic results." The effects, what happens to life and property, constitute development of the remainder of the paragraph.

All life—and consequently all good literature—is concerned with why something begins to exist and why it exists the way it does. A cause is the reason. An effect is the result of the operation of a cause. Cause and effect are necessarily related: Shakespeare's Macbeth killed Duncan because of ambition and greed; the effect of the murder is the substance of a tragedy that leads to Macbeth's total ruin. Such a statement about *Macbeth* indicates that the total cause of any event is complex and involves an intricate joining of preceding forces and events; the total effects of any given cause extend beyond immediate results.

cavalier

This term has several meanings as an adjective and noun: (1) haughty and disdainful; (2) offhand, casual, and unceremonious; (3) a horseman, especially a mounted soldier; (4) a courtly, gallant gentleman; (5) a woman's escort, or beau. In literary history, *Cavalier* refers to a follower of Charles I of England in his struggles with Parliament. The work of Cavalier poets (Carew, Lovelace, Suckling) is notable for its grace, polish, arrogance, and licentiousness. See CAROLINE.

Celtic

This term refers to a branch of language (including Irish, Gaelic, Manx, Cornish, Welsh, and Breton) that survives in Ireland, in parts of Scotland and England, in Wales, and in Brittany. *Celtic* also refers to Celts, members of an *Indo-European family now represented by the Irish, Welsh, etc., but once dominant in central and western Europe. The *Celtic renaissance* is a term applied to the late nineteenth-century movement aimed at preservation of the Celtic language, reconstruction of Celtic history, and stimulus of a new literature primarily Irish in subject matter and spirit. Among important writers of this cause were W. B. Yeats, J. M. Synge, Lady Gregory, and Padraic Colum. See FOLK DRAMA.

censorship

The repression of material on moral, ethical, religious, or political grounds. The struggle for freedom of expression by writers forms a substantial part of literary history, ranging from the arguments of Aristophanes in the fourth century B.C. to the rating of films in the late twentieth century. Possibly the most eloquent attack on *censorship* ever written was Milton's *Areopagitica:*

> As good almost kill a man as kill a good book: who kills a man kills a reasonable creature, God's image; but he who destroys a good book kills reason itself. . . . A good book is the precious lifeblood of a master spirit, embalmed and treasured up on purpose to a life beyond life.

chanson

A chanson is now interpreted to mean any poem written in a simple form and style and intended to be sung. The term, which is French derived from Latin, appears often in the phrase *chanson de geste* ("a song of great deeds"), an early form of French *epic dealing with legendary or historical characters such as Charlemagne.

chapbook

A small book or pamphlet of *popular ballads and *tales, sold during the eighteenth century to people on the street by peddlers, or chapmen. Chapbooks included murder cases, travel tales, accounts of witchcraft, strange occurrences, and legends. Today, *chapbook* is used in the title of numerous small books and pamphlets dealing with miscellaneous subjects.

character

This term has several meanings, the most common of which is "the aggregate of traits and features that form the nature of some person or animal." *Character* also refers to moral qualities and ethical standards and principles. In literature, *character* has several other specific meanings, notably that of a person represented in a story, novel, play, etc. In seventeenth- and eighteenth-century England, a character was a formal *sketch or descriptive analysis of a particular virtue or vice as represented in a person, what is now more often called a character sketch.

characterization

The creation of *images of imaginary persons in drama,

narrative poetry, the novel, and the short story is called characterization. In effective narrative literature, fictional persons, through characterization, become so credible that they exist for the reader as real people. See BELIEF.

Every reader is interested in people, or should be, because people are the most important single factor in individual lives. In fiction, a reader, primarily interested in the individuals concerned, has a natural tendency to identify with the "hero" and to hate the "villain" or to feel "for" or "with" one individual or group and "against" another.

It is difficult to identify with a character whom one does not know or understand. This is why characterization is important in fiction. Before a writer can make his reader sympathize with or oppose a character, that character must come alive. The reader wants to be able to visualize him— to see him act and hear him talk. Characterization, no mere by-product, is an essential part of *plot. Character generates (causes) plot and plot results from, and is dependent upon, character. See CAUSE AND EFFECT.

Writers use any or all of several basic means of characterization: a character is revealed by (1) his actions, (2) his speech, (3) his thoughts, (4) his physical appearance, (5) what other characters say or think of him. A *flat character is a minor participant in fiction, one who is characterized briefly by only one or two of these basic methods. A *round character is one fully developed by four or five of these methods and thus takes on such added dimensions that, as readers, we come to know and to understand him as a living, breathing human being. See VERISIMILITUDE.

Without characterization, no *thesis, no *plot, and no *setting can develop genuine interest for a reader or cause him to care what happens, or does not happen, to whom, and why.

charade

A parlor game in which players take turns at acting out in *pantomime a word or phrase. By extension, *charade* has come to mean "pretense," as, for example, Lady Macbeth's sleepwalking scene in Shakespeare's *Macbeth*.

Chaucerian stanza

A seven-line *stanza in iambic *pentameter, sometimes called *rhyme royal because the form was once associated with James

I of Scotland. This is a Chaucerian stanza from book 1 of Chaucer's *Troilus and Criseyde:*

> You lovers who now bathe in happiness,
> If in your veins a pitying drop there be,
> Reflect upon the outlived heaviness
> That you have suffered, and the adversity
> Of other folk; remember feelingly
> How you, too, Love dared sometimes to displease,
> Or else you won him with too great an ease.

chef d'oeuvre

In art, literature, and music, *chef d'oeuvre* means a masterpiece. In French, the meaning is "leading work." The chef d'oeuvre of John Milton, for example, is considered to be *Paradise Lost.*

chiasmus

A form of *antithesis, a reversal in the order of words so that the second half of a statement balances the first half in inverted word order. This line from Coleridge is an example of chiasmus:

> Flowers are lovely, love is flowerlike.

chivalry

Derived from *chevalier,* a French word meaning "horseman" or "knight," *chivalry* is a term for the customs and rules of medieval knighthood, the sum of ideal qualifications of a knight, including valor, generosity, courtesy to women and to one's foes, loyalty, and, above all, skill in the use of arms. The manners and morals incorporated in chivalry approximated a medieval religious code for the so-called upper classes. The exploits of chivalrous warriors were the subject matter of many *romances of the Middle Ages. In *The Canterbury Tales,* Chaucer portrayed a "parfit [perfect] gentle knight," and Spenser filled his *The Faerie Queene* with a colorful procession of courteous and heroic men riding over plains and through forests. Commonplaces in romantic literature are chivalrous warriors faithful to God and king, true to their ladyloves, helpful to all persons in distress, and deadly to tyrants, giants, and monsters. Scott's *Ivanhoe* and Tennyson's *Idylls of the King* carry on the idealistic traditions of chivalry, but more realistic concepts may be found in Malory's *Morte d'Arthur* and in the mocking passages of Cervantes' *Don Quixote* and Mark Twain's *A Connecticut Yankee in King Arthur's Court.*

choriambus

A metrical foot of four syllables, two short between two long ones. This foot is occasionally used in a verse form known as choriambics. This line from Swinburne's *Choriambics* provides an illustration:

Swéet thĕ / kĭssĕs ŏf deáth / sét ŏn thў lĭps.

chorus

A group of persons singing in unison. In ancient Greece, however, a chorus meant a group of singers and dancers who participated in religious festivals and dramatic performances and who, as actors, commented on the deeds of characters and interpreted for audiences the significance of events. By Elizabethan times, this active role of the chorus was handled by a single actor who recited both *prologue and *epilogue and occasionally provided commentary between acts. In Shakespeare's *King Lear,* the Fool plays a choruslike role in his comments on the action of the play. A "chorus" character appears in T. S. Eliot's *Murder in the Cathedral.* In novels, both Thomas Hardy and Sir Walter Scott often used rustic characters in the role of choruses.

chrestomathy

A collection of literary passages, often by one author. (See ANTHOLOGY.) *A Mencken Chrestomathy,* for example, contains selections from the book and magazine writings of H. L. Mencken.

chronicle

From a Greek word meaning "time," *chronicle* refers to a record of events and is an approximate *synonym of history. The first outstanding book of English prose is considered to be *The Anglo-Saxon Chronicle,* begun under King Alfred in the ninth century and covering history from 60 B.C. to the twelfth century. The term *chronicle* is usually employed in reference to any systematic account or narration of events that contains little or no interpretation and analysis.

chronicle play

A *drama based on historical material usually consisting of loosely connected *episodes arranged in order of time. Chronicle plays flourished in *Elizabethan times, partly because they taught history to uneducated audiences, partly because they made much use of pageantry, battles, and other spectacular dramatic elements. Several of Shakespeare's greatest works are chronicle plays, although the term *history play* is sometimes applied to those dramas, like *Henry V,* which are considered neither *tragedy nor *comedy.

cinquain

A group of five. In poetry, *cinquain* is applied to any *stanza of five lines. In form, a cinquain is analogous to the Japanese *tanka.

classic

As a noun, *classic* means a work of literature that is universally recognized for its outstanding and enduring qualities. Thus, the *Iliad* is a classic in world literature, *Hamlet* in English literature, *The Scarlet Letter* in American literature, etc. Arnold Bennett, English novelist and essayist, has written a clear explanation of why a classic is a classic:

> A classic is a work which gives pleasure to the minority which is intensely and permanently interested in literature. It lives on because the minority, eager to renew the sensation of pleasure, is eternally curious and is therefore engaged in an eternal process of rediscovery. A classic does not survive for any ethical reason. It does not survive because it conforms to certain canons, or because neglect would kill it. It survives because it is a source of pleasure and because the passionate few can no more neglect it than a bee can neglect a flower.

The term *classics* is usually applied to the literature of ancient Greece and Rome. The adjective *classical* means "of recognized excellence" or "in the established tradition." See CLASSICISM.

classicism

This term refers to a body of doctrine apparently derived from the qualities of early Greek and Roman culture as reflected in art and especially in literature. Classicism stands for certain ideas and attitudes such as formal elegance, correctness, simplicity, restraint, order, dignity, and proportion. Often contrasted with *realism and *romanticism, classicism places emphasis upon qualities for which the early Greeks were notable: clear, direct, simple expression of ideas in balanced and well-proportioned form; restraint of emotion and passion; an ability to think and to communicate objectively rather than subjectively. No writer can be classified as a perfect example of classicism because no writer can be so dispassionate, so calm, so objective as to forsake all of his strictly human qualities and attitudes. However, certain qualities apparent in the classical works of Homer and Virgil are traceable in much of the writing of Ben Jonson, John Milton, Alexander Pope, Matthew Arnold, and T. S. Eliot.

clerihew

A light verse form named after its inventor, E. Clerihew Bentley, an English writer. A clerihew contains pseudobiographical references to the person being *lampooned. For example, here is a clerihew composed by Bentley when he was studying chemistry:

> Sir Humphry Davy
> Abominated gravy.
> He lived in the odium
> Of having discovered sodium.

cliff-hanger

A *melodramatic adventure serial (in films or magazines) in which each installment ends in *suspense. That is, the viewer or reader is left hanging in suspense (just as portrayed characters are sometimes left on the brink of a precipice) so that interest in the eventual outcome will be sustained. The term *cliff-hanger* is applied to any event, situation, or contest in which the outcome is uncertain up to the last moment.

climate of opinion

The prevailing attitudes, standards, temper, outlook, and environmental conditions characterizing a period or a group of people. For example, the climate of opinion in Elizabethan England was nationalistic, venturesome, and hopeful. The climate of opinion in colonial America is now considered to have been pioneering, calculating, and God-fearing.

climax

The moment in a play, novel, short story, or narrative poem at which a *crisis comes to its point of greatest intensity and is in some manner resolved is called a climax. The term is an index of emotional response from reader or spectator and is also a designation of the turning point in action. See ACT, ANTICLIMAX, CRISIS.

cloak-and-dagger

This phrase applies to a play or novel that deals with espionage or intrigue and is highly dramatic and romantic. An allied form of drama and fiction is called cloak-and-sword, a type of writing in which characters actually wear cloaks and swords, exhibit courtly manners, and engage in duels. Dumas's *The Three Musketeers* is an example of cloak-and-sword (or cloak-and-dagger) romance.

closed couplet

A *couplet (two lines), rhyming *aa,* that expresses a complete, independent statement. Such a couplet is "closed" because its meaning does not depend upon what precedes or follows:

Hope springs eternal in the human breast;
Man never is, but always to be, blessed. (Pope)

closet drama

A *play, usually in verse, more appropriate for reading than for acting. Notable examples are Milton's *Samson Agonistes* and Browning's *Pippa Passes.*

cockney

A native of the East End district of London, England. Persons born within the range of sound of the bells of Bow Church in this area traditionally are called cockney and have a distinct *dialect, such as the pronunciation of *lady* as *lidey.* Cockney is sometimes associated with poor taste, low birth, and rudeness of manner. Such writers as Keats and Shelley were once called members of the Cockney School because they allegedly exhibited poor taste in some of their diction and rhyming.

coda

From a Latin word meaning "tail," *coda* refers to a largely independent passage at the end of a literary or musical *composition. A coda, or tailpiece, is designed to bring a work to a successful conclusion by serving as a summation of preceding *themes or *motifs.

codex

From a Latin word meaning "block of wood" or "tree trunk." A codex was originally a wooden tablet made suitable for writing with a coat of wax. When wood was replaced by parchment and paper, the term was retained for manuscript pages held together by stitching. *Codices* is a term now applied to manuscript volumes of any kind.

coffee-table book
A coffee table is a low bench usually placed in a prominent position in a living room. *Coffee-table book* is a disparaging term applied to a large and usually expensive art book or similar volume displayed as a *status symbol on social occasions.

cognitive meaning
A term applied to words and statements that are capable of being perceived and consequently known; that is, to comments about reality as experienced by most people. "Water is wet" and "Two times three equals six" are statements with cognitive meaning, ideas that do not express attitude or emotion. The phrase *cognitive meaning* is important in literature because some critics hold that poetry, for example, has no cognitive meaning, that it is neither false nor true, that it expresses and arouses emotions only, that poetry does not "mean" but "is." In other words, *cognitive meaning* is the antonym of *emotive meaning.

coinage
In a general sense, *coinage* refers to anything that is made, invented, or fabricated. In literature, *coinage* refers to words consciously and arbitrarily manufactured, as contrasted with words that have entered the language through long-standing, natural processes. For example, H. L. Mencken fabricated the word *ecdysiast* as the name of an exotic dancer who removed articles of clothing while performing. This coinage and many others now enrich the language. See NEOLOGISM.

coincidence
Two or more events or circumstances occurring at one time without any obvious causal connection create a coincidence. Despite the appearance of chance in everyone's life—an influence which seems to appear and reappear—effective writers shy away from coincidence. Good literature provides a *cause for any *effect and thus prevents the reader's judging it as "improbable" or "impossible" or "preposterous." (See BELIEF.)

In addition to irritating readers, repeated use of coincidence (mere chance) stretches the odds of life too much; a string of fortuitous events exceeds probability and becomes banal and unbelievable. A tightly knit chain of *cause and effect eliminates need for coincidence. An effective piece of narration makes less use of coincidence than life itself does simply because "life is stranger than fiction dares to be." See VERISIMILITUDE.

collage

The technique of composing a work of art by pasting together on a single surface materials not normally associated with one another, such as newspaper clippings, bottle tops or labels, theater tickets, etc. In literature, collage is illustrated in the work of such writers as John Milton, Charles Lamb, James Joyce, T. S. Eliot, and Ezra Pound, who have inserted *allusions, foreign expressions, and quotations from other writers into their essays and poems.

collate

This term means to bring together in order to compare. It refers to the critical examination of a statement or text of a manuscript so as to note points of agreement, or disagreement, between copies of that statement or text. *Collate* also means to place together in proper order the sheets of a *manuscript, pamphlet, or book. A collation is a careful comparison of two or more texts, editions, or printings. In older novels and plays, *collation* is sometimes used as the name for a "light meal."

collective unconscious

This is a term from psychology, largely *Jungian psychology, that applies to racially inherited ideas and concepts that allegedly persist in one's individual unconscious mind. Jung and his followers have held that typical characteristics of man's mind and spirit are conditioned by race, nation, family, and the spirit of the age in which he lives. These are combined with unique personal qualities. This psychological theory contends that the personal and the collective elements of man's *psyche are closely interrelated and that man is moved on the unconscious level to many attitudes and reactions over which he has no direct control.

colophon

From a Greek word meaning "summit" or "finishing touch," *colophon* refers to information supplied at the end of a book about its printer, publisher, the date and place of publication, the type used, etc. More often, *colophon* is used to refer to the distinctive sign, or *emblem, of a publisher. When a publisher's emblem appears at the front of a book (usually on the title page), it is called an *imprint.

color

This word of several meanings is used in literature to refer to a writing style that is vivid (with abundant details, fast-moving) and is filled with striking *images. *Color* is also applied to the slant of a writer, his opinions and attitudes. (See BIAS.) For instance, the work of Henry James is said to have been colored by his attitudes toward wealth, social position, and culture.

comedy

A ludicrous, farcical, or amusing event or series of events designed to provide enjoyment and produce smiles or laughter. More specifically, *comedy* (from Greek words meaning "merrymaking" and "singing") refers to any literary selection written in a light, familiar, bantering, or satirical style. Even more specifically, the term applies to a *play of light and amusing character that has a happy ending.

The pattern of dramatic comedy is the reverse of *tragedy. Comedy begins in difficulty (or rapidly involves its characters in amusingly difficult situations) and invariably ends happily; tragedy may, and often does, begin in happy circumstances and always ends in disaster. Not all comedies are humorous and lighthearted, although the great majority are. Occasionally, a comedy can be serious in *tone and intent as, for example, Dante's *Divine Comedy,* but even this is a comedy of a special sort because its *action begins in Hell and ends in Heaven. Comedy differs from *burlesque and *farce in that it has a more closely knit *plot, more sensible and intelligent *dialogue, and more plausible *characterization. In general, a comedy secures its effects by stressing some oddity or incongruity of character, speech, or action. When these effects are crude, the comedy is termed "low"; when they are subtle and thoughtful, the comedy is called "high." Other types of comedy are numerous; three may be mentioned: (1) comedy of *humors,* involving characters whose actions are controlled by some *whim or *humor; (2) comedy of *manners,* involving the *conventions and manners of artificial, sophisticated society; (3) comedy of *intrigue* or *situation,* depending upon plot more than characterization (such as Shakespeare's *The Comedy of Errors*).

comic relief

A humorous scene, incident, or remark occurring in the midst of a serious or tragic literary selection is referred to as comic relief. Such an intrusion is deliberately designed by a playwright or novelist to relieve emotional intensity and simultaneously to heighten, increase, and highlight the seriousness or tragedy of the action. Such an *episode, or *interlude, can enrich the tragic implications of a story, as no one knew better than Shakespeare. He provided comic relief in many of his plays, notably with the role of Mercutio in *Romeo and Juliet,* the gravedigger scene in *Hamlet,* and the episode of the drunken porter in *Macbeth.*

commedia dell'arte

Popular Italian comedy developed during the period from the sixteenth to the eighteenth century, in which masked entertainers improvised dialogue and action from a *plot *outline based on themes associated with *stock situations and *stock characters. The term literally means "comedy of art." The characters and action in a Punch-and-Judy show constitute an example of this type of comic drama.

common measure

Designated by the abbreviation C.M. and frequently appearing with hymns, common measure consists of lines of fixed iambic meter that end in exact rhymes. Also called "common time" and the "hymnal stanza," common measure is most often applied to a group of four iambic lines rhyming *abab* or *abcb.*

commonplace book

A book in which quotations in prose and verse are entered as remarks and ideas for further consideration. The writer of a commonplace book, as distinguished from the keeper of a *diary or author of a *journal, may make irregular entries concerning various topics. A commonplace book may consist entirely of an author's own sayings or wholly of excerpts from the writings and comments of others. Jefferson and

Emerson compiled commonplace books of genuine interest to themselves and to later readers.

commonwealth
This term refers to a group of sovereign states and their associated dependencies, as, for example, the British Commonwealth of Nations. Certain states of the United States refer to themselves as commonwealths rather than as states: the Commonwealth of Virginia. In English literary history, the term (with a capital letter) refers to the period between the execution of Charles I in 1649 and the restoration of the monarchy under Charles II in 1660. During most of this time, England was governed by Parliament under the direction of Oliver Cromwell, the Puritan leader, with John Milton as Latin Secretary of the Commonwealth government.

compensation
A form of substitution, a means of supplying omissions in verse. Compensation usually involves unstressed syllables, the absence of which is compensated for by a rest, or pause, as in Tennyson's lines:
>Break, break, break
>On thy cold grey stones, O Sea!

Despite the fact that the second of these lines has seven syllables and the first only three, the lines are metrically equivalent because of pauses following each of the words in the first line.

complaint
A *lyric poem that comments on the misery of the speaker (the poet), usually involving either the fickleness of his beloved, the dreadful state of the world, or his general unhappiness. Well-known complaints are Chaucer's *To His Empty Purse* and Surrey's *Complaint of a Lover Rebuked.*

complication
A difficult issue or situation, appearing sometimes suddenly, which changes existing plans, methods, or attitudes. In literature, a complication consists of a detail of *character or *situation entering into and twisting or changing the main thread of a *plot. Specifically, in plays and stories it is that part of the narrative in which entanglement of affairs caused by the *conflict of opposing forces is developed and explained. Complication, usually the middle part of a story or play, develops the conflict already set forth: it "ties the

knot tighter" by placing further obstacles in the path of the
*protagonist, by mentioning further misunderstandings, by
raising additional problems. The second act of a five-act
tragedy is often called "the act of complication." See ACT.

composition

The act of composition is the formation of a whole by
creating, ordering, and arranging its parts. A composition is
any literary, musical, or artistic product which reveals some
plan and form. Every literary selection is a composition in
one form or another: poem, essay, novel, play, short story,
letter, biography, etc. In schools, the term is applied to any
written exercise but especially to a piece of writing which
exhibits a plan, care in preparation, and a definite *purpose
or *thesis.

comstockery

Moral censorship of the fine arts and literature. Comstock-
ery (named after Anthony Comstock, an American writer
and reformer) is often intense, overly zealous condemnation
and attempted suppression of outspoken works that are not
necessarily salacious. See CENSORSHIP.

conceit

A fanciful *image, an elaborate *metaphor in which a writer describes a person or idea by use of an *analogy which
often seems farfetched and even startling. A beautiful woman, for example, is discussed as a rose or as a marble statue.
Some conceits are merely fanciful, some remarkably ingenious, some artificial, some highly intellectual; some seem
appropriate, striking, effective; others appear false and misleading. Effective or not, conceits have been common in
literature, especially poetry, from the time of Petrarch
(1304–1374) to the present.

John Donne, noting that his love was about to destroy a
flea which had extracted blood from both himself and her,
wrote:

> Oh, stay, three lives in one flea spare,
> Where we almost, yea, more than married are.
> This flea is you and I, and this
> Our marriage bed, and marriage temple is.

Shakespeare uses several conceits and simultaneously
satirizes them in the opening of one of his sonnets:

> My mistress' eyes are nothing like the sun;

Coral is far more red than her lips' red;
If snow be white, why then her breasts are dun;
If hairs be wires, black wires grow on her head.

concreteness

Effective writers achieve concreteness in their work by giving it a quality of reality, specific elements that the reader can see, hear, feel, smell, or taste. Even emotions and sensations are made to seem tangible. A literary artist ordinarily does not merely "tell" about the characters he portrays; he "shows" them in their actions and thoughts.

For example, Shakespeare, in describing the intensity and brooding countenance of Cassius in *Julius Caesar,* not only notes these characteristics but writes "Yond Cassius has a lean and hungry look." Thus are made vivid and unmistakable the unhappiness and frustration of a man who "thinks too much." For another example, "jealousy" is referred to in *Othello* as "the green-eyed monster"; in *Romeo and Juliet,* the hero remarks that no one can understand the depth of his love for Juliet because no one has ever loved as he does: "He jests at scars that never felt a wound."

Writers possess the ability to abstract and to generalize and frequently use these powers. But their aim is to move, not merely inform; to portray, not merely philosophize. They make *abstractions on occasion, but more often they leave abstraction and conclusions for the reader to draw for himself. In most writing, the primary aim of the author is to make the reader *feel* and then to *think;* as the French writer Guy de Maupassant put it, "The public is composed of numerous groups who cry to us [authors]: 'Console me, amuse me, make me sad, make me sympathetic, make me dream, make me laugh, make me shudder, make me weep, make me think.' " Normally, only writing which possesses concreteness can achieve these effects. See ABSTRACT DICTION, ABSTRACTION, BELIEF.

condensation

From Latin words meaning "to thicken together," *condensation* applies to a shortened version of a longer work, especially a novel or play. See ABRIDGED, ABSTRACT, APERÇU, BRIEF, CONSPECTUS, EPITOME, PRÉCIS, REDACTION, RÉSUMÉ, SUMMARY, SYNOPSIS.

confession

This term means an acknowledgment, an avowal, a disclosure of some sort. In a literary application, *confession* does not necessarily imply an admission of sin or wrongdoing. De Quincey's *Confessions of an English Opium Eater* and the *Confessions of Saint Augustine* resemble *autobiography far more than they do the vulgar forms of "confession stories" found in *pulp magazines. Rousseau's *Confessions* and George Moore's *Confessions of a Young Man* disclose autobiographical details not usually revealed, but they primarily express their authors' most profound convictions and deepest thoughts.

A *confessional* usually refers to a place set apart for the hearing of confessions by a priest.

confidant

A confidant (feminine, *confidante*) is a person to whom secrets and intimate thoughts are entrusted, an intimate friend or acquaintance with whom one feels free to discuss secret or private matters. Dramatists and novelists have often used a confidant rather than employing an *aside or *soliloquy to reveal the thoughts of major characters and to summarize events not shown onstage or not revealed in a *flashback. Usually a minor character, a confidant thus enables a writer to show the *protagonist in more intimate detail than otherwise would be possible: as confidant, Dr. Watson reveals much about Sherlock Holmes, Horatio about Hamlet, and Lady Macbeth about her husband.

conflict

The opposition of persons or forces upon which the *action depends in drama and fiction is called conflict. Dramatic conflict is the struggle which grows out of the interplay of opposing forces (ideas, interests, wills) in a *plot; conflict may be termed the material from which a plot is constructed.

One type of conflict is *elemental,* or *physical:* a struggle between man and the physical world. It represents man versus forces of nature: the difficulties and dangers, for example, faced by explorers, navigators, astronauts. Rain, cold, heat, wild beasts in the jungle, treacherous tides—these are constant obstacles to mankind. Such elemental conflicts are frequently found in films, in melodramatic television plays, and in *pulp magazines; occasionally, combined with other ingredients, they appear in narrative or dramatic masterpieces.

Another type of conflict is *social:* a struggle between man and man. Much popular fiction is based on social conflict: two men trying to win the love of a girl; the competition of businessmen; a girl having difficulties with her parents over her conduct; racial and religious prejudices, etc.

A third kind of conflict is *internal,* or *psychological:* a struggle between desires within a person. External forces may be important and other characters may appear in the narrative, but the focus is always upon the central figure's inner turmoil.

A variant form of social conflict is a *protagonist's struggle against society, as in some of the novels of Dickens, George Eliot, and Theodore Dreiser. A fifth kind of conflict is man's struggle against fate and destiny as, for example, in a play by Sophocles or a novel by Thomas Hardy. But most conflicts are basically physical, social, or internal—or combinations of these three. Conrad's *Youth* contains elements of all three kinds of conflict, but the primary one is physical; so, too, Stevenson's *Treasure Island* is primarily, although not wholly, a plotted narrative based on physical conflict. All of Hardy's novels contain elements of each kind of conflict, but the dominant struggle is usually social (between man and man or between man and society). The great tragedies of *Macbeth* and *Hamlet* contain elements of each kind of conflict, but the basic one in each instance is internal.

connotation

The suggestions and associations which have surrounded a word as contrasted with its bare, literal meaning, its *denotation. For example, the denotative meaning of *gold* is "a malleable, ductile, yellow trivalent and univalent metallic element," but its connotative meaning is associated with color, riches, power, happiness, greed, luxury, evil, and misery. These suggestions and implications beyond the core meaning of *gold* constitute its connotation, its "plus" or "added" associations. A mother is "a female parent," but everyone adds his private and personal meanings to the word as well as group meanings of national or racial origin and even universal concepts of the term.

To a good writer, both denotations and connotations are important. He uses words with exact and specific meanings, but he knows that insensitiveness to the connotative values of words will rob his work of charm and effectiveness. If he never uses connotation, his writing will be flatter, more insipid, than it should be.

Scientists and philosophers tend to use words in their denotative meanings; literary artists rely upon connotation for beautiful effects and deepest meanings. An essayist (Robert Thouless) has illustrated this distinction by quoting these lines from Keats's *The Eve of St. Agnes:*

> Full on this casement shone the wintry moon
> And threw warm gules on Madeline's fair breast.

He then shows how all beauty and richness are destroyed by substituting neutral, denotative words:

> Full on this window shone the wintry moon,
> Making red marks on Jane's uncolored chest.

consonance

Having a general meaning of "accord" and "agreement," *consonance* is used in *prosody to refer to the correspondence of consonants, especially those at the end of a word. A kind of *rhyme, consonance is illustrated in a phrase such as "dis*cuss* and then dis*miss*." See ALLITERATION, ASSONANCE.

conspectus

A survey; a general or comprehensive view; a *digest or *summary that retains the overall pattern of a larger work but condenses its contents sharply. See ABRIDGED, ABSTRACT, APERÇU, BRIEF, EPITOME, PRÉCIS, REDACTION, RÉSUMÉ, SUMMARY, SYNOPSIS.

conte

A French term, *conte* originally applied to any *short story or *tale, especially one dealing with legendary, extraordinary, and highly imaginative events. In general use, *conte* is but a name for a compact, brief story, such as those written by Guy de Maupassant.

context

The part, or parts, of a passage of writing or speaking preceding or following a particular word or group of words is referred to as *context*. The context of a group of words is nearly always so intimately connected as to throw light upon not only the meaning of individual words but the sense and purpose of an entire passage or selection.

The surroundings of any statement often change, extend, or amend the meaning which seems apparent in the statement itself. For example, Cardinal Newman's famous essay *Definition of a Gentleman* begins with this statement: "Hence it is that it is almost a definition of a gentleman to say he is one who never inflicts pain." But it is unfair and unwise to quote Newman's definition without recalling the *almost* in the statement; the author explains in the context, in every statement which follows, that even one who inflicts no pain is not an ideal gentleman unless he holds religious convictions.

Certain passages in the Bible and in many other great works of literature in themselves seem cruel or obscene but, taken in context, have different meanings. One basic test for pornography is determining the intent, purpose, and character of an entire work—the complete selection in context—rather than focusing upon a particular passage notable for its profanity or obscenity. "Quoting out of context" and "reading out of context" are considered serious faults in literary criticism.

contrapuntal

Primarily a term used in music, *contrapuntal* means "composed of two or more independent melodies sounded together." A term derived from Latin words meaning "point against point," *contrapuntal* is an adjectival form of *counterpoint. The method by which one theme in a novel, for example, is developed and balanced against another is contrapuntal and constitutes a kind of counterpoint. Another example is Shakespeare's use of contrapuntal character development in contrasting Hamlet's indecisiveness with his desire for revenge.

controlling image

A *metaphor or *image which persists throughout a literary work and determines its form and nature. The controlling image of Thurber's *The Secret Life of Walter Mitty,* for example, is that of a timid, depressed, and badgered man who seeks to escape humdrum routine. The controlling image of much of Faulkner's writing is decadence; of Hemingway's, courage under pressure.

convention

A literary practice which has become an established means of expression, an accepted technique. Literature makes use of scores of conventions, such as the fainting heroine of sentimental fiction, the despair of a rejected lover, a bragging coward as a *stock character, the set pattern of rhyme in much poetry, love at first sight, the *fading of an image on a motion-picture screen to indicate a lapse of time, etc. When a set of conventions is characteristic of a group of writers, the word *tradition* is used: the *classical* tradition, the *pastoral* tradition, the *Puritan* tradition, etc. See BELIEF, DRAMATIC CONVENTION.

copy

In its most general sense, *copy* means an imitation, transcript, or reproduction of an original, but in literature it refers to any *composition, whether handwritten or typed, that is intended for printing. In journalism, *copy* applies to the appeal or newsworthiness of a person or event ("A human interest story is always good copy").

copyright

The exclusive right, granted by law for a fixed period, to produce, dispose of, and otherwise control copies of a literary and artistic work. In the United States, a copyright extends for twenty-eight years, is renewable once, and thus controls for fifty-six years. In England, regardless of the date of initial publication and copyright, protection continues for fifty years after the author's death.

coronach

A funeral *dirge, a poem or song of lamentation. A Gaelic word, *coronach* means "a crying out together." Canto 3 of Sir Walter Scott's *The Lady of the Lake* is called "Coronach," one stanza of which begins:
> The hand of the reaper
> Takes the ears that are hoary,
> But the voice of the weeper
> Wails manhood in glory.

Corpus Christi

Literally, the body of Christ. A Corpus Christi play was a medieval religious drama performed as part of a procession on the fiftieth day after Easter.

cosmic

Immeasurably extended in time or space. *Cosmic* is used to

refer to events and concepts such as those in Dante's *Divine Comedy* and Milton's *Paradise Lost* that are vast, universal, and even outside the earth.

coterie

A group of persons associated because of similar interests and purposes. One of the most famous coteries in literature was called the Sons of Ben, a group of seventeenth-century poets who attempted to continue the literary ideals of Ben Jonson (1572–1637), the Elizabethan playwright. The *beat generation is a somewhat loose but populous kind of coterie. See CABAL.

counterplot

A secondary *theme in a play or novel used as a variation of the principal theme or in contrast to it. A counterplot (also called a subplot) constitutes a related but separate action. Counterplots appear in several of Shakespeare's plays, such as *Hamlet, King Lear,* and *Henry IV.* In the last-named, the activities of Falstaff and his companions are the counterplot, whereas the principal theme is the putting down of a political rebellion. In *Hamlet,* the struggle between Laertes and Hamlet is the counterplot to the primary conflict between Hamlet and Claudius. In *King Lear,* the dominant figure of the counterplot (Edmund) actually determines the outcome of the principal action.

counterpoint

In music, counterpoint is the art of combining melodies; in literature, counterpoint is the art and technique of playing off complementary and opposing *characters, *themes, or *plots against each other. In a novel entitled *Point Counter Point,* Aldous Huxley moves from one set of individuals to another, balancing each life against its "counterpoint." The lives of these people repeat the same patterns in different forms. See CONTRAPUNTAL.

coup de théâtre

A "stroke concerning the theater," coup de théâtre is an unexpected, surprising turn in a play which produces an amazing or sensational effect. In an Elizabethan play, *The White Devil,* a character is shot by his sister and mistress. The audience, expecting his death, is shocked when the "wounded" man, discovering that neither woman intends to follow him in death, leaps to his feet shouting, "I am not wounded."

couplet
A pair of successive lines of verse, especially a pair that rhyme and are of the same metrical length.

> Words are like leaves; and where they most
> abound,
> Much fruit of sense beneath is rarely found. (Pope)

See CLOSED COUPLET, DISTICH.

courtesy book
A book defining and explaining the ideals, training, duties, and conduct of persons planning or intending to serve at court in medieval times. A courtesy book, usually written in *dialogue, explains, for instance, the etiquette of *courtly love and the duties and responsibilities of a courtier. See ETIQUETTE BOOK.

courtly love
The chivalric, romantic code and philosophy of love and lovemaking. Courtly love was illicit, secret, discreet, never promiscuous, and always dedicated. A system of courtly love is revealed in Chaucer's *Troilus and Criseyde* and in several romances about King Arthur, Queen Guinevere, and Lancelot. See ARTHURIAN.

Coventry
A city in central England with many historic associations. One of the most important series of *mystery plays was called the Coventry Mysteries because they were first and most often produced in Coventry. To "send someone to Coventry" is to refuse to associate with him, to ignore him, although the phrase may have originated during periods when political prisoners were sent to Coventry for safekeeping.

Cowleyan ode
A poem in which the rhyme scheme and stanzaic pattern are irregular. This form of *lyric was named after Abraham Cowley (1618–1667), an English poet who first used it. The best-known Cowleyan ode in English is Wordsworth's *Ode*

on *Intimations of Immortality from Recollections of Early Childhood;* the first lines of the first stanza read:

> There was a time when meadow, grove,
>   and stream,
> The earth, and every common sight,
> To me did seem
> Appareled in celestial light,
> The glory and the freshness of a dream.

crisis

A turning point, for better or worse, in an acute disease, a love affair, a military campaign, or any activity. The term can refer to the point of time when it is decided whether a course of action or an affair shall be stopped, be modified, or proceed and also applies to an emotionally significant event or radical change of status in an individual's life.

In *drama and *fiction, a crisis occurs when opposing forces creating *conflict interlock in a decisive *action on which the *plot will turn. Such a brief period of time may occur more than once in a given novel or play, each crisis resulting in a climax; a crisis is essentially a structural element of plot, whereas a climax (always produced by a crisis) is primarily an index of emotional response from reader or spectator. One of several major crises in *Hamlet* occurs in act 3, scene 2, when Claudius sees the play-within-a-play. The resulting climax consists of Claudius's emotion, fright, and guilty departure. See ACT, CLIMAX.

criticism

Thoughtful, many-sided evaluation and analysis. *Criticism* comes from Greek *kritikos,* meaning a "judge." Thus criticism is a process which weighs, evaluates, judges. Contrary to some opinion, it does not deal only with faults. Sound criticism mentions good qualities as well as bad, virtues as well as faults. It does not set out to praise or condemn; rather it weighs faults and excellencies and then passes a considered judgment.

In his *Principles of Literary Criticism,* I. A. Richards says:

> The qualifications of a good critic are three. He must be an adept at experiencing, without eccentricities, the state of mind relevant to the work of art he is judging. Second, he must be able to distinguish experiences from

one another as regards their less superficial features. Third, he must be a sound judge of values.

Subjective criticism judges a literary work solely in terms of the critic's personal reaction to it. *Impressionistic* criticism, like subjective criticism, is primarily concerned with a critic's reactions and impressions. *Ethical* criticism applies principles of morality; *historical* criticism reconstructs the standards and settings of the period in which a work was produced; *biographical* criticism centers on the author rather than the work; *comparative* criticism sets up parallels between different works; *objective* criticism is nonexistent since, as Anatole France once wrote:

> The good critic is he who recounts the adventures of his soul in the presence of masterpieces. Objective criticism no more exists than objective art, and those [critics] who suppose that they are putting anything but themselves into their work are the dupes of the most fallacious illusion.

critique

An *article or *essay evaluating a literary or other work of art. *Critique* is but another name for a review. However, the best-known title using the word is Kant's *Critique of Pure Reason,* which, although a review, is also a demonstrated system concerning man's a priori knowledge in scientific matters and a vigorous argument which removes religion and immortality from the sphere of reasoning and places them in the realm of faith.

curse

This word, derived from an *Old English term meaning to "call down wrath," is a *malediction, the expression of a wish that evil, misfortune, or doom shall befall someone. *Curse* also applies to retribution for evil as in the most famous instance in all literature, "the curse of Cain." God's curse upon Cain, who murdered his brother Abel, is stated in Genesis 4: "And now art thou cursed from the earth, which hath opened her mouth to receive thy brother's blood from thy hand. When thou tillest the ground, it shall not henceforth yield unto thee her strength; a fugitive and a vagabond shalt thou be in the earth." See IMPRECATION.

curtain

In the theater, a curtain is a set of hanging drapery for concealing part or all of a stage from audience view. *Curtain* is applied also to the end of a *scene or *act, which is indicated by the falling or closing of a curtain. A curtain *call* is the appearance of performers at the end of a theatrical performance in response to applause. A curtain *lecture* is a scolding administered in private by one person to another. A curtain *line* is the last line of *dialogue in a scene or act. Curtain *music* is music played before the raising of a theater curtain or before the beginning of a performance or act. A curtain *raiser* is a short play presented before the main performance. A curtain *speech* is the final statement of an act or scene or a brief speech by an actor, author, or producer following a performance.

cycle

Originally meaning "circle," *cycle* is applied to any group of poems, plays, or narratives about a central figure, theme, or major event. Accounts of the Trojan War, the Charlemagne *epics, and the *romances associated with King Arthur and the *Knights of the Round Table are cycles.

cynicism

Distrust, doubt, or contempt for accepted standards of conduct, especially honesty and morality. A cynical writer (such as Oscar Wilde or George Bernard Shaw) holds a low opinion of mankind in general or at least disbelieves in the sincerity of human motives. Any individualistic writer who scorns ordinarily accepted standards and ideals is considered a cynic. Well-known novels that exhibit cynicism are Samuel Butler's *The Way of All Flesh,* Somerset Maugham's *Of Human Bondage,* and Sinclair Lewis's *Main Street.* See MENIPPEAN.

dactyl

A metrical foot of three syllables, one stressed syllable followed by two unstressed ones, as in the words *Washington, yesterday,* and *humanly.* Each of the first three feet in both lines of this excerpt from Browning's *The Lost Leader* is a dactyl:

Júst fŏr ă / hándfŭl ŏf / sílvĕr hĕ / léft ŭs
Júst fŏr ă / ríbaňd tŏ / stíck iň hĭis / cóat.

Dark Ages

This phrase is sometimes loosely applied to the whole of the Middle Ages from about A.D. 476 to the *Renaissance. Scholars avoid the term because it is vague and because the period thus covered was actually one of considerable activity in intellectual, cultural, scientific, and artistic pursuits. The phrase is primarily a reference to the earlier part of the Middle Ages (from the fifth to the eleventh century).

dead metaphor

A term used to refer to a word that began as a *metaphor (an implied comparison) but is now accepted in a literal meaning, such as *telecast* (a television broadcast). The term is applied also to metaphors that are archaic or obsolete, such as *baker's dozen* for *thirteen.*

decadence

In a general sense, *decadence* refers to any period in literary or art history considered inferior to a preceding period. The period following Shakespeare, for example, was notable for such decadent qualities as sensationalism, loss of poetic power, and a lowered standard of morality.

decasyllable
A word or a line of verse containing ten syllables. This line from Pope's *An Essay on Criticism* is decasyllabic:
> True ease in writing comes from art, not chance.

decorum
An observance or requirement of polite society or anything that is proper and fitting. In literature, *decorum* is a critical term describing that which is suitable to a subject, character, or setting. In *Paradise Lost,* for instance, fallen angels speak in a dignified, highly rhetorical style that fits the occasion. In *Huckleberry Finn,* characters speak and act in informal, colloquial ways that are appropriate to their stations in life and therefore are "decorous."

deduction
Two common methods of thinking are deduction and *induction. The former seeks to establish a specific conclusion by showing that it conforms to, is allied with, or "leads down from" a general truth or principle, a *premise. In deduction, movement of thought, expressed or implied, is always from the general to the particular. For example, if one accepts the general principle that most Danes have blue eyes, it may be deduced that Hans, a Dane, probably has blue eyes.

Induction seeks to establish a general truth, a principle, a premise. The inductive process begins by using observations of a number of facts; it classifies these facts, looks for similarities among them, and from a supposedly sufficient number of those particulars draws a conclusion or leads "into" or "up to" a principle. Once stated, the principle is supported by other facts and particulars: movement of thought is always from the particular to the general. For instance, if one knows hundreds of Danes, most of whom have blue eyes, he may conclude (induce) from these specific cases that most Danes have blue eyes.

Through induction (inductive reasoning) the laws (principles, generalized statements) of science have been arrived at. Through deduction (deductive reasoning) they are applied in particular situations—the development of a vaccine or the manufacture and launching of space rockets. As in science, so in writing: all literature is based upon deductive or inductive processes of thought. See ARGUMENTATION, SYLLOGISM.

deism

The religion of those who believe in the existence of God on the evidence of nature and reason only. Followers of deism reject the divinity of Jesus Christ, supernatural revelations, and the inspiration of the *Bible. Deists believe that God created the world but has since remained indifferent to creation. Deism arose from the scientific movement which developed after the discoveries and theories of Copernicus, Columbus, Galileo, and others.

The effects of this "natural religion," or rationalistic *point of view, on literature have been great. Strong evidences of deism are apparent in Pope's *An Essay on Man,* in much of the poetry of Wordsworth and Shelley, in Gibbon's *The Decline and Fall of the Roman Empire,* and in Thomas Paine's *The Age of Reason.* Much of the literature of the Revolutionary period in America is deistic, notably some of the writings of Benjamin Franklin and Thomas Jefferson.

déjà vu

A French phrase meaning "already seen." *Déjà vu* is used to refer to a trite, unoriginal story situation or to dated film making. In psychology, *déjà vu* applies to the illusion of having previously experienced something being encountered for the first time.

delusion

A false belief or opinion. Literature is filled with descriptions of persons whose minds and judgments are mistaken in some way. For example, Don Quixote, deluded by his reading of romances of *chivalry, decks himself in rusty armor and cardboard helmet to roam the world as a knight-errant. Shakespeare's Othello, for another instance, suffers a delusion about his wife's faithfulness and innocence with a resulting unwarranted jealousy that leads to tragedy. In psychiatry, *delusion* refers to a persistent, dominating mental conception that is false and unreasonable. See ILLUSION.

denotation

The specific, exact, and concrete meaning of a word independent of any associated or secondary meanings. See CONNOTATION.

denouement
This term, derived from a French word meaning "to untie," refers to the outcome or result of any complex situation or sequence of events. More specifically, it is applied to the final outcome or unraveling of the main dramatic *complications in a play, novel, or other work of literature. Denouement is an ingenious untying of the knot of an *intrigue that involves some explanation of the secrets and misunderstandings connected with the *plot. In drama, *denouement* is the term most often applied to comedies, *catastrophe to tragedies.

description
A *form of discourse which tells how something looks, tastes, smells, sounds, feels, or acts. It deals with things, people, animals, places, scenes, moods, and impressions. The primary purposes of description are to portray a sense impression and to indicate a *mood. It tries to make the impression or mood as vivid, as real, as lifelike for the reader as it was for the writer when he received the impression or observed the mood.

Description is not often an independent form of writing. Except in travel "literature," it rarely stands alone. Often, however, a paragraph of description appears in a longer work, such as this one from O. Henry's short story *A Municipal Report:*

> Eight-sixty-one Jessamine Street was a decayed mansion. Thirty yards back from the street it stood, outmerged in a splendid grove of trees and untrimmed shrubbery. A row of box bushes overflowed and almost hid the paling fence from sight; the gate was kept closed by a rope noose that encircled the gate-post and the first paling of the gate. But when you got inside you saw that 861 was a shell, a shadow, a ghost of former grandeur and excellence.

Description is most effective when used in short passages as an aid in explaining or narrating something. But although its part is minor, its function is important. The great value of description is that it brings something to life; it creates a vivid impression for the reader or hearer. Everyone lives in a world of *images, not *abstractions, and responds to the graphic and the concrete. Good description, always graphic and concrete, is made so by the use of abundant details.

Depth and richness of description depend upon the ability of the writer to receive, select, and express details. Some details are based upon visual reproduction—color, movement, and form—and others convey impressions of tastes, touches, smells, and sounds. Nevertheless, to catalog all pertinent information about an object is not to describe it. The result of this process is only a mass of raw material from which the reader must formulate his own impression. The writer of good description uses plentiful detail, but he tries to produce a single effect, a *dominant impression. His primary purpose is to convey the impressions which he received when he saw or felt or tasted or smelled whatever it is that he is describing. These impressions form a pattern which must be supported by details but not obscured by them. See BELIEF, CHARACTERIZATION, EXTRANEOUS, SETTING, VERISIMILITUDE.

detective story

A narrative (*short story or *novel) in which a *mystery is unraveled by a detective through the assembly and interpretation of clues. The detective story had its origin in Edgar Allan Poe's *The Murders in the Rue Morgue* in 1841; Poe firmly established the type in several other tales of similar sort. *Conventions of this form of light entertainment include such details as the perfection of the crime, the stupidity of police, the brilliance or diligence of the detective, and a striking *denouement. A basic rule of the detective story is that clues from which a solution can be obtained must be given to the reader precisely as and when the detective receives them. In a sharply limited sense, Sophocles and Shakespeare might be called detective story writers, since *Oedipus Rex* and *Hamlet* involve a *hero trying to clarify a situation involving a murder.

Among notable writers of this form may be mentioned Poe, Sir Arthur Conan Doyle (the Sherlock Holmes stories), S. S. Van Dine (Philo Vance), Ellery Queen, Dashiell Hammett, and Dorothy Sayers.

determinism

The philosophical doctrine that all facts and events are determined by outside causes, that results and effects are controlled by natural laws. Determinists believe that human choices and decisions are regulated by external sources and that man's will is free and therefore able to function only in the sense that it is uncompelled. Determinism is related to *naturalism in that both theories embrace the idea that what a person thinks, does, and says is directed by heredity and environment over which he has little or no control.

deus ex machina

A Latin phrase meaning "god from a machine." The term is a name for the literary device of resolving the arrangements of a *plot by the intervention of outside or supernatural forces or by an unexpected and unprepared-for trick or *coincidence. *Deus ex machina* is often used to refer to any artificial, forced, or improbable method used to untangle the difficulties of a play or novel. An example occurs in *The Threepenny Opera,* a comic work in which Mac the Knife is saved from hanging by a proclamation from Queen Victoria.

deuteragonist

In classical Greek drama, the character second in importance to the protagonist, especially one serving as the antagonist. (See AGON, ANTAGONIST, PROTAGONIST, TRITAGONIST.) In *The Adventures of Huckleberry Finn,* the slave Jim is the deuteragonist and Tom Sawyer is the tritagonist.

devil's advocate (disciple)

One who, for the sake of argument, presents or defends an opposing point of view or an evil cause. Both *devil's advocate* (supporter) and *devil's disciple* (follower) refer to an adverse critic, to a detractor, to one who argues against a plan or idea considered sound and good. In Roman Catholicism, the phrase is applied to an official appointed to present arguments against the beatification or canonization of a person as a saint. In this sense, a devil's advocate is not a whitewasher of the wicked but a blackener of the good. One of George Bernard Shaw's plays that illustrates this role is entitled *The Devil's Disciple.*

dialect

The language of a particular district, class, or group of persons; the sounds, grammar, and diction employed by people distinguished from other persons either geographically or socially. A major technique of *characterization is the use by persons in a narrative of distinct varieties of language that indicate their educational, social, and geographical status. When a novelist or playwright reproduces the sounds, word choices, and speech rhythms of characters, he gives an illusion of reality to fictional characters. Without exception, all writers of *dialogue generally acknowledged to be proficient have differentiated between characters through the skillful use of dialect.

dialogue

This word means "a conversation," "a speaking together." Dialogue involves an exchange of opinions or ideas and is used in narrative poetry, short stories, novels, and plays to reveal characters and to advance action. Some works of literature are composed wholly of conversation: a dialogue of Plato, for example.

diary

A daily record, especially of the writer's (keeper's) own attitudes, observations, and experiences. *Diary* also refers to a book for keeping such a record. As an intimate record of thoughts and events, a diary is not usually intended for publication, but many famous ones have been published: those of Samuel Pepys, Jonathan Swift, and William Byrd, for example. See AUTOBIOGRAPHY, BIOGRAPHY.

diatribe

A bitter, sharp, and abusive attack upon and criticism of some person, act, or condition. Originally a diatribe was a *dialogue about some matter of philosophy, but as such conversations became more violent and faultfinding, the term assumed its present meaning.

dibrach

A poetic foot of two unaccented (short) syllables. A dibrach is also called a *pyrrhic foot.

diction

The style of speaking and writing as reflected in the choice and use of words. Diction refers to the selection and arrangement of words in statements and to the accuracy, emphasis, and distinction with which they are spoken and written.

dictionary

A book containing a selection of the words of a language, arranged alphabetically, providing information about spelling, pronunciation, meanings, origins, etc. Sometimes a dictionary is restricted to word lists of special interest, such as dictionaries of art, of science, of medicine, etc.

A modern dictionary is not an "authority" in any exact meaning of the word. It does not prescribe or dictate, except in the sense that it records and frequently explains the comparative standing of words and phrases as regards national, reputable, and current usage.

didacticism

From a Greek word meaning "to teach," *didacticism* means the practice, art, or science of providing instruction. In literature, *didacticism* refers to the use of writing for teaching, for offering guidance in moral, religious, and ethical matters. Since all literature exists in order to communicate, the didacticism of a given selection depends upon the purpose of the author. If a writer's primary intention is to provide instruction, his work is didactic; if he is concerned more with artistic qualities and techniques than with a message, his work, no matter how instructive, is considered nondidactic. For instance, Upton Sinclair's *The Jungle* is a novel of didacticism because the author was intent upon pointing out the social and economic injustices then prevailing in the meat-packing industry. Hawthorne's *The Scarlet Letter* teaches much about the universal subject of sin, but it is primarily a psychological *romance notable for its narrative appeal. See PROPAGANDA.

digest

A collection of classified, condensed matter, usually dealing with historical, literary, scientific, or legal concerns. In legal language, a digest is an *abstract (summary statement) of some body of law. As a verb, *digest* means "to condense, abridge, summarize." See ABRIDGED, ABRIDGMENT.

digression

When applied to writing, *digression* refers to a passage or section that departs from the central *theme or basic *plot of a selection. To some readers, lengthy or seemingly unimportant passages of *description in a novel appear to be digressions. An *epic simile is a form of digression. Laurence Sterne's *Tristram Shandy* contains a section entitled "Digression on Digressions."

dilettante

A person who takes up an activity, art, pursuit, or subject

merely for amusement and in a superficial, desultory way. A dilettante is a dabbler, an amateur who pursues an art as a pastime but not with serious intent. The term is also applied to a lover of the fine arts, especially music and painting.

dime novel
A cheap, *melodramatic, or sensational work of fiction, usually paperbound. (Dime novels were sold for ten cents during the period of their greatest popularity, 1850–1920.)

dimeter
A verse (line) of two metrical feet. Thomas Hardy's poem *The Robin* is in dimeter:

When Í / dĕscend
Tŏwards / thĕir brínk
Ĭ stánd / and look
And stoóp / and drínk.

Dionysia
Dramatic festivals held periodically in honor of Dionysus, in classical mythology the god of wine, drama, and fertility. Dionysus was the Greek name for Bacchus; Bacchanalia was the Latin (Roman) name for Dionysia. In Dionysian orgies Greek drama was born, both *tragedy and *comedy. In the latter days of Greek power and through the Roman era, Dionysia were characterized by debauchery and drunkenness; hence the word *bacchanalian* (drunken) and the current use of *Dionysian* to describe any ribald, intoxicated, and convivial orgy.

dirge
A lyrical poem or song expressing mourning for the dead. *Dirge* is a term now applied to any kind of solemn, mournful music. (See ELEGY, THRENODY.) In Shakespeare's *The Tempest*, Ariel sings a dirge for Ferdinand's lost father:

Full fathom five thy father lies;
Of his bones are coral made;
Those are pearls that were his eyes:
Nothing of him that doth fade,
But doth suffer a sea-change
Into something rich and strange.
Sea nymphs hourly ring his knell:

> Ding-dong.
> Hark! now I hear them—Ding-dong, bell.

disbelief

Refusal to believe or to accept something as true. The incredulity of readers is a constant concern of all writers, because unless they can secure acceptance for the characters they portray and the actions they narrate, their work fails to communicate. See BELIEF, SUSPENSION OF DISBELIEF, VERISIMILITUDE.

dissertation

A formal treatise, a learned *essay or *thesis. *Dissertation* (derived from a Latin term meaning "discussion") can be applied to any formal discourse in speech or writing, but it has also been loosely used in the title of a discursive *personal essay, Charles Lamb's *A Dissertation upon Roast Pig.*

dissonance

A harsh or inharmonious sound. In this sense, *dissonance* is a synonym for *cacophony. (Also, see CONSONANCE, an antonym for *dissonance.)* On occasion, a writer may deliberately employ a combination of harsh-sounding words in order to create a desired effect, as in these lines from a poem by Gerard Manley Hopkins:

> For how to the heart's cheering
> The down-dugged ground-hugged grey
> Hovers off, the jay-blue heavens appearing
> Of pied and peeled May!

distich

A synonym for *couplet, a distich is a pair of verse lines making complete sense. Usually, the lines of a distich rhyme, as in this couplet from Milton's *Il Penseroso:*

> These pleasures, Melancholy, give,
> And I with thee will choose to live.

dithyramb

Originally, a dithyramb was a choral song or chant sung during festivals and sacrifices dedicated to Dionysus. (See DIONYSIA.) The term is now applied to literary expression, both verse and prose, that employs unrestrained, passionate, wild, or excited language. Dithyrambic verse appears in Dryden's *Alexander's Feast,* a chorus of which reads:

83

With ravished ears
The monarch hears,
Assumes the god,
Affects to nod,
And seems to shake the spheres.

ditty

A loosely applied term that refers to a poem designed for singing and to any short, simple song. The name is most often used for popular melodies and for songs sung by sailors.

divine afflatus

Poetic inspiration; an elevation of mind and spirit preceding creative composition during which the poet (or other writer) is felt to be receiving aid from a divine source. *Divine afflatus* is now largely used in a contemptuous sense to imply that the receiver of such an alleged gift overvalues the worth of his efforts. See AFFLATUS.

document

A written or printed paper that provides information or evidence of some sort. Historians, biographers, and some novelists rely on documents as the *source of their own writing. See PRIMARY SOURCE, SECONDARY SOURCE.

documentation

The use of documentary evidence; the citing of *documents as proof or backing for statements made. A formally written paper is said to be documented when it is accompanied by *footnotes and a *bibliography. All histories, biographies, and formal essays rely to some extent upon documentation, the citation of authority for statements expressed and conclusions reached.

doggerel

A term applied to verse that is crudely written, loose or irregular in measure, and that usually exhibits comic or burlesque qualities. Doggerel is any poorly executed attempt at poetry that deals with trite subject matter, is overly sentimental, and is monotonous in form. The *epitaph on Shakespeare's tomb is doggerel, sometimes cited as unworthy of his genius and possibly not composed by him:

Good friend, for Jesus' sake forbear

To dig the dust enclosed here!
Blest be the man that spares these stones,
And cursed be he that moves my bones.

dogma

A settled and established opinion, belief, or principle. Dogma is also a specific doctrine or tenet laid down by some authority such as a church, a society, a monarch, or a government. Dogma is not necessarily faulty or harmful, but dogmatism (the arrogant assertion of opinions as truths) is rare in worthwhile literature. In *The Way of All Flesh*, Samuel Butler wrote, "It is in the uncompromisingness with which dogma is held and not in the dogma or want of dogma that the danger lies."

domestic tragedy

A dramatic composition dealing with a serious and somber theme that involves middle-class or lower-class characters, settings, and conflicts. A domestic tragedy is not concerned with the problems of persons of high rank but with events in the lives of everyday, contemporary people. Since the eighteenth century, dramatists have slowly but increasingly become aware that tragic events do occur in the lives of others than heroes of lofty estate. Plays dealing with the fate of lowly people are more common in the twentieth century than ever before, among them such domestic tragedies as O'Neill's *Desire under the Elms,* Arthur Miller's *The Death of a Salesman,* and Tennessee Williams's *The Glass Menagerie.*

dominant impression

The most important and influential effect upon a reader of a literary selection. (See CONTROLLING IMAGE, EXTRANEOUS.) The dominant impression of one reader may differ from that of another, but many readers will agree that the dominant impression received from *Othello* is that of the power of jealousy to destroy one's character; from *Macbeth,* the ruinous effects of ambition and ruthlessness; from *King Lear,* the destructive force of fury and the redemptive qualities of unselfishness and forgiveness.

Doric

The best synonyms for *Doric* are *simple* and *unpretentious.* The term is derived from Doris, a small country in Greece, the inhabitants of which spoke in a rustic "Doric" *dialect. The first *pastoral poets wrote in this dialect; centuries later, John Milton used "Doric lay" in *Lycidas* as a synonym for "pastoral poem": "With eager thought warbling his Doric lay." Because the Doric dialect was rustic and because Doric architecture is notable for strength and simplicity, such unpretentious selections of literature as several of Wordsworth's "nature" poems are referred to as Doric.

double-decker novel

A double-decker is something with two decks or tiers, such as a ship, bed, bus, sandwich, or cake. *Double-decker novel* is a term that refers to any narrative work of great or excessive length. In the nineteenth century the term applied to the serial (in installments) publication of a work, the final issue of which appeared in two parts.

double entendre

A French phrase referring to a word or phrase with a "double meaning." Usually, one of the two possible meanings of a double entendre is indelicate, risqué, or suggestive. In *Macbeth,* Lady Macbeth, making plans for the visit of Duncan, remarks, "He that's coming must be provided for." She was speaking as hostess and as assassin-to-be. See EQUIVOQUE.

double rhyme

A rhyme of two syllables of which the second is unstressed, such as *motion* and *notion.* An example of double rhyme appears in these lines:

> Others aver, to him, that Handel
> Is scarcely fit to hold a candle.

(See FEMININE RHYME.) The work of Ogden Nash, for example, is filled with double and even triple rhymes (*fortunate* and *importunate*).

double talk

Speech using nonsense syllables in rapid *patter along with standard words. A variant form of double talk is the use of a nonexistent word in an otherwise sense-making statement.

drama

A composition in prose or verse presenting in *pantomime and *dialogue a narrative involving *conflict and usually designed for presentation on a stage. Drama, derived from a Greek word (*dran*) meaning "to do," "to act," was referred to by Aristotle as "imitated human action," a definition that remains serviceable. Drama presupposes a theater, actors, and an audience; in order to be fully experienced, a play should be seen and heard, not merely read.

Drama arose from religious ceremonies (see DIONYSIA); both *comedy and *tragedy evolved from such varied themes in those ceremonials as fertility, life, and death. Medieval drama largely evolved from rites commemorating the birth and resurrection of Jesus Christ. (See MIRACLE PLAY, MORALITY PLAY, MYSTERY PLAY.) Beginning with the Renaissance, dramatic elements were widened, developed, and emphasized in so many and diverse ways that drama today bears only a faint resemblance to its beginnings. Nevertheless, a play is fundamentally what it was more than 2,000 years ago: a picture of human life revealed in successive changes of events and told in dialogue and *action for the entertainment and instruction of an audience.

dramatic convention

A device employed in a play as a substitute for reality which the audience is supposed to accept as genuine and real. (See BELIEF, SUSPENSION OF DISBELIEF.) The *chorus in Greek plays is a dramatic convention. The *curtain which opens and closes the stage is a convention, as is the stage itself, which must be regarded as the actual scene or geographical setting of action. Actors must be accepted as real persons involved in a dramatic story. In real life, persons rarely talk to themselves in lengthy, rhetorical *monologues, another dramatic convention. A *soliloquy (the act of talking as if alone) is a dramatic convention. So is the *aside (a remark that the audience, but not other actors on the stage, is supposed to hear). Even the *theater itself is a convention by reason of its invisible fourth wall through which the audience views interior action.

Every type of literature makes use of generally accepted devices, but those of drama are more numerous. more imaginative, and more demanding of the viewer (or reader) than those of any other literary form.

dramatic illusion

An illusion is something that deceives by producing a false

impression. In psychological terms, an illusion is a perception (understanding, recognition) that represents what is perceived in a way different from the way it is in reality. A dramatic illusion refers to the conventions of plays (see DRAMATIC CONVENTION) that intentionally and necessarily present as real several persons, scenes, speeches, and acts that are actually illusory. When one witnesses a production of *Macbeth,* he sees it in a modern theater, but through a dramatic illusion he understands that the real setting is Scotland in the eleventh century. The audience at a production of a Shakespearean tragedy by dramatic illusion accepts a stage filled with dead and dying persons, but it knows that these dead persons will live and again die in other performances.

All literary illusions, including those of drama, involve something imagined; without them, literature would be impossible to create, understand, and enjoy. See ILLUSION.

dramatic irony
A condition in which the audience is made aware of information unknown to some of the actual characters in a play. This information may involve the real identity of a character, his true intentions, or the probable outcome of action; because the audience possesses knowledge which characters do not, it is able to measure words and deeds against a clear standard and understanding. A striking example of putting into a speaker's mouth words that have a different meaning for the audience occurs in *Macbeth* when the drunken porter jests about being the porter at the gate of Hell. In *Othello,* an *allusion to the villain as "honest Iago" is an instance of dramatic irony. In Sophocles's *Oedipus Rex,* Oedipus seeks throughout the play for the murderer of Laius, only to find that he himself is guilty. See IRONY.

dramatic monologue
A poetic form in which a single character, speaking to a silent auditor at a critical moment, reveals both a dramatic situation *and* himself. This kind of poem was brought to a high level of excellence by Robert Browning in such selections as *My Last Duchess* and *Soliloquy of the Spanish Cloister.* T. S. Eliot's *The Love Song of J. Alfred Prufrock* is a recent example of the dramatic monologue.

dramatic poetry
A term applied to poetry that employs dramatic form, such as

the *dramatic monologue. By extension, the term refers to plays written partly in verse and partly in prose (as were many of Shakespeare's productions) and to such poetic dramas as Shelley's *The Cenci* and Maxwell Anderson's *Winterset.* See CLOSET DRAMA.

dramatis personae

A Latin term ("masks of the drama") meaning "characters of the play." Frequently printed at the beginning of a published play or in the program for a live production is a list of characters with indications of their relationships.

dream vision

Also referred to as a "dream allegory," a dream vision is a device used in narrative verse that presents a story as though it were told by someone who falls asleep and dreams the events of the poem. This type of "vision literature" was especially popular during the Middle Ages. The term *dream allegory* is more exact when, as occurred frequently, physical struggles in the narrative involved moral and spiritual conflicts and when characters bore such names as Hypocrisy and Fear. *The Romance of the Rose* (thirteenth century), Dante's *Divine Comedy,* Chaucer's *The Book of the Duchess* (and other poems by Chaucer), and *Piers Plowman* are dream visions.

A dream allegory provides the framework (see FRAME STORY) for Bunyan's *Pilgrim's Progress* and Edward Bellamy's *Looking Backward.* In *Alice's Adventures in Wonderland,* Alice dreams about a world inside a rabbit hole. Joyce's *Finnegans Wake* is one long dream.

dumb show

(1) A scene enacted without words. Such performances were common in Elizabethan drama, where they were usually symbolic or allegorical interpretations of the main action of the play. (2) A *play-within-a-play presented partly in *pantomime, such as that appearing in *Hamlet,* act 3, scene 2.

duodecimo

A book size resulting when a sheet of paper is folded and cut so as to form twelve leaves (twenty-four pages). The term is derived from Latin *duodecim* ("twelve").

duologue

(1) A synonym for *dialogue, a conversation between two per-

sons. (2) A dramatic performance in the form of a dialogue limited to two speakers; a short scene with two actors only.

E

echo allusion

A form of *allusion (reference, mention) that varies a well-known saying. For example, Oscar Wilde wrote an echo allusion of Abraham Lincoln's famous utterance: " . . . but democracy means simply the bludgeoning of the people by the people for the people "

echo verse

Poetry (or, more likely, *doggerel) in which a line has its closing syllables echoed with a different meaning in the following line. These lines from Jonathan Swift's *A Gentle Echo on Woman* are illustrative:

Shepherd: Echo, I ween, will in the words reply,
　　　　　　　And quaintly answer questions: shall I try?
Echo: Try.
　　　　　What must we do our passion to express?
　　　　　Press.

eclogue

From a Greek word meaning "selection," *eclogue* refers to a *pastoral or *idyllic poem that praises country life. The best-known eclogue in English literature is Spenser's *The Shepheardes Calender*. W. H. Auden's *Age of Anxiety* and Robert Frost's *Build Soil* are examples of twentieth-century eclogues.

economy

In literature, *economy* refers to the efficient and sparing use of words to express ideas and emotions. *Economy* is a *synonym for conciseness and an antonym of verbosity. Such writers as Francis Bacon, Ralph Waldo Emerson, and Ernest Hemingway are noted for economy, whereas Henry Fielding, Charles Dickens, and Thomas Wolfe are not. In general, poetry is more likely to exhibit economy than prose is. In poetry, which consists of words in their best possible use, "each word must carry twenty other words upon its back."

edition

(1) The *format (shape and size) in which a literary work is published; (2) the whole number of impressions (copies) of a book, magazine, or newspaper printed from a set of type in one continuous run; (3) a version of any work (printed or not) that is publicly presented, as, for instance, the latest edition of a play or opera. *Edition,* from a Latin word meaning "to give out," is loosely and inexactly used in both publishing and general circles. If a new "printing" involves no changes in the text or illustrations, or only minor corrections, the result is not a new edition but an *impression.* A thorough revision resulting in a noticeably different version is a *new edition.* A *first edition is the book as it is (was) originally published.

editorializing

Setting forth a position or opinion on some subject; injecting personal interpretations or explanations into an otherwise objective, detached, or factual account. Literary artists obviously have attitudes, ideas, and points of view, but rarely are these now stated directly as pronouncements by the author. *Editorializing* does appear in numerous novels, essays, and poems of the eighteenth and nineteenth centuries, but the bulk of all literature of whatever period is designed to cause readers to form opinions and make inferences rather than tell them *what* to think or what authors believed. A standard rule implicit in the work of most writers is "Show, don't tell." *Editorializing* is prevalent in *essays and *articles of *persuasion and, of course, in newspaper editorials and columns.

editorial we

The plural pronoun *we* is often used by editors and other writers as a substitute for a repetitive *I*. The editorial *we*, a device well established in newspaper writing, occasionally appears in fiction and other forms of literature largely published prior to the twentieth century. More recent writers (and readers) consider this *convention both artificial and pretentious. See ENALLAGE.

Edwardian

An adjective applying to the reign of Edward VII of England, who ruled from 1901 to 1910. As a literary term, *Edwardian* is sometimes used to characterize the self-satisfaction of this period, or its extravagance and opulence. The Edwardian era was notable for the powerful reaction of its writers to the alleged propriety and conservatism of the *Victorian age. Distrust of authority and basic doubt concerning established principles of conduct and authority were hallmarks of the Edwardian period. It has been noted that, in this "English" era, the best poet writing in English may have been William Butler Yeats, an Irishman; the best dramatist, G. B. Shaw, another Irishman; and the best novelist, Joseph Conrad, an expatriated Pole.

effectiveness

A quality (or group of qualities) in writing which enables an author to produce effects and results intended or expected. (See CONTROLLING IMAGE, DOMINANT IMPRESSION.) The positive and even dynamic qualities which have the power to produce lasting effects include such diverse matters as insight, understanding, interest in and knowledge of human nature, technical skill, and, above all, powerful desire and ability to communicate directly, clearly, and imaginatively with and to the hearts and minds of readers.

ego, egoism

One's conscious self is one's ego; the word *ego* may also be defined as that trait or component of personality that most immediately and directly controls thoughts and behavior. That is, *ego* is the "I" or "self" of any person; *ego* is "a person" feeling, thinking, and distinguishing itself from the selves of others.

Ego can also mean "conceit" and "self-love," in which senses it is a *synonym for *egotism*. The ego and egotism of a writer like George Bernard Shaw were evidenced in his tendencies to make himself, his deeds and thoughts, the object of others' attention, interest, and conversation. Egoism also emphasizes concentration on oneself, implies self-interest, and is the opposite of altruism.

For many understandable reasons, most writers are egotists. All characters in literature who seek attention for themselves, who usually are scornful of others' interests and opinions, and who are generally self-assertive, self-important, and filled with self-esteem may be termed egotists, egoists, or persons with inflated egos.

Einfühlung

A German term which is an approximate *synonym for empathy (the projection of one's own feelings into an object, scene, or situation). (See EMPATHY, SYMPATHY.) In German, the word means "a feeling into." If, for instance, a reader actually "feels" like washing his hands along with Pontius Pilate or Lady Macbeth, he is experiencing Einfühlung.

elegant variation

A form of jargon; specifically, the practice of using different words and *metaphors as elaborate and artificial substitutes for a term being discussed. The coiner of the phrase, Sir Arthur Quiller-Couch, explains elegant variation in his *On the Art of Writing:*

> In an essay on Byron, Byron is (or ought to be) mentioned many times. But [the writer] has a blushing sense that to call Byron Byron twice on one page is indelicate. So Byron, after starting bravely as Byron, turns into "that great but unequal poet." [Later] he becomes "the gloomy master of Newstead"; overleaf he is reincarnated into "the meteoric darling of society"; and so proceeds through successive waters [forms, embodiments]—"this archrebel," "the author of *Childe Harold*," "the apostle of scorn," " . . . the martyr of Missolonghi," "the pageant-monger of a bleeding heart."

elegy (elegiac)

A mournful, melancholy poem, especially a funeral song or *lament for the dead. (See DIRGE, THRENODY.) Among well-known elegies are Gray's *Elegy Written in a Country Churchyard,* Shelley's *Adonais,* Tennyson's *In Memoriam,*

Milton's *Lycidas,* and Walt Whitman's *When Lilacs Last in the Dooryard Bloom'd.*

Elegiac, an adjective suggesting the expression of sorrow and regret, refers also to *meter. Elegiac meter consists of a line of dactylic *hexameter followed by one of *pentameter, as explained and illustrated in Coleridge's lines:

> In the hexameter rises the fountain's silvery column;
> In the pentameter aye falling in melody back.

The elegiac *quatrain in verse is iambic pentameter rhyming alternately, as in these lines from Gray's *Elegy:*

> Can storied urn or animated bust
> Back to its mansion call the fleeting breath?
> Can Honor's voice provoke the silent dust,
> Or Flattery soothe the dull cold ear of Death?

elision

From a Latin term meaning "a striking out," *elision* refers to the omission of a vowel at the end of one word when the next word begins with a vowel and also to the dropping of a vowel, consonant, or entire syllable in pronunciation. Elision may also involve the striking out of an entire passage. (See ABRIDGED, UNABRIDGED.) Elided words common in literature include *I'll, doesn't, th', ne'er, o'er, e'er.*

Elizabethan

In English history and literature, the name given to that part of the *Renaissance which occurred during the reign of Elizabeth I (1558–1603). It was an era of religious controversy, commercial growth, and nationalistic expansion during which *drama and *lyric poetry reached their highest levels.

ellipsis

(1) The omission of a word or words that a reader must supply for full understanding; (2) a mark (or marks) to indicate the omission or suppression of words, phrases, etc. The bracketed (nonappearing) word in these lines from Pope's *An Essay on Criticism* illustrates ellipsis:

> Authors are partial to their wit, 'tis true,
> But are not critics [partial] to their
>   judgment too?

The ellipsis periods shown in the quotation from Quiller-Couch under ELEGANT VARIATION are elliptical marks indicating the omission of words.

Elysium

In classical mythology, Elysium (or the Elysian fields) was the home of the blessed after death. In literature, *Elysium* refers to any place or state of perfect happiness, as suggested in these lines from Keats's *Lines on the Mermaid Tavern:*

> Souls of Poets dead and gone,
> What Elysium have ye known,
> Happy field or mossy cavern,
> Choicer than the Mermaid Tavern?

emblem

A sign, design, figure, or *symbol that identifies or represents something, such as the emblem of a society or organization. Spenser's *The Shepheardes Calender* shows the influence of emblems. The casket scene in Shakespeare's *The Merchant of Venice* is a form of emblem literature.

An emblem book is a collection of emblems in book form usually dealing with particular *themes. Such books contained pictures, the symbolic meaning of which was expressed in accompanying verse or prose.

emotive meaning

The emotion that a reader or listener associates with a word or phrase. An emotive meaning is one with an emotional *connotation of approval or disapproval. Literature is filled with emotive meanings because it is made up of language designed to excite emotion. See COGNITIVE MEANING, CONNOTATION, DENOTATION.

empathy

Identification with an object and sharing in its physical and emotional sensations. Empathy involves ascribing the feelings and attitudes present in oneself to the plight of characters in a literary work and the conditions of their lives. When a reader physically and emotionally feels hunger, cold, and misery as he reads of the overworked and half-starved central character in Dickens's *David Copperfield,* he is experiencing empathy. Keats revealed his empathic nature when he wrote that "if a Sparrow comes before my Window, I take part in its existence and pick about the gravel." Burns's poem *To a Mouse* ("Wee, sleekit, cow'rin', tim'rous beastie") is a poem built upon empathy. See EINFÜHLUNG, SYMPATHY.

emphasis

The stress laid upon, or the significance and importance attached to, a *character, *setting, or *theme. *Emphasis* refers to the intensity and force of expression with which a writer develops an idea, reveals a character, unfolds a plot, or stresses a concept. See CONTROLLING IMAGE, DOMINANT IMPRESSION, EFFECTIVENESS.

empiricism

The practice of drawing rules of behavior and practice not from theory but from experience; the doctrine that all knowledge is derived from the act of living. An empirical method of writing is "experimental," especially important in *naturalism and in certain *avant-garde approaches, such as *Theater of the Absurd. An empirical judgment of literature is considered "untrained," "without proper foundation."

enallage

The substitution of one grammatical form for another, such as the plural for the singular in *editorial we. The best-known example of enallage in literature occurs in Shakespeare's *Richard III:* "But me no buts."

encomium

An expression of praise; a poem or speech that pays tribute to someone. Encomium is a synonym for *eulogy. Encomiastic verse praises or glorifies people, ideas, or objects, as in these lines from Wordsworth's *Ode to Duty:*

> Stern Lawgiver! yet thou dost wear
> The Godhead's most benignant grace;
> Nor know we anything so fair
> As is the smile upon thy face.

end rhyme

*Rhyme that occurs at the end of verses (lines) of poetry. This duplication of similar sounds at the ends of lines is normally expected in English verse. See FEMININE RHYME, INTERNAL RHYME, RHYME.

end-stopped line

A line of poetry in which a grammatical pause (such as the end of a phrase or clause) coincides with the end of the line. Each of the twelve lines is end-stopped in Bradstreet's *To My Dear and Loving Husband,* which begins:

> If ever two were one, then surely we.
> If ever man were loved by wife, then thee;
> If ever wife was happy in a man,
> Compare with me ye women if you can.

See RUN-ON LINE.

English sonnet

Better known as the Shakespearean sonnet, an English sonnet is a fourteen-line poem with a *rhyme scheme of *abab, cdcd, efef, gg.* See SONNET, SHAKESPEAREAN SONNET.

enjambement

The running on of thought from one line, couplet (pair of lines), or *stanza to the next. Enjambement, a French term equivalent to "striding over," occurs with the use of *run-on lines. These lines from Milton's *Paradise Lost* illustrate enjambement:

> But see! the angry victor hath recalled
> His ministers of vengeance and pursuit
> Back to the gates of Heaven . . .

Enlightenment

Another term for the *Age of Reason, a philosophical movement of the seventeenth and eighteenth centuries which stressed the powers of human reason and was marked by political, religious, and educational unrest.

enthymeme

A *syllogism (argument) in which one *premise (proposition) is unexpressed. An enthymeme is illustrated in the statement "All men are mortal; therefore, Shakespeare was mortal." The omitted premise is "Shakespeare was a man."

entr'acte

(1) The interval between two acts of a theatrical or operatic performance or (2) the entertainment provided during this peiod. *Entr'acte,* a French term, also refers to a piece of music or a short *sketch prepared for use on such an occasion.

envoi

Also spelled *envoy,* an envoi is a postscript to a prose composition (see CODA) or a short *stanza concluding a poem. For an example of an envoi in verse, see BALLADE.

epic

A lengthy narrative poem in which action, characters, and language are on a heroic level and style is exalted and even majestic. Major characteristics of an epic are (1) a setting remote in time and place, (2) an objective, lofty, dignified style, (3) a simple plot, (4) a central incident (or series of incidents) dealing with legendary or traditional material, (5) a theme involving universal human problems, (6) a towering hero of great stature, (7) superhuman strength of body, character, or mind, (8) supernatural forces entering the *action. Among noted epics are the *Iliad* and the *Odyssey* by Homer; the Spanish *Cid; Beowulf;* Virgil's *Aeneid;* Dante's *Divine Comedy;* Milton's *Paradise Lost;* Longfellow's *Hiawatha;* Benét's *John Brown's Body.*

epic simile

A *simile (likeness, comparison) developed in a lengthy passage. As an elaborated comparison, an epic simile is longer, more detailed, and more ornate than a simple *metaphor. The object, image, or picture developed in an epic simile creates an impression that temporarily at least obscures the principal thread of the story. The epic simile, patterned after the elaborate *digressions appearing in Homer's work, is sometimes referred to as the *Homeric simile.

Epicurean

A term referring to the philosophy of Epicurus, a third-century-B.C. Greek thinker, who held that the highest good in life is pleasure, pleasure being broadly interpreted as freedom from pain or disturbance. Literature is called *Epicurean* when it emphasizes a search for pleasure as, for instance, in some of the works of Oscar Wilde and A. C. Swinburne. Epicureans actually avoided hedonism through their belief that pleasure derives from such qualities and traits as honesty, integrity, and prudence.

epigone

An undistinguished imitator or follower of an important literary artist. *Epigone* is from a Greek phrase meaning "born afterward." In a sense, every dramatist since Shakespeare has been something of an epigone, as every epic poet since John Milton has been.

epigram

A witty, ingenious, and pointed saying that is expressed tersely. (Originally, an epigram meant an inscription, or *epitaph.) Coleridge once defined an epigram as "A dwarfish whole, / Its body brevity, and wit its soul." Francis Bacon's remark "I would live to study and not study to live" is an epigram. See ADAGE, APHORISM, APOTHEGM.

epilogue

(1) A concluding part added to such a literary work as a novel, play, or long poem; (2) a speech to be delivered at the conclusion of a dramatic performance. An epilogue is related to the peroration (eloquent conclusion) of a speech and is contrasted with *prologue (introductory speech). See APPENDIX, CODA.

epiphany

Spelled with a capital letter, Epiphany is the name of a Christian festival, observed on January 6, commemorating the revelation of Jesus Christ to gentiles through the Wise Men (Magi). In literature, *epiphany* means an intuitive and sudden insight into the reality and basic meaning of an event; the term also refers to a literary work, or part of a work, that symbolically presents such a moment of perception and revelation. In this latter meaning, *epiphany* was used by James Joyce as a term for "a sudden spiritual manifestation," first revealed in his *Stephen Hero,* which was expanded into *Portrait of the Artist as a Young Man.*

episode

An incidental event or happening within a longer prose or verse narrative. An episode occasionally is a *digression but usually is a unified narrative passage integrated within the main plot.

episodic

An adjective which refers to a literary work made up of a number of thematically related but loosely connected scenes, incidents, or stories. Tennyson's *Idylls of the King* is episodic in structure, and so are many *double-decker novels, especially those of the eighteenth and nineteenth centuries.

epistle

A letter, especially a formal one characterized by *didacticism.

An epistle differs from an ordinary or conventional letter in that it is consciously literary and is deliberately planned for publication. The term *epistle* is applied to several books of the *Bible, to formal letters of dedication, and to published comments on political and religious matters.

epistolary
A term usually applied to a novel written in the form of a series of letters; also, epistolary friendships are prominent in literary history. The epistolary form of a novel allows the author to present several points of view without injecting himself into the narrative, but the structure seems awkward and unreal to many modern readers. The first epistolary novel in English was Richardson's *Pamela* (1740).

epitaph
A brief poem or other form of writing praising a deceased person; a commemorative inscription on a tomb or monument. Many writers, notably Dr. Johnson and John Milton, wrote dignified and moving tributes to the dead in the form of epitaphs, and Shakespeare possibly wrote an epitaph for his own tomb (see DOGGEREL). John Gay's grim self-epitaph on his tomb in Westminster Abbey is as follows:
> Life is a jest and all things show it.
> I thought so once, and now I know it.

epitasis
A term once used to designate the rising *action of a play, that part of a drama, following the protasis, in which the main action is developed. (For the position of epitasis in drama, see ACT, COMPLICATION.) The term applies to dramatic action in a play, novel, or short story that is in preparation for the *catastrophe.

epithalamion
A bridal song; a poem in honor of a bride and bridegroom. The best-known marriage hymn (song, poem) in English is Spenser's *Epithalamion.* The most famous epithalamion in world literature is the Biblical Song of Solomon (Song of Songs).

epithet
A word or phrase applied to a person or thing to show a quality or characteristic, such as the "Age of Reason," "William the Conqueror," and "Richard the Lionhearted." An epithet may involve abuse or contempt but is not necessarily a form of *in-

vective. Homer used many epithets, including "rosy-fingered dawn," "swift-footed Achilles," and "all-seeing Jove."

epitome
(1) A *summary or condensed statement, especially of a literary work. See ABRIDGMENT, ABSTRACT. (2) A representative of some greater subject, body, or quality that is typical of the whole, as in these lines from Dryden's *Absalom and Achitophel:*
> A man so various, that he seemed to be
> Not one, but all mankind's Epitome.

epode
From a Greek term meaning "additional song" or "after-song," *epode* means (1) a kind of lyric verse in which a long line (or stanza) is followed by a short one; (2) the *stanza sung by a Greek *chorus while standing still. See ANTISTROPHE, STROPHE.

eponym
The name of someone so commonly associated with a specific characteristic or quality that the name itself stands for the attribute. Eponyms include the following: Caesar for *dictator,* Marquis de Sade for *sadism,* Helen for *beauty,* Bluebeard for *woman killer,* Hercules for *great strength.* See PATRONYM.

equivoque
(1) A play on words; (2) an evasive answer that can be interpreted in more than one way. Equivoque is illustrated in a statement such as "Nothing is too good for this man." If an equivoque is deliberately misleading, it becomes *equivocation. See DOUBLE ENTENDRE.

Eros
The ancient Greek god of love, identified by the Romans and later peoples as Cupid. Spelled with a small letter, *eros* is a synonym for desire and sensuous love; in psychiatry, *eros* refers to the *libido.

eroticism
The sexual or amatory (lovemaking) quality or character of literature. *Eroticism* refers to the use of sexually arousing or suggestive *allusions, *settings, and *situations and to the condi-

tion of being sexually aroused or excited. Erotic literature ranges from the sentimental to the pornographic, but erotica (literature dealing with sexual love) deals with fleshly desire, attraction, and fulfillment. Shakespeare's *Hamlet, Romeo and Juliet,* and *Antony and Cleopatra* have a "love interest," but emphasis on sexual drive and desire varies in intensity in ascending order of their listing here.

Erziehungsroman

A synonym for *Bildungsroman, a novel about the formative years of the central character. *Roman,* a French word for "novel," is combined with German *Erziehung,* which means "upbringing." See KÜNSTLERROMAN.

escapism

The desire or tendency to avoid reality and to seek entertainment and release in fantasy or imaginative situations. The appeal of escapism is suggested in this comment from Sir Philip Sidney's *Defence of Poesy:* "He cometh unto you with a tale which holdeth children from play and old men from the chimney-corner." Escape literature enables the reader to forget or put aside his troubles and to live vicariously in another world. Although sometimes of inferior quality, television shows, detective and mystery stories, films, and radio programs provide diversion from the tediousness and the anxieties of daily living.

essay

A short literary *composition on a particular *theme or topic, usually in prose and generally thoughtful and interpretive. Because the term *essay* is applied loosely and widely, no fully acceptable definition is possible. Some essays are descriptive, narrative, or argumentative; some are whimsical, humorous, or satiric; some are biographical, critical, or historical; some are objective, some subjective.

One basic division is helpful: "formal" and "informal" compositions. See FAMILIAR ESSAY, FORMAL ESSAY, INFORMAL ESSAY, PERSONAL ESSAY.

Montaigne first used the word *essay* in 1580 for informal reflections on himself and mankind in general. Francis Bacon's *Essays* (1597) were written as "counsels for the successful conduct of life and the management of men." Since the seventeenth century, English essayists, such as Addison, Goldsmith, Lamb, Hazlitt, Steele, and Chesterton, have poured out prose compositions on various topics. Essayists of other countries, including the United States, have been no less prolific.

*Articles in magazines, editorials (see EDITORIALIZING), columns, *book reviews, and some forms of *criticism are also essays of a sort.

ethos

(1) The *moral* element in dramatic literature that determines a character's actions rather than his thought or emotion; (2) the character (principles, beliefs, traditions) of a person, group, community, or nation; (3) the major customs and practices of a society; (4) the fundamental spirit of a culture. Thus, for example, one speaks of the democratic ethos of the American people.

etiquette book

Another name for *courtesy book. *Etiquette* is a more apt word than *courtesy* to describe a book that deals with the conventional requirements of social behavior and the accepted codes of usage prevailing in polite society. By extension, Lord Chesterfield's *Letters to His Son* is a kind of etiquette (or courtesy) book, and so is much of Benjamin Franklin's *Autobiography,* a work undertaken to instruct the author's son about business, society, and ways of living.

etymology

(1) The study of the origins of words; (2) an account of the history of a particular word. *Etymology,* derived from Greek terms meaning "true sense" and "word," is simply defined as a study of historical linguistic changes in words. See FOLK ETYMOLOGY.

eulogy

A formal *composition or speech in praise of someone, especially an *oration in honor of a deceased person. *Eulogy* also means "high praise" and is a *synonym for *encomium. Related terms are *dirge, elegy, monody, panegyric,* and *threnody.* One of the best-known eulogies in literature is Mark Antony's "funeral oration" for Brutus as it appears in Shakespeare's *Julius Caesar:*

> This was the noblest Roman of them all.
> All the conspirators, save only he,
> Did that they did in envy of great Caesar;

He only, in a general honest thought
And common good to all, made one of them.
His life was gentle, and the elements
So mix'd in him that Nature might stand up
And say to all the world, "This was a man!"

euphemism

The use of an indirect, mild, or vague word or expression
for one thought to be coarse, offensive, or blunt. *Euphe-mism* is from a Greek phrase meaning "the use of words of
good repute or omen." In recent years, effective writers
who mean "prison" are likely to say so and not "correction-al institution." If they mean "dead," they will not likely
write "deceased" or "the late." Euphemisms are usually
vague and wordy, as is evident in this comment by Eliza-beth Barrett Browning on the insanity of a fellow poet:
"Discord fell on the music of his soul; the sweet sounds and
wandering lights departed from him." See PARRHESIA.

euphony

A pleasant-sounding, harmonious combination of sounds. *Eu-phony*, from a Greek word meaning "sweet-voiced," is an
antonym of *cacophony. All good poetry is euphonious
except when an author deliberately strives to achieve a
harsh, strident effect. The following lines from Tennyson's
Lotus-Eaters have a pleasing sound:
There is sweet music here that softer falls
Than petals from blown roses on the grass,
Or night-dews on still waters between walls
Of shadowy granite, in a gleaming pass...
And in the stream the long-leaved flowers weep,
And from the craggy ledge the poppy hangs in
sleep.

Euphuism

An affected and artificial style of writing or speaking which
flourished during the sixteenth centry. Euphuism takes its
name from John Lyly's *Euphues*, which was designed to reveal
how elegant and polished English prose could be. The principal
characteristics of euphuism are excessive use of *alliteration,
*antithesis, *allusions to mythological and real persons, and
*conceits. See BAROQUE, FINE WRITING, PRECIOSITY, PURPLE
PROSE.

ex cathedra

A Latin phrase that means "from the chair." The term is used to mean "with authority" and "from the seat, or source, of authority." A papal *bull, for instance, is an ex cathedra statement.

excursus

A detailed discussion of some point in a book, especially such a statement appearing as an *appendix. An excursus is usually considered a formal, lengthy *digression from a principal theme or narrative account. A lengthy explanatory *footnote, which frequently appears in a work of history or *biography, is an excursus.

exegesis

Critical interpretation and explanation of a literary work. *Exegesis* is usually applied to an analysis of an unusually difficult passage in poetry or prose; the term refers especially to interpretations and explanations of selections from the *Bible. See EXPLICATION.

exemplum

A Latin word meaning "example," *exemplum* is used in English to apply to an anecdote that illustrates or supports a moral issue or that teaches a lesson of some sort. An example of such a moralized tale is Chaucer's *The Pardoner's Tale,* a kind of narrative sermon intended to prove that the love of money is the root of all evil. See ANECDOTE, DIDACTICISM, FABLE, INCIDENT.

existentialism

The belief that man forms his essence, his essential being, in the course and pattern of the life he elects to lead. *Existentialism* is a loose term with several meanings, but it is normally applied to writing that emphasizes man's responsibility for forming his own nature and that stresses the prime importance of personal decisions, personal freedom, and personal goals. The doctrine of existentialism holds that man is completely responsible for himself because he has a free will to do exactly as he pleases. If man follows social, political, or moral conventions and refuses to make his own decisions and choices, existentialists claim that he is contemptible.

Existentialism had its beginnings in the work of a Danish

theologian, Søren Kierkegaard, in the nineteenth century, but it owes its greatest popularity and influence to the French novelist-philosopher Jean-Paul Sartre, who declared that "man is alone in a godless universe." Sartre and his post–World War II followers insist that the universe is meaningless, a concept that produces anxiety, loneliness, acute discomfort, and despair.

Sartre's existentialism, like that of Albert Camus, Simone de Beauvoir, Samuel Beckett, and Franz Kafka, among others, is largely atheistic, but a form of Christian existentialism which holds that possibilities for altering human nature and society are great has been set forth by such writers as Jacques Maritain, Paul Tillich, and Gabriel Marcel. Both groups of existentialists are (1) concerned with man's essential being and nature, (2) convinced that thought and reason are insufficient to understand and cope with the mysteries of living, (3) conscious that anguish and despair are the common lot of everyone, and (4) fixed in the belief that a sense of morality depends upon positive and active participation in life.

exordium

The beginning of anything. In literature, *exordium* refers to the introductory part of an essay, formal article, or speech. See INVOCATION, PRELUDE.

explication

Explanation, interpretation; the act of making meaning clear and plain. *Explication* appears in the phrase *explication de texte* ("explanation of text"), an approach to literary *criticism involving close and detailed study, analysis, and *exposition of the text of a selection. In such explication, a critic concentrates on language, style, and the interrelations of parts to the whole so as to make plain the meaning and *symbolism of the text.

exposition

In writing, exposition is that *form of discourse that explains, defines, and interprets. It embraces all *composition, both oral and written, that does not primarily describe an object (*description), tell a story (*narration), or maintain a position (*argumentation). *Exposition* is also applied to the beginning portion of a *plot in which background information is set forth. For example, Shakespeare provides details about characters and situation at the beginning of each of his plays, notably *Henry V, Richard III, Romeo and Juliet,* and *Othello.*

Magazine articles, editorials, and essays usually consist almost wholly of exposition; plays, novels, short stories, and a considerable quantity of poetry contain some exposition along with other more dominant elements of discourse.

expressionism

A term with several meanings variously applied to different forms of artistic work, *expressionism* is impossible to define exactly and succinctly. In the so-called fine arts (painting, sculpture, etc.) it involves techniques in which forms derived from nature are exaggerated or distorted and in which colors are intensified to express emotion. In drama, *expressionism* applies to a style of playwriting and production emphasizing emotional content, the subjective reactions of characters, and symbolic or abstract representations of reality. In novels and short stories, *expressionism* involves the presentation of an objective outer world through the intensified impressions and moods of characters. In poetry, the movement is evidenced by distortions of objects and by dislocations of generally accepted ideas of time and space.

In brief (but not with total accuracy), expressionism in modern literature can be referred to as any deliberate distortion of reality. The following selections are notable for expressionistic tendencies and techniques: Strindberg's *Dream Play;* Eugene O'Neill's *The Emperor Jones;* Tennessee Williams's *The Glass Menagerie;* James Joyce's *Ulysses* and *Finnegans Wake;* T. S. Eliot's *The Waste Land.* See ANGST, IMPRESSIONISM, REALISM, THEATER OF THE ABSURD.

extraneous

An adjective meaning "irrelevant," "not pertinent or applicable," "unneeded and unnecessary." *Extraneous* applies to material in literary selections that appears to be "introduced from without" and that does not fit properly into the principal *theme, *conflict, or *setting of the selection itself. A *digression is often extraneous, but in well-constructed literary works, nothing that does not contribute to the author's purpose and the hoped-for *dominant impression of the reader is allowed to intrude. Edgar Allan Poe once wrote:

> A skillful literary artist has constructed a tale. If wise, he has not fashioned his thoughts to accommodate his

incidents; but having conceived, with deliberate care, a certain unique or single *effect* to be wrought out, he then invents such incidents—he then combines such events as may best aid him in establishing this preconceived effect. If his very initial sentence tend not to the outbringing of this effect, then he has failed in his first step. In the whole composition there should be no word written, of which the tendency, direct or indirect, is not to the one pre-established design.

extrasensory

An adjective meaning "not perceptible by the normal senses," "supernatural." An extrasensory perception is something "felt" or "sensed" by intuition rather than through sight, sound, hearing, etc. Effective writers try to "show" what they mean, but they and the characters whom they develop rely constantly on inner feelings and emotions directly traceable to what they receive through extraordinary insights. See AFFLATUS.

extravaganza

In the nineteenth century, *extravaganza* was applied to the elaborate production of any fanciful subject, especially a fairy tale, employing song and dance. Currently, an extravaganza is a dramatic or musical composition (such as comic opera or a musical comedy) notable for its light theme, loose structure, and elaborate costuming and staging. See BURLESQUE, CARICATURE, MUSICAL COMEDY.

eye rhyme

Also called sight rhyme, eye rhyme is a form of agreement apparent in spelling but not in sound. Examples of eye rhyme (half rhyme, *slant rhyme) are *love* and *move; have* and *grave; watch* and *patch; bead* and *bread.*

F

fable

A short, simple story, usually with animals as characters, designed to teach a moral truth. (See ALLEGORY, APOLOGUE, BESTIARY, PARABLE.) Fables with animals as principal characters are sometimes called beast fables, such as Kipling's *Jungle Books* and *Just So Stories,* Joel Chandler Harris's stories from Uncle Remus, and George Orwell's *Animal Farm. Fable* is also occasionally applied to stories about supernatural persons, to accounts of extraordinary events, to legends and myths generally, and to outright falsehoods.

fabliau

A sort of smoking-room story, popular with medieval French and English poets. A fabliau, always humorous and frequently ribald, conventionally was told in eight-syllable verse that satirized the faults of clergymen and women. Fabliaux are less serious than fables but do present moral lessons through bawdy situations. Chaucer's *Canterbury Tales* includes several fabliaux: stories by the Friar, the Miller, the Reeve, the Cook, the Manciple, etc.

facsimile

An exact copy of a book, manuscript, or painting. *Facsimile,* a synonym for *replica* and *reproduction,* is related to *ver-batim. Facsimile* also applies to the transmission of printed and visual materials by radio and telegraph.

fairy tale

A story about elves, dragons, sprites, hobgoblins, and other magical creatures. These supernatural "spirits" are usually represented as having mischievous temperaments, unusual wisdom, and power to regulate the affairs of man in whatever fashion they choose. The most famous writers or compilers of fairy tales were the Grimm brothers (Germany) and Hans Christian Andersen (Denmark). The term *fairy tale* is also applied to a misleading or incredible account, belief, or statement.

fallacy

From a Latin word meaning "to deceive," *fallacy* names a false or misleading notion, belief, or argument. In logic, a fallacy is any of various kinds of erroneous reasoning that make arguments unsound. Literature is peopled with characters who entertain fallacious ideas that lead to comic or tragic situations. For example, both Don Quixote and Othello were ruled by fallacies, with vastly different outcomes. See DEDUCTION, INDUCTION, LOGIC, PATHETIC FALLACY, SYLLOGISM.

falling action

The part of a play that follows the *climax (the moment of highest and most intense interest). Falling action is equivalent to the *resolution or *denouement of a drama, which leads to the *catastrophe. See ACT, ACTION.

familiar essay

A term applied to the more intimate and subjective kind of *personal essay. (See ESSAY.) A familiar essay is light in manner and tone, often humorous, occasionally whimsical, and always deft and polished in its approach to personal experiences, problems, and prejudices. Among noted familiar essayists may be mentioned Oliver Goldsmith, Charles Lamb, Robert Louis Stevenson, and E. B. White.

fancy

This word is often considered a synonym for *imagination,* the forming of mental images of what is not actually present in the senses. In modern literary criticism, however, imagination is considered "creative" and "organic," whereas fancy is considered "logical," "mechanic," or "factitious." This distinction was first noted by Coleridge in his *Biographia Literaria:*

> The *fancy* brings together images which have no connection natural or moral, but are yoked together by the poet by means of some accidental coincidence.

Fancy also has a meaning of superficial love or liking for something attractive, as is suggested by a song from Shakespeare's *The Merchant of Venice:* "Tell me where is fancy bred. / Or in the heart or in the head?"

fantasy

Extravagant and unrestrained imagination; the forming of weird or grotesque mental *images. *Fantasy* is applied to a literary work the action of which occurs in a nonexistent and unreal world (such as fairyland) and to a selection that involves incredible characters (as Maeterlinck's *The Blue Bird* does). *Science fiction and *utopian stories are forms of fantasy.

farce

A farce is (1) a foolish show, a ridiculous sham; (2) a light, humorous *play in which the *plot depends upon a carefully exploited situation rather than upon character development. A farce is usually considered to be a boisterous *comedy involving ludicrous *action and *dialogue. Farce is a mainstay of many television and motion-picture comedians, but farcical scenes occur in such well-wrought plays as *The Taming of the Shrew, Twelfth Night,* and *A Midsummer Night's Dream.*

fatalism

(1) Acceptance of all things and events as inevitable; submission to *fate; (2) the philosophical doctrine that all happenings are the result of predestination. The lives of major characters in nearly all of Thomas Hardy's works (*The Return of the Native, Jude the Obscure,* etc.) are ruled and regulated by both meanings of *fatalism* cited here.

fate

A word meaning "destiny," "fortune," "lot." Although often used lightly, *fate* emphasizes the irrationality and impersonal (cold) character of events. Approximate synonyms for *fate* occasionally appearing in literature include *karma, kismet, chance,* and *luck.*

"The three Fates" and "the cruel Fates" are phrases also appearing in literary works. Ancient Greeks and Romans believed that these Fates controlled the birth, life, and death of everyone: Clotho (who held the distaff), Lachesis (who spun the thread of life), and Atropos (who cut the thread when life was ended).

feminine ending

An unaccented syllable at the end of a line of poetry. In the following line from Shakespeare's *The Merchant of Venice,* the *-ats* of *ducats* constitutes an unstressed eleventh syllable in a line of iambic pentameter:

And Í / bĕ pléased / tŏ gíve /
tĕn thóus/ănd dúcăts.

feminine rhyme

A rhyme extending over two or more syllables. Feminine rhyme is "double" if it includes two syllables, "triple" if it includes three. In a humorous poem by John Millington Synge, feminine two-syllable rhymes include *sister* and *blister, liver* and *give her.* A three-syllable rhyme is illustrated by *hampering* and *pampering.* See DOUBLE RHYME, MASCULINE ENDING.

Festschrift

A term composed of two German words meaning "feast" or "festival" and "a writing." A Festschrift is a volume of *essays, *articles, and *sketches contributed by several authors in honor of someone, usually a colleague or friend, and published on the occasion of an important occurrence, such as the retirement of the person being honored.

fetishism

Belief in, or use of, some object regarded with awe as being the embodiment or residing place of a powerful spirit or force. The magical and ecstatic rites associated with voodooism, for instance, are a form of fetishism. In psychiatry, the term refers to a compulsive use of some object or part of the body as a stimulus in the act of attaining sexual pleasure (a lock of hair, a shoe, underclothing, one's feet, etc.). In literature, a fetish is any idea or object that calls forth unqualified respect, reverence, or devotion; for example, feudal knights made a fetish of duty and loyalty to their leader.

feudalism

The social and economic system prevailing in Western Europe during a large part of the *medieval period. The entire system was based upon force, with every landholder the tenant and servant of some greater landlord. As rent, various groups (barons, knights, etc.) paid to their superiors "service" which consisted of military aid, or actual property, or both. Socially, two principal groups existed: (1) knights, higher clergy, lords and (2) free renters, serfs, peasants.

Feudalism, which broke down in the fifteenth century, was primarily responsible for the ideals of *chivalry and was powerfully influential in medieval *romances and romantic *epics. An exceptionally clear picture of the social, ecclesiastical, and political order of feudalism is revealed in Chaucer's *The Canterbury Tales.*

fiction

From a Latin word meaning "to make," "to mold," fiction is imagined and invented literary *composition. Fiction may or may not be based on history and fact, but its distinguishing characteristic is that it is fashioned to entertain and, somewhat secondarily, to instruct. Effective fiction makes readers *think,* but the primary purpose of all fiction, effective or ineffective, is to make readers *feel.* The term is usually applied to *novels and *short stories, but *drama, the *epic, *fables, *fairy tales, *folklore, and *parables contain fictional elements. *Nonfiction includes *autobiography, *biography, the *essay, and history, but, as currently written, these types frequently contain strong fictional components. See NARRATION.

figurative, literal

These words, often confused, have directly opposite meanings. *Figurative* means "not literal," that is, metaphorical, ornate, rhetorical, and based on or making use of *figures of speech. *Literal* means "true to fact," "actual," "not exaggerated," "in accordance with strict meaning." See CONNOTATION, DENOTATION.

figurative language

Deliberate and intentional departure from normal word meanings or word order so as to gain freshness and strength of expression. Figurative language is writing (or speech) that makes use of one or more figures of speech, such as *metaphors and *similes. The basic purposes of figurative language are to employ ornamental devices for comparing dissimilar things and for creating sounds and *images. See CONNOTATION, DENOTATION, FIGURES OF SPEECH.

figures of speech

Expressive uses of language in which words are used in other than their literal senses so as to suggest and produce pictures or *images in a reader's (hearer's) mind. Figures of speech may be divided into three classes: (1) *imagined similarities,* such as those in an *allegory, *allusion, *conceit, *simile; (2) *suggestive associations* in which one word is linked with another as, for example, *golden* with *youth, happiness,* and *wealth:* *hypallage, *hyperbole, *metonymy, and *synecdoche; (3) *appeals to the ear and eye,* as in *alliteration, *anacoluthon, and *onomatopoeia.

Figures of speech may also be grouped into (1) "figures of thought" in which words retain their meanings but not their rhetorical patterns, as in an *apostrophe, and (2) *tropes, in which words undergo a definite change in meaning, as in a *metaphor.

Another useful classification of figures of speech is (1) those that actually involve a comparison (*analogy, *personification, *trope) and (2) those that do not normally compare anything (*hyperbole, *litotes, *irony).

fin de siècle

A French expression meaning "end of the century." The term is generally used to mean a period free from social and political conventions and traditions, a meaning derived from the transitional era of the 1890s, when writers were trying to escape the "bonds" of Victorianism. (See VICTORIAN.) Because the artistic temper of this period was confused, fin de siècle now has such opposed meanings as "decadent" and "up-to-date." See DECADENCE, EDWARDIAN.

fine arts

Visual arts such as architecture, painting, sculpture, watercolor, and ceramics. The fine arts are those created with concern for aesthetic values rather than utility (the practical arts, useful arts). Every fine art is subject to judgments concerning its beauty and meaningfulness.

fine writing

Composition which is mistakenly thought to be free from all impurities because it has been polished to perfection. Actually, fine writing is affected and overcareful as a result of the use of pompous and polysyllabic words, *euphemisms, etc. See AFFECTATION, EUPHUISM, RHETORIC.

first edition

(1) The whole number of copies of a literary work printed first, from the same *type, and issued (published) together; (2) an individual copy of a work from this number; (3) the first printing of a newspaper for a given date. See EDITION.

five-act formula

A term applied to the custom of writing plays in five acts of approximately equal length and playing time. In the nineteenth century, a German novelist and journalist, Gustav Freytag, described the structure of a five-act play as a pyramid, with action rising and falling as suggested under the entry ACT.

flashback

A scene inserted into a *play, *novel, or *short story representing an earlier event. A flashback is a narrative device that flashes back to the presentation of an incident that occurred prior to the opening scene of a literary work. Such a flashback may be developed through a reverie, a recollection by a character, a dream sequence, or dialogue. Nearly all of Edna Ferber's *Ice Palace* consists of a flashback; Arthur Miller's *Death of a Salesman,* Thornton Wilder's *The Bridge of San Luis Rey,* the film *Citizen Kane,* and Somerset Maugham's *Cakes and Ale* make extensive use of flashbacks. See IN MEDIAS RES.

flat character

A term coined by E. M. Forster (in *Aspects of the Novel,* 1927) to designate a person who appears in a literary work as little more than a name or as someone who is presented with a single trait. A flat character is not fully developed, lacks complexity, never surprises the reader by what he does or says, and may be referred to as a *type or *caricature. Conversely, a *round character has depth, complexity, full development, and is capable of convincingly surprising the reader time and again. All great works of literature that present characters at all contain both flat and round characters, just as life itself does. Macbeth is a round character; King Duncan is a flat character. See FOIL.

focus

A central point of attention, activity, or attraction. In every literary work, the author selects an individual, a group, a situation, or an idea and directs his and the reader's attention to it. In a short story, focus is usually not shifted from one person or situation, but in a novel, play, or long narrative poem, the center of attention may be altered many times. See CONTROLLING IMAGE, DOMINANT IMPRESSION, THEME.

foil

A person or thing that, by contrast, makes another seem better or more prominent. Using one character as a foil to another brings out the qualities of both. For example, the Fool is a foil in *King Lear;* Hotspur and even Falstaff are foils to Prince Hal in *Henry IV.* Several dozen princes, princesses, and counts are foils in Tolstoi's *War and Peace.* See FLAT CHARACTER.

folio

A term with several meanings, the most common of which is that of a book with a large *format, one having pages more than 30 centimeters (about 12 inches) in height. *Folio* also means (1) a sheet of paper folded once to make two leaves (four pages) of a book; (2) a page number of a book.

Shakespeare's plays were first collected and published in 1623 in a folio edition, so called because of the size of the pages of the volume.

folk ballad

An anonymous storytelling poem handed down orally from generation to generation. See BALLAD, POPULAR BALLAD.

folk drama

In a general sense, folk drama consists of dramatic activities of the folk (the so-called common people), in popular festivals and religious rites. In medieval England, the meaning of the term was widened to include plays about such popular folk heroes as Saint George and Robin Hood. The term *folk drama* now refers to plays written by dramatists on folk themes that reveal the attitudes, problems, language, and customs of "everyday" people rather than those of high estate. Much of the drama of the Irish literary movement—plays by Lady Gregory, J. M. Synge, and others—belongs in this classification, and so do the "peasant plays" of Pirandello as well as plays by such American writers as Paul Green that reflect the lives of mountain people and Negroes.

folk epic
A composition by an unknown author, or authors; a selection assumed to be the work of a group of unknown persons. A folk epic, synonymous with popular epic, grew out of early national history, was founded on primitive beliefs, and focused attention on a noble hero. See ART EPIC, EPIC, LITERARY EPIC.

folk etymology
A fanciful explanation for the origin and derivation of words. Folk etymology consists of false or unlearned modification of words (*Welsh rarebit* from *Welsh rabbit*) and of irrelevant *analogy (*bridegroom* from *bridegome*). See ETYMOLOGY.

folklore
The long-standing and traditional beliefs, legends, and customs of a people. *Folklore,* derived from *Anglo-Saxon *folc* ("people") and *lar* ("learning"), once embraced only orally transmitted materials but now includes written accounts of traditions, literature, craftsmanship, and folk habits. Much folklore is contained in *ballads, *beast epics, *fairy tales, *maxims, *myths, old wives' tales, and riddles. In the United States, folklore covers such diverse items as *Amerind materials, work songs, chanteys, Negro spirituals, and *tall tales.

folktale
A legend or narrative originating in, and traditional among, a people, especially one forming part of an oral *tradition. The term covers a wide range of materials from outright *myths to *fairy tales. *The Thousand and One Nights* is a famous collection of folktales. Some of the stories about Paul Bunyan, Davy Crockett, Pocahontas, Johnny Appleseed, and Daniel Boone are folktales.

fool
A silly or stupid person. In *drama, a fool is a court jester, a professional clown who sometimes hides wit and under-

standing beneath a cloak of foolishness. In some literary works, like *Twelfth Night* and *King Lear,* the simplicity of such a *stock character causes his remarks to clarify and deepen the underlying meanings of events. Wherever a fool appears in literature, his basic role is that of a *foil.

foot

A group of syllables constituting a metrical unit of verse, a set pattern of stressed and unstressed sounds. In English, a foot most often consists of accented and unaccented syllables in one of five principal groupings:

1. The *iambic* foot (or *iamb*) consists of an unstressed syllable followed by a stressed (long) syllable: *today, about, repeat.* Most English verse falls into an iambic pattern.

2. The *trochaic* foot (*trochee*) consists of a stressed syllable followed by an unstressed (short) syllable: *meter, pleasant, daily.*

3. The *anapestic* foot (*anapest*) consists of two unstressed syllables followed by a stressed syllable: *intercede, for the nonce.*

4. The *dactylic* foot (*dactyl*) consists of a stressed syllable followed by two unstressed syllables: *silvery, national, penitent.*

5. The *spondaic* foot (*spondee*) consists of two stressed syllables: *thirteen, deadbeat.*

These lines from Coleridge are illustrative:

Trōchĕe / trĭps frŏm / lōng tŏ / shōrt;
From long to long in solemn sort
Slōw Spōn/deē staĺks; / strōng foōt! /
   yēt iĺ / ăblē
Evĕr tŏ / cōme ŭp wĭth / Dāctyĺ trī/syllăblĕ.
Ĭam̄/bĭcs mārch / frŏm shōrt / tŏ lōng;
Wĭth ă leāp / ănd ă boūnd /
   thĕ swĭft Ăn/ăpaĕsts thrōng.

For comment on less common kinds of feet, see AMPHI-BRACH, AMPHIMACER, ANTIBACCHIUS, BACCHIC, PYRRHIC.

footnote

An explanatory or proof-citing note or comment referring to a specific part of the main text of a work. A footnote, so-called because it is normally placed at the bottom (foot) of a page, is usually indicated in the text by a superior number. By extension, *footnote* refers to any minor but related comment upon, or afterthought to, a main statement. See DOCUMENTATION, SOURCE.

foreshadowing

Showing, indicating, or suggesting beforehand. In a literary work, foreshadowing provides a hint of what is to occur later. For instance, the early appearance, conversation, and actions of the three witches in *Macbeth* foreshadow the *atmosphere of danger and gloom that runs throughout the play. See NARRATIVE HOOK, PROLEPSIS.

foreword

Introductory remarks in a book, article, or other type of *composition. *Foreword* is synonymous with *preface* in that both provide comments upon, or explanations of, what is to follow and both are usually less formal in tone than the following text. *Foreword* is a less learned word than preface, *prologue, and prolegomenon, but each of these terms names introductory remarks designed to put a reader into a proper frame of mind for understanding and appreciating the work he is about to read. Also see EXORDIUM, PREAMBLE.

form

The manner and style of arranging and coordinating the parts of a *composition, the structural pattern of a work of art. *Verse form* applies to the organization of rhythmic units in a line; *stanza form* applies to the organization of verses in a poem; *novel form* applies to the arrangement of *incidents and *episodes in chapters or other divisions, etc.

In literature, such expressions as *ballad form, elegy form, short-story form,* and the like apply to categories called *genres.

Form is more than an external scheme imposed upon subject matter; it should be considered the entire structural integration of expression and thought. The form of a successful literary work is shaped from within more than it is imposed from without. As a result, in genuine works of literature shape (form) and substance are one. See GENRE, STRUCTURE, STYLE.

formal essay

A serious, carefully organized, logically developed *composition designed to inform or persuade. See ESSAY.

format

The general physical appearance and makeup of a book, magazine, or newspaper: shape, size, typeface, binding, quality of paper, margins, bulk, etc. *Format* has been extended in meaning to refer to the organization, type, style, or plan of such diverse items as buildings, meetings, business operations, and social activities.

formula

In literature, *formula* means a fixed and conventional method of developing a *plot. A stereotyped plot pattern appears in many motion pictures, television plays, *Western stories, and *slick magazines. Well-known formulas (formulae) include the "redemption" theme (a dissolute or wayward person recovers his manhood); the Cinderella story (a poor, virtuous girl wins her man from a rich, predatory rival); the "country bumpkin" plot (an unsophisticated person defeats a "city slicker" rival), etc.

In a sense, all literary selections follow a formula of some sort, but genuine literature does not do so slavishly and always exhibits qualities and ingredients that transcend hackneyed situations and stereotyped action and characterization.

fourteener

A verse form, especially an *iambic line, consisting of fourteen syllables. George Chapman's translation of the *Iliad* (which inspired Keats's *On First Looking into Chapman's Homer*) was written in this meter. See HEPTAMETER, SEPTENARY.

frame story

A story within a narrative setting, or frame. (See STORY-WITHIN-A-STORY.) The *convention of using a framework for separate narratives has been employed for many centuries. Certain stories in *The Thousand and One Nights* interrupt other stories being related. Boccaccio's *The Decameron* is a collection of 100 tales developed on a central framework. The general setting of Chaucer's *The Canterbury Tales* is a frame; stories the pilgrims tell along the way are frame stories.

free verse
Verse that lacks regular meter and line length but relies upon natural rhythms. Free verse is "free" from fixed metrical patterns but does reveal the *cadences that result from alternation of stressed and unstressed syllables. Some writers and critics contend that free verse by its very irregularity provides added force to thought and expression. Conversely, Robert Frost once remarked, "Writing free verse is like playing tennis with the net down." For further discussion, see VERS LIBRE.

Freudianism
The doctrines and psychoanalytic theories of Sigmund Freud (1856–1939), an Austrian physician (neurologist), with regard to the diagnosis and treatment of neurotic and psychopathic states, the interpretation of dreams, etc. The influences upon literature of Freud's exploration of the subconscious and his emphasis on the sex drive of human beings have been profound and long-lasting. A Freudian writer searches for *symbols in his characters' dreams, speech, and actions. Such a follower of Freudianism is concerned with developing the *libido, repressed anxieties, and inmost thoughts of characters. Strong elements of Freudianism appear in James Joyce's *Ulysses* and *Finnegans Wake,* in several of the plays of Eugene O'Neill, Tennessee Williams, and Edward Albee, and in much of the work of William Faulkner. See JUNGIAN, SURREALISM.

fundamental image
A central figure or object around which a literary work is organized. When a writer singles out an aspect or feature of an object or idea being described or discussed, he develops a fundamental image intended to reduce a possibly complex whole to a unifying base. In describing the Battle of Waterloo, Victor Hugo used the shape of the letter A to explain the positions of opposing armies. Another fundamental image is illustrated in this paragraph from Thomas Hardy's *The Dynasts:*

> The nether sky opens, and Europe is disclosed as a prone and emaciated figure, the Alps shaping like a backbone, and the branching mountain chains like ribs, the peninsular plateau of Spain forming a head. Broad

and lengthy lowlands stretch from the north of France across Russia like a grey-green garment hemmed by the Ural Mountains and the glistening Arctic Ocean. See CONTROLLING IMAGE, DOMINANT IMPRESSION.

fustian

(1) A stout fabric of cotton and flax; (2) inflated, exaggerated, turgid language. Although fustian is mentioned often as wearing apparel in Thomas Hardy's Wessex novels, the term is most often applied in literature in its second sense of *bombast and ranting language. These lines appear in Pope's *Epistle to Dr. Arbuthnot:*

Means not, but blunders round about a meaning;
And he whose fustian's so sublimely bad,
It is not poetry, but prose run mad.

Gallicism

A French expression or *idiom used in another language. A statement such as *je ne sais quoi* ("I don't know what") employed in English to mean "an indefinable, elusive, or pleasing quality" is a Gallicism. The term, which also applies to any French linguistic characteristic or pecularity, is derived from Gaul, an ancient name for France.

gasconade

Boastful talk, extravagant bluster. *Gasconade* is derived from Gascony, a former province in France, the natives of which were considered boasters and braggarts. Vainglorious *fiction and *cloak-and-dagger literature often contain gasconade. See MILES GLORIOSUS.

general semantics

A systematic study of the relations between words and people's actions, of the connections between words (as symbols) and human behavior. (See SEMANTICS, WORD.) General semantics is concerned with word meanings in more than their "dictionary sense"; it involves several kinds of verbal and nonverbal meanings and the importance of those meanings in private lives and public affairs.

General semanticists claim that the meanings of words reside in the person who uses them or responds to them. For example, a student of general semantics has suggested that one cannot find in a dictionary the meaning of a particular sunset;

that the true meaning of *sunset* lies in oneself, in one's thoughts and feelings, in what one says, thinks, and does about a sunset. That is, general semantics asserts that the true meanings of words are no more in the words themselves than the meaning of an elm tree is in an elm. The thoughts and images of many poets and novelists reflect this concept of word meanings. For example, a literary artist, instead of a general semanticist (the late Wendell Johnson), might have written that the meanings of *a green meadow* are "the children who chase butterflies across it, the artist who paints it, the cows which graze upon it, or the old soldier who remembers the battle that once was fought across its green slopes."

genre

A category or class of artistic endeavor having a particular form, technique, or content. *Genre,* a word from French, is a synonym for *type* and *kind.* Among genres in literature are included the *novel, the *short story, the *essay, the *epic, etc. The term *genre* is somewhat loose and general; for instance, *poetry* suggests a genre, but so do *lyric, *pastoral, *ode, *elegy, and *sonnet.

In painting, *genre* is applied to works that deal with everyday life in realistic techniques. See FORM, TYPE.

genteelism

From a Latin word meaning "well-bred" and a French word meaning "elegant," *genteelism* is applied to literary works notable for their polished style and graceful form. In current literary criticism, *genteelism* is often used with mocking or scornful reference to what are considered false standards of refinement. (See AFFECTATION.) The term can be a synonym for *euphemism, as illustrated in the use of *limb* for *leg* and *serviette* for *napkin.* The phrase *genteel tradition* is applied to attitudes of correctness and conventionality in writing more common in the eighteenth and nineteenth centuries than they are today.

Georgian

An adjective applying to the reigns of the four Georges (1714–1830), with particular reference to the styles of architecture, crafts, and arts current in England during that period. In literature, *Georgian* is a vague term of doubtful usefulness since it has been loosely applied to all British writers living in that era as well as to authors during the later reign of George V (1910–1936) and even that of George VI (1936–1952).

georgic

An adjective meaning "agricultural," *georgic* is used as a noun to designate a poem about farming and allied aspects of rural life. The *Georgics* of Virgil (first century B.C.) deals with such topics as rural life, weather forecasting, animal husbandry, and beekeeping.

gest (geste)

An old-fashioned name for a *metrical romance involving warfare and adventure. *Gest*, derived from a Latin word meaning "deeds" or "exploits," now occurs more often in the form of *geste* (see CHANSON). A thirteenth-century collection of stories, the *Gesta Romanorum* (deeds of the Romans), has been widely used as a source book by later writers, including Shakespeare.

gestalt

A unified whole; a pattern or form that has a *structure not accounted for by the sum of its parts. Gestalt psychology teaches that physiological and mental acts do not occur through reflexes, stimuli, and sensations but through gestalts (wholes) operating separately and independently. In literature, *gestalt* applies to a manner of *composition, such as that illustrated by Coleridge's insistence that poetry and prose exhibit a characteristic "construction" (or gestalt). (See FORM.) By this theory, a poem is a composition in patterned language not explained by the rhythm, rhyme, stanzaic structure, etc., that function distinctly, although interrelatedly. See INTENTIONAL FALLACY.

gleeman

A wandering entertainer, a strolling singer or minstrel. See JONGLEUR, SCOP, SKALD, TROUBADOUR.

gloss

An explanation or definition of a difficult, unusual, or technical word or passage. A gloss may appear as a *footnote, as a note in the margin of a *manuscript, or in a special kind of *appendix called a glossary. The word *gloss* is sometimes used in the sense of providing a false appearance or explanation; to "gloss over" something is to excuse or explain it away. See ANNOTATION, VARIORUM.

gnomic

An adjective applied to terse statements of general truth; a characteristic of writing that is didactic, moralistic, aphoristic, and sententious. *Gnomic*, derived from a Greek term meaning "judgment," "opinion," or "wisdom," is applied to all *maxims, to some *fables and *proverbs, and to many of the "wise" statements of Francis Bacon, Benjamin Franklin, Emerson, Thoreau, and Robert Frost.

In ancient Greece, a group of "gnomic poets" dealt with ethical and philosophical matters in pithy sayings and excessive moralizing. Gnomic elements appear in modern poetry, such as that by Carl Sandburg, W. H. Auden, and Archibald MacLeish.

Gongorism

An affected, artificial, and heavily ornamented style of writing. Gongorism, derived from the name of an early seventeenth-century Spanish poet, Góngora, makes use of *bombast, *conceits, *paradoxes, and *puns and has some of the characteristics of *Euphuism.

Gothic

An adjective of varied meanings derived from *Goth,* the name of a Germanic tribe of ancient and medieval times. *Gothic* refers to (1) a style of architecture originating in France and persisting from the twelfth to the sixteenth century, characterized by ribbed vaults, pointed arches, flying buttresses, ornamental gables, and fine woodwork and masonry; (2) anything pertaining to the *Middle Ages and therefore erroneously considered crude and barbaric; (3) a style in literature characterized by gloomy *settings, violent or grotesque *action, and a *mood of decay, degeneration, and *decadence.

The Gothic novel was a late eighteenth- and early nineteenth-century kind of *fiction noted for the qualities indicated in the third definition above. Popular romantic and thrill-evoking works in this *genre include Walpole's *The Castle of Otranto,* Radcliffe's *The Mysteries of Udolpho,* Lewis's *The Monk,* and Mary Shelley's *Frankenstein.*

Götterdämmerung

A German term formed from words meaning "gods" and "twilight," usually translated "twilight of the gods." In English, the expression is used to refer to collapse and destruction accompanied by disorder and violence. The resounding defeat of Austrian and Russian armies in the Battle of Austerlitz, as described in Tolstoi's *War and Peace,* has often been referred to as a Götterdämmerung.

Grail, Holy

A cup (chalice), or dish, which, in medieval *legend, was used by Jesus Christ at the Last Supper and in which were received the last drops of His blood at the Cross. The Holy Grail, which appears often in literature as a *symbol for Christian purity, formed a cycle of tales. Search for the Holy Grail was the source of many adventures of the *Knights of the Round Table. The framework of Tennyson's *Idylls of the King* firmly fixes the legendary history of the cup to the *Arthurian cycle of romance and adventure.

Graveyard School

A phrase used to refer to a group of eighteenth-century English poets who wrote gloomy poems about death and life after death. These writers, reacting against others who avoided all thoughts of death, the grave, and "the mystery of the future," tried to create an *atmosphere of "pleasing gloom." Gray's *Elegy Written in a Country Churchyard* is a restrained example of graveyard poetry which, as one critic has said, reflected "the joy of gloom, the fondness for bathing one's temples in the dank night air, and the musical delight of the screech owl's shriek." The expression *graveyard writing* is sometimes applied to work that is pessimistic, foreboding, and despairing of man's fate.

Grub Street

The former name of a London street in Cripplegate (changed in the nineteenth century to Milton Street). In his *Dictionary,* Samuel Johnson notes that this street was "much inhabited by writers of small histories, dictionaries, and temporary poems, whence any mean production is called *grub-street.*" The term is applied to any form of literary hackwork (routine writing done for money only).

Grundy, Mrs.

A conventional, narrow-minded person critical of any breach of propriety. The name is taken from that of a nonappearing character in an eighteenth-century play by Thomas Morton, concerning whom questions such as "What will Mrs. Grundy say?" and "What will Mrs. Grundy think?" are constantly asked. Mrs. Grundy is a *symbol of social *convention.

H

hack
A person who, solely for money, exploits his creative ability in the production of unimaginative work. See GRUB STREET.

hagiography
Writing about, and critical study of, the lives and legends of saints. Hagiography is a subtype of *biography. *Hagiology* is a related term with the same meaning as *hagiography*.

haiku
A form of Japanese verse usually employing *allusions and comparisons. A haiku is composed of three lines containing a fixed number of syllables, usually seventeen or nineteen:

  O cricket, from your cheery cry
  No one could ever guess
  How quickly you must die.
See IMAGISM, TANKA.

half rhyme
Imperfect rhyme, the result of *assonance or *consonance: *years, yours; somewhere, summer.* See NEAR RHYME, RHYME, SLANT RHYME.

hamartia
An error in judgment. Hamartia, derived from a Greek word meaning "fault," is sometimes known as "the tragic flaw" because it represents a fatal weakness that causes the

downfall of a *protagonist in *tragedy. This hamartia may be caused by inherited weakness, by faulty character traits, or by poor judgment; whatever the cause, the result is action, or inaction, that leads to destruction and death. (See CAUSE AND EFFECT, TRAGEDY.) Rashness is the character flaw that caused Oedipus to kill his father; ignorance led to his marrying his own mother. The hamartia (or tragic flaw) of Macbeth is ambition; of Othello, jealousy. See HUBRIS.

harangue
A passionate and vehement speech, especially one delivered to a crowd and designed to rouse emotions. In Shakespeare's *Julius Caesar,* Antony's speech over the body of Caesar is an example of the harangue. The term has been extended in meaning to include any long and pompous speech or heated oral attack. Adolf Hitler achieved and temporarily maintained political eminence by haranguing public gatherings. See DIATRIBE, TIRADE.

head rhyme
A *synonym of *alliteration. Head rhyme is based on *assonance or *consonance. The line "Apt alliteration's artful aid" is an example of head rhyme, or "beginning rhyme," which may occur in successive words or successive lines of verse.

Hellenism
(1) Imitation or adoption of ancient Greek customs, art, thought, etc.; (2) the characteristics of Greek culture from the fourth to the first century B.C.: (3) ancient Greek culture and ideals. *Hellenism,* from a Greek word meaning "similarity to the Greeks," is a loose and broad term, for it refers to admiration (and to admirers) of Greek art, architecture, sculpture, philosophy, tribal customs, and language—indeed to everything concerning ancient Greek civilization. Related words are *Hellene* (a Greek), *Hellenic, Hellenize* (to make Greek in character), *Hellenist* (a person who adopts Greek speech, customs, etc.), and *Hellenistic.*

hemistich
A half line of verse or a line of less than the usual length. *Hemistich* refers to that part of a line of poetry preceding or following a *caesura (pause, break). These lines from Pope's *An Essay on Criticism* are illustrative:

131

Trust not yourself; // but your defects to know,
Make use of ev'ry friend—// and ev'ry foe.

hendecasyllabic
Adjective applied to a line of verse of eleven syllables. *Hendecasyllabic* is derived from a Greek term meaning "eleven" and another Greek word from which *syllable* is formed. A line from Tennyson illustrates hendecasyllabic verse: "Like the skater on ice that hardly bears him."

hendiadys
A figure of speech in which a complex idea is expressed by two words joined by *and*. *Hendiadys* is Greek for "one by means of two" or "one through two." The device occurs in this passage from the Psalms: "Such as sit in darkness and in the shadow of death, being fast bound in misery and iron." The idea of the last three words is one: the iron (shackles) *is* the misery.

heptameter
A line of verse consisting of seven *feet. This is a line in heptameter from Walt Whitman's *When Lilacs Last in the Dooryard Bloom'd:*
Ever / return/ing spring, / trini/ty sure /
to me / you bring.

hero, heroine
In classical mythology, a hero was a man of godlike prowess and goodness who came to be honored as a divinity. Later, a hero was a warrior-chieftain of special strength, ability, and courage. Still later, a hero was an immortal being, a demigod. For several centuries, a hero has been considered a man of physical or moral courage, admired for bravery and noble deeds. A heroine is a female hero.

Somewhat incorrectly, *hero* and *heroine* are sometimes considered the principal characters in a story, film, play, or novel. See AGON, ANTAGONIST, PROTAGONIST.

heroic couplet
Two rhyming lines of verse in iambic *pentameter. This simplest form of English *stanza is so called because it was frequently used for *epic poetry and poetic *drama. This is a heroic couplet from Pope's *Essay on Man:*
Laugh where we must, be candid where we can;
But vindicate the ways of God to man.

heroic drama
A form of *tragedy and *tragicomedy that developed in England late in the seventeenth century. Heroic drama, often in verse, was characterized by *bombast in dialogue, violent *conflict, and *spectacles involving passionate love and savage warfare. Dryden's *The Conquest of Granada* is an example of this type.

heroic line
An iambic *pentameter line, called heroic because used so often in *epic poetry and other narratives involving heroes engaged in adventure, warfare, and death.

heroic stanza
A *quatrain (four lines) in iambic pentameter. Gray's *Elegy Written in a Country Churchyard* is composed in heroic stanzas:

Far from the madding crowd's ignoble strife,
Their sober wishes never learned to stray;
Along the cool sequestered vale of life
They kept the noiseless tenor of their way.

heuristic
An adjective applying to any course of action that stimulates interest, furthers investigation, and causes one to discover something for himself. *Heuristics,* the science or technique of finding things, comes from a Greek term meaning "to discover." The major purpose of most great literature is heuristic in that it is designed to enable readers to find out for themselves the real meaning of life and living.

hexameter
A line of verse consisting of six *feet. Longfellow's *Evangeline* is written in hexameter:

This is the / forest pri/meval. The / murmuring /
pines and the / hemlocks
Bearded with / moss, and in / garments green, /
indis/tinct in the / twilight

historical novel
A narrative in *novel form characterized by an imaginative reconstruction of historical personages and events. Writers

have combined *fiction and history for many centuries, but Sir Walter Scott firmly established the *type in *Ivanhoe, Kenilworth,* etc. Prominent historical novels include Thackeray's *Henry Esmond,* Dickens's *A Tale of Two Cities,* Tolstoi's *War and Peace,* Dumas's *The Count of Monte Cristo,* Hervey Allen's *Anthony Adverse,* and Margaret Mitchell's *Gone with the Wind.*

historical play

A *drama dealing with events from history, especially critical and crucial episodes in the career of a ruler or outstanding military personage. A historical (or history) play is synonymous with chronicle play, although the latter is more likely to deal with incidents involving only one major character and to make greater use of pageantry (coronations, battle scenes, state funerals) than the former. See CHRONICLE PLAY.

holograph

(1) Something wholly written by the person in whose name it appears; (2) a document such as a deed, will, or letter in the author's handwriting. The holograph of James Joyce's *Finnegans Wake* has proved important to literary scholars and critics because it reveals the creative process at work. See ALLONYM.

Homeric

A term referring to the eighth-century-B.C. Greek epic poet, the reputed author of the *Iliad* and *Odyssey.* Because of the stature of this writer and the majesty and grandeur of his works, *Homeric* is used to mean "imposing," "grand," "of heroic dimensions." For instance, Homeric laughter is loud, hearty, and room-shaking.

A Homeric epithet is a descriptive phrase that accents a dominant trait of a character, such as "swift-footed Achilles," "Odysseus, sacker of cities," and "laughter-loving Aphrodite." See EPITHET.

A Homeric simile is an extended figure of speech, a figurative comparison which develops parallel likenesses over several lines of verse. See EPIC SIMILE.

homostrophic

Following an identical stanzaic pattern throughout a selection. *Homostrophic,* literally meaning "one *strophe," is a synonym of *Horatian when applied to odes and other long poems. Keats's *Ode to Autumn* is a homostrophic poem consisting of three stanzas of eleven lines each, each line five feet in length. See HORATIAN, PINDARIC.

Horatian

A reference to Horace (65–8 B.C.), Roman poet and satirist. In literature, *Horatian* applies to the poetic style and diction of Horace. An ode is Horatian when each of its stanzas follows the same metrical pattern, as, for instance, Keats's *Ode to a Nightingale* does. See HOMOSTROPHIC, PINDARIC.

hubris

Arrogance; excessive self-pride and self-confidence. *Hubris,* a Greek term for "insolence," referred to the emotions in Greek tragic heroes that led them to ignore warnings from the gods and thus invite *catastrophe. Hubris is that form of *hamartia or *tragic flaw that stems from overbearing pride and self-assumed superiority. In Sophocles's *Antigone,* Creon rejects warnings from the blind prophet Tiresias, and consequently suffers the death of Antigone and the self-destruction of his wife and son. The play ends with these words about hubris from the leader of the *chorus:

> Wisdom is the supreme part of happiness; and reverence toward the gods must be inviolate. Great words of prideful men are ever punished with great blows and, in old age, teach the chastened to be wise.

Hudibrastic

Referring to *Hudibras,* by Samuel Butler, a seventeenth-century *mock heroic poem. *Hudibrastic* implies a playful, *burlesque style, such as that of much *doggerel. Hudibrastic verse is humorous or satiric and is filled with "wise" sayings and farfetched rhymes. Here are a few lines from *Hudibras* itself:

> Beside, he was a shrewd philosopher,
> And had read every text and gloss over;
> Whate'er the crabbed'st author hath
> He understood by implicit faith;
> Whatever skeptic could inquire for,
> For every *why* he had a *wherefore;*
> Knew more than forty of them do,
> As far as words and terms could go.

humanism

Any system of thought or action in which human interests,

values, and dignity are held to be dominant. Humanism implies devotion to the concerns of mankind; it is an attitude of mind that concentrates upon the activities of man rather than upon the supernatural world, the world of nature, or the so-called animal kingdom. Historically, humanism was a *Renaissance doctrine, born in fourteenth-century Italy, which stressed the essential worth, dignity, and potential of man as contrasted with an older view that man was wicked, worthless, and doomed to destruction both in this life and in that to come. Renaissance humanists, deriving their beliefs from study of ancient poets, historians, and philosophers, came to believe that man was indeed the center of the universe and that he was capable of living a life of reason, dignity, morality, and even happiness. In a more specific sense, humanism involves devotion at any time, including the present, to those studies that deal with the life, thought, and literature of ancient Greece and Rome. Advocates of humanism in literary history range from Petrarch, Thomas More, Erasmus, and Sir Philip Sidney to Shakespeare, Milton, and Goethe.

humanities

A term applied specifically to the classical languages and literatures of Greece and Rome and more broadly to subjects distinct from the physical and social sciences: art, literature, music, and philosophy. See QUADRIVIUM, SEVEN LIBERAL ARTS, TRIVIUM.

humor

A comic quality causing amusement. *Humor* is also applied to the faculties of seeing, understanding, or expressing what is amusing and laughter-producing and to a mood or frame of mind ("in a good humor today"). Humor consists primarily of the recognition and expression of peculiarities, oddities, and absurdities in a situation or action.

Humor is not always light and mirth-provoking, despite its ever-present capacity for perceiving and stating what is amusing or ridiculous. George Eliot, a nineteenth-century English novelist not noted for humor, wrote, "Humor is thinking in jest while feeling in earnest." Joseph Addison once said that Good Sense was the father of Wit and that Humor was the offspring of Wit and Mirth. For a discussion of differences between wit and humor, see WIT.

136

humors

In ancient and medieval physiology, four liquids of the body—blood, phlegm, yellow bile, black bile—were called humors. These liquids were allied with four elements: the blood, like air, was warm and moist; phlegm, like water, was cold and moist; yellow bile, like fire, was hot and dry; black bile, like earth, was cold and dry. In these ancient beliefs, one's emotional and physical condition was affected by the condition of one's humors. Good health and a perfect temperament resulted when no one humor was dominant. This conception of humors in Elizabethan times came to mean "mood," "disposition," or "peculiarity" and is helpful in understanding such characters as, for example, Hamlet, King Lear, Lady Macbeth, Jaques, and scores of other Shakespearean personages. In *Every Man out of His Humour,* a satirical comedy (1599) by Ben Jonson, appear these lines:

> The choler, melancholy, phlegm and blood . . .
> Receive the name of humours. Now thus far
> It may by metaphor apply itself
> Unto the general disposition:
> As when some one peculiar quality
> Doth so possess a man that it doth draw
> All his effects, his spirits, and his powers,
> In their confluxions, all to run one way,
> This may be truly said to be a humour.

hymn

A *song or *ode in praise or honor of God or any deity, of a nation, or of an ideal. A typical hymn is a lyric poem in verse form designed to be sung, and hence a direct means of emotional expression. In literature, hymns are often songs of praise in honor of any outstanding or exalted person, such as Ben Jonson's *Hymn to Diana.* Shelley's *Hymn to Intellectual Beauty* is an example of a tribute to an ideal. Oliver Wendell Holmes and John Greenleaf Whittier were notable American writers of hymns on religious and moral themes.

hypallage

A *figure of speech in which an *epithet (descriptive term) is applied not to an apparently appropriate noun but to another. Hypallage occurs in Virgil's phrase "the trumpet's Tuscan blare" (rather than the more usual "Tuscan trumpet's blare") and in Keats's line in *Ode to a Nightingale:* "The murmurous haunt of flies on summer eves" (rather than "the haunt of murmurous flies"). See METONYMY, OXYMORON.

hyperbaton

A *figure of speech in which words are transposed from their natural order. *Hyperbaton* is employed to increase *emphasis, as in Shelley's "Hail to thee, blithe Spirit! / Bird thou never wert" (*To a Skylark*) and in Shakespeare's *Othello:* "Yet I'll not shed her blood, / Nor scar that whiter skin of hers than snow."

hyperbole

Obvious and deliberate exaggeration; an extravagant statement. Hyperbole is a figure of speech not intended to be taken literally. Exaggeration for the sake of *emphasis is a common poetic and dramatic device: in *Hamlet,* Shakespeare wrote, "If thou prate of mountains let them throw millions of acres on us . . . " and in *Macbeth:*

> No; this my hand will rather
> The multitudinous seas incarnadine,
> Making the green one red.

See IRONY, LITOTES.

hysteron proteron

A *figure of speech in which what logically should come last comes first. *Hysteron proteron* is from Greek words meaning "later earlier." Examples: *bred and born* for *born and bred, thunder and lightning* for *lightning and thunder.* See HYPERBATON.

iambus

A poetic foot of two syllables, the first unaccented, the second accented. The iambus is the most common metrical foot in English. *Iamb* is a shortened form of *iambus,* the adjectival form of which is *iambic.* These lines by Richard Lovelace consist of iambic feet:

> Ĭ coúld / nŏt lóve / thĕe, Déar / sŏ múch
> Lŏved Í / nŏt hón/ŏr moŕe.

icon

An *image, picture, or other representation. In some religious sects, an *icon* refers to a painting or related likeness of some sacred personage such as Christ, the Virgin Mary, an angel, or a saint.

ictus

The accent, or stress, that falls on a syllable. *Ictus* does not refer to the accented syllable but to the accent (stress) itself. See ACCENT.

id

A psychoanalytical term referring to that part of the *psyche (spirit) that is the source of instinctive energy (action). According to analysts, one's id provides impulses that seek satisfaction in pleasure and is controlled, if it is controlled, by one's *ego and *superego (social ideals, conscience). The term *id* (and its implications) appears often in twentieth-century literature. See FREUDIANISM, JUNGIAN, LIBIDO.

identical rhyme

Rhyme created by the repetition of a word. The device is illustrated in lines 2 and 4 of this *stanza from Coleridge's *The Rime of the Ancient Mariner:*

> He holds him with his skinny hand;
> "There was a ship," quoth he.
> "Hold off! unhand me, grey-beard loon!"
> Eftsoons his hand dropt he.

The recurrence of two words which sound exactly alike but have different spellings and meanings is called rime riche; it is shown in these lines from Chaucer's *The Canterbury Tales:*

> The hooly blisful martir for to seke [seek],
> That hem hath holpen whan that they were
> seeke [sick].

ideograph

A written symbol that represents an idea or object directly rather than a particular word or speech sound. The Chinese language, for instance, is written in ideographs. A stick figure, a diagrammatic drawing representing a human or animal, often used in statistical work, is an ideograph.

idiolect

The language or speech pattern of an individual at a particular period of his life. Because no such thing as total conformity in pronunciation, for instance, is possible, every speaker of every language has an idiolect, his individual way of pronouncing that differs, however slightly, from the pronunciation of everyone else.

idiom

(1) A language, dialect, or style of speaking peculiar to a people; (2) the constructions or expressions of one language whose structure is not matched in another language. The word *idiom* meant, in original Greek, "a private citizen, something belonging to a private citizen, personal." By extension, *idiom* has come to mean "individual" and "peculiar." Idiomatic usage in English, for example, refers to expressions that conform to no grammatical precedents or

principles but are laws unto themselves. *Idiom* has been widened in meaning to apply to a distinct style or character, such as the modern idiom or the idiom of *naturalism or *existentialism or *polyphonic prose, etc.

idola
False *images of the mind. *Idola* is the plural of *idolum,* or *idol,* something to which strong attachment is given and which is an object of passionate devotion. In his *Novum Organum* (1620), Francis Bacon classified the principal fallacies of people into *idola tribus, specus, fori, theatri* ("idols of the tribe, cave, market, theater").

idyll
A composition in prose or verse describing *pastoral scenes and events or any simple, appealing, and charming *incident; also spelled *idyl.* An *idyll* is an idealized story of happy innocence. The *Idylls* of Theocritus, a third-century-B.C. poet, described the primitive, rustic life of Sicilians. Tennyson's *Idylls of the King* lacks descriptions of rustic life, but in *tone and *mood is idyllic (simple, poetic, pleasing). John G. Whittier's *Maud Muller* is a well-nigh perfect example of an idyll. See ARCADIA, GEORGIC, PASTORAL.

ignis fatuus
Also referred to as "will-o'-the-wisp" and "friar's lantern," *ignis fatuus* is a Latin term meaning "foolish fire." The phrase applies to a flitting phosphorescent light seen at night over marshy ground, caused by the combustion of gas from decomposed organic matter. In literature, *ignis fatuus* is used to refer to something that is misleading and deluding, as in the Earl of Rochester's lines:

Reason, which fifty times to one does err,
Reason, an ignis fatuus of the mind.

illiteracy
A word or expression not accepted in either informal or formal speech and writing, such as *disremembered* and *youse.* Characteristic of uneducated speech, illiteracies appear in literature in the dialogue of persons being characterized as unlettered or ignorant. In a more general sense, *illiteracy* means the lack of ability to read and write.

illuminated manuscript
Sheets that contain writing and are decorated with color.

Before the invention of printing (fifteenth century), devotional, religious, and other texts were copied on paper, parchment, or other writing surfaces by scribes in monasteries. Capital letters were drawn in combinations of colors (gold, red, blue, etc.), and pages were embellished by floral designs and representations of religious figures. See CALLIGRAPHY, INCUNABULA, MANUSCRIPT.

illusion

(1) An impression of what is perceived that is other than true; (2) a false mental *image or conception which may be something imagined or a misinterpretation of a real appearance. An illusion may be harmful but quite often is harmless, pleasing, and even useful. For instance, an audience at a play has to experience illusions of reality in order to grasp what is happening. See BELIEF, CONVENTION, DELUSION, DISBELIEF, DRAMATIC ILLUSION, SUSPENSION OF DISBELIEF.

image

(1) A physical representation of a person, animal, or object that is painted, sculptured, photographed, or otherwise made visible; (2) the mental impression or visualized likeness summoned up by a word, phrase, or sentence. An author can use *figurative language (such as *metaphors and *similes) to create images as vivid as the physical presence of objects and ideas themselves. When Andrew Marvell wrote in *To His Coy Mistress:*

> But at my back I always hear
> Time's wingèd chariot hurrying near;
> And yonder all before us lie
> Deserts of vast eternity . . .

he was describing the transience of life and mystery of the future in the images of a hurrying vehicle and limitless deserts.

The image is a distinctive and essential element, a basic ingredient, of nearly all imaginative prose and poetry. See CONCRETENESS, CONNOTATION, FIGURATIVE LANGUAGE, IMAGERY, METAPHOR, SIMILE, SYMBOL, TROPE.

imagery

The forming of mental *images, figures, or likenesses of things; the use of language to represent actions, persons, objects, and ideas descriptively. Any effective writer, especially a poet, is a maker of pictures in words, but he can, and does, appeal to

senses other than sight. For instance, Edgar Allan Poe combined both a visual and a nonvisual image in
> Along the ramparts plumed and pallid
> A wingèd odour went away.

Coleridge resorted to auditory imagery in these lines:
> And now 'twas like all instruments,
> Now like a lonely flute;
> And now it is an angel's song,
> That makes the heavens be mute.

Also, imagery can be both figurative and literal, as in these lines from a sonnet by Wordsworth:
> It is a beauteous evening, calm and free,
> The holy time is quiet as a Nun
> Breathless with adoration; the broad sun
> Is sinking down in its tranquillity.

See CONNOTATION, FIGURATIVE LANGUAGE, IMAGE, METAPHOR, SIMILE, SYMBOL, TROPE.

imaginative writing

Composition which is dependent upon the formation and expression of mental *images and concepts stored in the memory and upon the ability to recombine former experiences and observations in the creation of new impressions aimed at a specific goal. In general, *poems, *plays, *short stories, and *novels are judged to be imaginative writing, although many such selections are based upon observed realities and recorded facts. *Biography, history, *essays, and *articles are usually judged to be less imaginative than so-called creative or fictional writing, but many selections in these *genres are heavily dependent upon their author's ability to see inner relationships through powers of the mind that constitute imagination. See FANCY.

imagism

The theory and practice of a group of early twentieth-century poets in Great Britain and the United States who believed that poetry should employ the language of common speech, have complete freedom in subject matter, create new rhythms, and present clear, precise, and concentrated *images. Ezra Pound, Richard Aldington, and Amy Lowell were adherents of imagism and were known as imagists. Carl Sandburg's *Fog* ("The fog comes / on little cat feet") is an imagist poem.

143

imitative words

Expressions that imitate the sound made or associated with the referent (the object or action named). An imitative word, such as *buzz* or *clattered,* is also referred to as *onomatopoeia, which occurs in these lines from Alfred Noyes's *The Highwayman:*

> Tlot-tlot; tlot-tlot! Had they heard it?
> The horse-hoofs ringing clear;
> Tlot-tlot; tlot-tlot, in the distance?
> Were they deaf that they did not hear?

A notable example of imitative words appears in Tennyson's *The Princess:*

> The moan of doves in immemorial elms,
> And murmuring of innumerable bees.

imperfect rhyme

Resemblance in the sound of words that is not true or exact. Imperfect rhyme, also known as approximate rhyme, *half rhyme, *near rhyme, and *slant rhyme, is illustrated in lines 1 and 3, 2 and 4 of this passage from William Butler Yeats:

> Heart-smitten with emotion I sink *down*
> My heart recovering with covered *eyes;*
> Wherever I had looked I had looked *upon*
> My permanent or impermanent *images.*

imprecation

A curse; the calling down of evil upon someone. (See CURSE.) An imprecation occurs in *King Lear* (act 1, scene 4) when Lear, thinking that Cordelia does not truly love him, says:

> Hear, Nature! hear, dear goddess, hear!
> Suspend thy purpose, if thou didst intend
> To make this creature fruitful!
> Into her womb convey sterility!
> Dry up in her the organs of increase,
> And from her derogate body never spring
> A babe to honour her! If she must teem,
> Create her child of spleen, that it may live
> And be a thwart disnatur'd torment to her! . . .
> Turn all her mother's pains and benefits
> To laughter and contempt, that she may feel
> How sharper than a serpent's tooth it is
> To have a thankless child!

impression
(1) the process, or result, of printing from *type; (2) a printed copy from type or plates; (3) one of a number of printings made at different times from the same set of type. See EDITION.

impressionism
A literary practice which does not stress reality but rather the impressions of the author (or one of his characters). *Impressionism* may also be defined as an artistic theory which claims that the dominant purpose of literature is to explain effects upon intellect, feelings, and conscience rather than to provide detailed descriptions of objective *settings and events. Impressionism is a personal style of writing in which the author develops characters and paints scenes as they appear to him at a given moment rather than as they are (or may be) in actuality. For instance, the so-called camera-eye passages in John Dos Passos' *U.S.A.* are impressionistic. In Joyce's *Portrait of the Artist as a Young Man,* much is revealed about Stephen Dedalus's feelings but little about his physical surroundings and activities. See EXPRESSIONISM, IMAGISM, STREAM OF CONSCIOUSNESS, SYMBOLISM.

imprimatur
An official license to print or publish a *book, *pamphlet, etc. *Imprimatur* is a Latin term meaning "let it be printed" or "let it be made by pressing upon something." Specifically, an imprimatur is a license issued by a censor of the Roman Catholic Church. See NIHIL OBSTAT.

imprint
Information (publisher's name, place and date of publication) appearing on the title page (or elsewhere) in a book. *Imprint* also has the meaning of fixing firmly in the mind or memory; for example, a great work of literature makes an imprint on readers. See COLOPHON.

impropriety
Something that is incorrect, inappropriate, not suitable. In language, an impropriety is an erroneous expression, the improper use of a word, such as saying or writing *literal* when *figurative* is meant or saying *eats* for *food.*

incantation

(1) The chanting of words thought to have magical power or (2) words that possess a charm or cast a spell. Incantation is illustrated by the mumblings and chants of the witches in *Macbeth*. Ariel's song ("Full fathom five thy father lies") from Shakespeare's *The Tempest* is an incantation as well as a *dirge.

incident

An event or occurrence; a distinct piece of *action. An incident is a short narrative dealing with a single situation. When incidents are strung together in connected fashion, they become *episodes in a *plot.

incremental repetition

A form of iteration (uttering repeatedly) occurring in writing, especially in the *ballad. *Incremental* refers to "addition," "gain," and "the process of increasing"; coupled with "repetition" it suggests "cumulative growth." An important structural device of the ballad, incremental repetition applies to the use of *refrains but even more to the repetition of *stanzas with increments—either additions or changes in key words to indicate advancement of the story. The opening stanzas of a *popular ballad, *The Demon Lover,* illustrate incremental repetition:

"Oh where have you been, my long, long love,
This long seven years and more?"
"O I'm come to seek my former vows
Ye granted me before."

O hold your tongue of your former vows,
For they will breed sad strife;
O hold your tongue of your former vows,
For I am become a wife."

incunabula

Books produced in the earliest stages (before 1500) of printing from movable type. Incunabula comes from a Latin word meaning "swaddling clothes" and is a synonym for cradle books. A famous incunabulum (singular) is Caxton's edition of *The Canterbury Tales,* printed in 1478.

index

An alphabetical listing (with page numbers) of all topics treated in a book, appearing in, or constituting, the back matter of a work. An index should be distinguished from a table of contents because of its position in a book, its primary purpose, and its detail. The plural of *index* is *indexes* or *indices*. Sometimes referred to as "the Index" is *Index Librorum Prohibitorum* (list of prohibited or forbidden books), published for adherents of the Roman Catholic faith.

induction

A form of reasoning (thinking) from the specific to the general. Induction tries to establish a general truth from the observation of specific facts. From a sufficient number of these facts, or particulars, the inductive process of reasoning reaches a principle or conclusion. For instance, a novelist may provide a dozen or several hundred "facts" about the actions, thoughts, and comments of a given character. From these particulars, general ideas and understandings about the personality and characteristics of that individual are induced by both author and reader. Most narratives in prose and poetry involve the process of induction, although a *problem novel or play may begin with a general thesis (belief) and then provide supporting details. See DEDUCTION.

Induction is also an *archaism (an outmoded term) for an introduction, *preamble, or *prologue. (See FRAME STORY.) In *A Mirror for Magistrates,* Thomas Sackville's Induction (1563) describes how the poet was led into Hell, where exist the souls of those whose lives form the subject matter of the *Mirror* itself. In *The Taming of the Shrew,* Shakespeare, in a prefatory section called Induction, presents a drunken tinker, Christopher Sly, who becomes convinced that he is a nobleman; for him, a play, the *Shrew* itself, is presented.

informal essay

A *composition without set *form or obvious pattern which also goes by the names of *familiar essay, light essay, and *personal essay. Subject matter for an informal essay is infinite; it may reflect any of a thousand *moods or feelings. In his preface to *Essais,* Montaigne clearly explained the purpose and aim of this form of writing:

> Reader, lo is here a well-meaning book.... I have proposed unto myself no other than a familiar and private end. I have no respect or consideration at all, either to thy service, or to my glory.... I desire ... to be delineated in mine own genuine, simple, and ordinary fashion, without contention, art, or study....

Although informal essays make no pretensions to learning or instruction, nevertheless the best of them are stylistically polished and imply far more than they state. For example, Swift's *A Modest Proposal* and Defoe's *Shortest Way with the Dissenters* are ironic and thought-provoking informal essays.

in medias res

A Latin phrase meaning "in the middle of things." The term applies to the literary device of beginning a narrative well along in the sequence of events. The device, a *convention in *epic poetry and often used in novels, short stories, drama, and narrative poetry, is designed to attract immediate attention and secure prompt interest. For example, Homer's *Iliad* begins in the final year of the Trojan War, the beginning of which is recounted later in the epic. When a story is begun at some point other than its chronological opening, a *flashback (or series of flashbacks) is also employed.

innuendo

A word derived from a Latin term suggesting a "hint" and used in English to refer to an indirect suggestion or intimation of some kind. An innuendo is a way of implying something without actually stating it. In Robert Frost's *Mending Wall,* there is an innuendo that "good fences" perpetuate prejudice, prevent understanding, and avoid companionship more than they make "good neighbors":

> He will not go behind his father's saying,
> And he likes having thought of it so well
> He says again, "Good fences make good
> neighbors."

intentional fallacy

A term used to describe the so-called error of judging the meaning and success of a literary work in terms of the author's expressed purpose in writing it. (See AFFECTIVE FALLACY.) In this phrase, *intentional* does not mean "deliberate" but instead refers to the intention of the writer. Two modern critics (Wimsatt and Beardsley) have claimed that "the poem is not the critic's own and not the author's. It is detached from the author at [its] birth and goes about the world beyond his power to 'intend' about it or control it." See FALLACY.

interior monologue

A form of writing which represents the inner thoughts of a character. It records the internal, emotional experience of an individual, reaching downward to unspoken levels where *images represent emotions and sensations. The Molly Bloom section at the end of James Joyce's *Ulysses* is an example of interior monologue in which the author seems not to exist and the reader directly "overhears" the thought flowing through the character's mind. In plays by Eugene O'Neill and novels by William Faulkner, the authors present, guide, and even comment on impressions passing through the minds of characters. See STREAM OF CONSCIOUSNESS, a related term which applies more to subject matter than to the technique (interior monologue) of presenting inner thoughts (see MONOLOGUE).

interlude

(1) An intervening episode, incident, space, or period of time; (2) a short dramatic sketch introduced between the acts of plays or given as part of another entertainment. *Interlude,* which comes from Latin words meaning "between play," is applied to any interruption of the main plot of a novel or play and to a break in a lecture or essay.

internal rhyme

Correspondence in sound created by two or more words in the same line of verse; rhyme falling in the middle as well as at the end of the same metrical line. (See LEONINE VERSE.) Internal rhyme appears in the first and third of these lines from Shelley's *The Cloud:*

> I silently *laugh* at my own *cenotaph,*
> And out of the caverns of rain,
> Like a child from the *womb,* like a ghost
> from the *tomb,*
> I arise and unbuild it again.

intrigue

Deceitful plans, underhanded plotting. *Intrigue* involves crafty or secret dealings and is applied, for example, to plays that have intricate plots. *The Way of the World,* by William Congreve, is a comedy of intrigue.

inversion

Reversal of the usual or natural order of words. (See ANAS-

TROPHE.) Inversion occurs often in poetry for *emphasis and also to accommodate *meter, as in Coleridge's *Kubla Khan:*
> A damsel with a dulcimer
> In a vision once I saw.

invocation

The act of calling upon a deity, spirit, or person for protection, aid, inspiration, or assistance of some kind. Invocation (derived from a Latin term meaning "to call") has become a literary *convention in which a writer, usually a poet, calls on a *muse for help and divine guidance. At the beginning of *Paradise Lost,* John Milton directs an invocation to Urania, the muse of astronomy and epic poetry:
> Sing, Heavenly Muse ... I thence
> Invoke thy aid to my adventrous song,
> That with no middle flight intends to soar
> Above the Aonian mount ...

Ionic

(1) A metrical foot with two long and two short syllables. Ionic meter is rare in verse written in English but is frequent in the Latin odes of Horace; (2) a term applying to one of the classical orders in ancient Greek architecture: fluted columns, molded bases, richly ornamented figures, etc. See DORIC.

irony

A *figure of speech in which the literal (*denotative) meaning of a word or statement is the opposite of that intended. In literature, irony is a technique of indicating an intention or attitude opposed to what is actually stated. Aristotle defined *irony* as "a dissembling toward the inner core of truth"; Cicero supplied a simpler and more helpful explanation: "Irony is the saying of one thing and meaning another." Sometimes called the most ironic writing in all literature is Jonathan Swift's *A Modest Proposal,* in which the author "recommends" that the Irish sell their babies to English landlords for food. Among devices by which irony is achieved are *hyperbole, *litotes, *sarcasm, *satire, and *understatement.

Socratic irony is so called because Socrates adopted another's point of view in order to reveal that person's weaknesses and eventually to ridicule him. Another form of irony with a special meaning is *dramatic irony.

Italian sonnet

A poetic form, also called Petrarchan, consisting of fourteen lines divided into an *octave (eight lines) and a *sestet (six lines), usually rhyming *abbaabba, cdecde* (or *cdcdcd*). One of the best-known of all Italian sonnets is Keats's "On First Looking into Chapman's Homer." See PETRARCHAN, SONNET.

italics

A style of printing types in which letters usually slope to the right. Italics are used in many literary selections to differentiate between varying kinds of material, to secure greater *emphasis, to denote words as words, etc. In hand-written *manuscripts, underlining is a method of italicizing words.

ivory tower

A place, situation, or attitude toward life that is remote from practical, worldly affairs. The phrase, first used by Sainte-Beuve, a nineteenth-century French literary critic, suggests aloofness, disdain for practical considerations, and indifference to everyday existence and to all matters that are outside one's restricted circle of interests. Poets, for example, have often been called ivory-tower dwellers, but in *A Defence of Poetry* Shelley referred to them as "the unacknowledged legislators of the world."

Jacobean

Referring or applying to the reign of King James I of England (1603–1625). *Jacobean,* a term applied to the literature (especially drama), furniture, art, and architecture of that period, is derived from Jacobus, the Latin form of James. The literature of this era was really a late flowering of Elizabethan writing, although toward the end of James's reign, *cynicism and *realism began to flourish. During this epoch, many of Shakespeare's greatest plays were written; John Donne, Ben Jonson, and Francis Bacon were at the peak of their creative powers; the King James Bible appeared in 1611. See BIBLE; ELIZABETHAN.

jeremiad

A mournful *complaint, an expression of sorrow, a lamentation denouncing evil. *Jeremiad,* named after the Old Testament prophet Jeremiah, refers to any literary work which contains prophecies of destruction or complaints about the state of society and the world. Jonathan Edwards's sermon *Sinners in the Hands of an Angry God* is a jeremiad.

jestbook

An *anthology (collection) of jokes and witticisms, satirical *anecdotes, *epigrams, and ribald stories. Jestbooks (or jokebooks) have been popular since the first one, *A Hundred Merry Tales,* appeared in England in the sixteenth century.

jig

A rapid, lively dance. The term appears in numerous eighteenth- and nineteenth-century novels dealing with rustic life, such as those by Thomas Hardy. In *Elizabethan times, a jig was an amusing dramatic *interlude with words sung to the accompaniment of dancing. In *Hamlet,* the title character says of Polonius: "He's for a jig or a tale of bawdry [obscenity]."

jingle

A piece of verse that repeats sounds, contains numerous rhymes, and frequently is humorous, lighthearted, and nonsensical. *Nursery rhymes ("Hickory, dickory, dock" and "To market, to market") are jingles.

jongleur

A wandering entertainer in medieval France and Norman England who sang songs, often of his own composition, and told stories. A jongleur resembled a *gleeman and *minstrel. See TROUBADOUR.

journal

(1) A newspaper or any *periodical published for a learned society, profession, organization, or legislative body; (2) a daily personal record of occurrences, observations, and experiences. (See AUTOBIOGRAPHY.) Notable journals have been kept by such writers as Daniel Defoe, Charles Darwin, and André Gide. The term has also been loosely applied to fictitious history (Defoe's *Journal of the Plague Year*) and to such writings as Boswell's *Journal of a Tour to the Hebrides* (travel) and Jonathan Swift's *Journal to Stella* (letters).

juncture

(1) A point of time, especially one that is critical or important because of circumstances; (2) a term in linguistics referring to a distinctive sound feature marking the boundary of a word or expression. For example, the word *well* requires a pause, before or after, in a statement such as "The person who can do this *well* deserves our thanks." If a pause (juncture) occurs before *well,* the adverb modifies *deserves;* if a pause occurs after *well,* the adverb modifies *can do.*

Jungian

A term referring to Carl Gustav Jung (1875–1961), a Swiss psychiatrist. Jung supported many of the ideas, theories, and methods of Freud (see FREUDIANISM), but he differed from his mentor in many important ways. Jungian psychology largely rejects the ideas of infantile sexuality and wish fulfillment that are a part of Freudianism and holds that Freud's psychoanalytic principles were overly concrete and one-sided. Jung introduced the concept of the *collective unconscious and was largely responsible for a theory of human types divided into introverted and extroverted kinds of behavior. Jungian psychology has been influential in the lives and works of many twentieth-century authors because it tries to explain irrational forces of the present day and to throw light on the primeval and often impersonal terrors that confront mankind.

Juvenalian

Resembling the Roman satirist Juvenal (A.D. 60–140). A Juvenalian writer (such as Jonathan Swift) is noted for his pungent *realism, or biting *satire, or both.

juvenilia

Literary compositions produced in an author's youth, typically marked by immaturity of style, thought, and subject matter. For instance, Lord Byron's *Hours of Idleness,* published when the writer was eighteen, was first entitled *Juvenilia.* The term is also applied to literary productions intended for the young.

kabuki

Popular drama of Japan, developed in the seventeenth century, that is characterized by elaborate costuming, stylized acting, and rhythmic dialogue. In Japanese, *kabuki* means "music and dancing with spirit and style." Kabuki is distinguished from *noh (or nō), the classical and lyrical drama of Japan.

karma

Destiny. See FATE.

keening

A wail or lamentation, especially a lament for the dead. A one-act play, *Riders to the Sea,* by John M. Synge, an Irish dramatist, is based upon the keening (mourning) of an old mother for her missing son. When her only other son is also drowned, the central character ceases to keen because she has nothing else to lose and nothing more to fear. See DIRGE.

kenning

A conventional, poetic phrase used for, or in addition to, the usual name of a person or object. Originally an Icelandic term, a kenning is a stock phrase, a picturesque metaphorical compound, such as *wave traveler* for *boat, the helmet of night* for *darkness,* and *whale's path* for *ocean.* See EPITHET, HOMERIC, METAPHOR.

King's English

Educated or "correct" English grammar and usage. Despite the fact that several English sovereigns have not been able to speak English at all, it has long been fitting to think of the ruler's language as above reproach; Chaucer wrote "God save the king, that is lord of this language." The King's (or Queen's) English is always "proper," and the phrase is sometimes used to mean "the linguistic currency of the realm."

kismet

One's appointed lot. See FATE.

Knights of the Round Table

A legendary order of knights created by King Arthur. (See ARTHURIAN; CHIVALRY; GRAIL, HOLY.) According to Sir Thomas Malory (1400–1471) and his *Morte d'Arthur*, 150 knights had seats at a table where none was at the "head." These knights ventured into all then-known countries in search of adventure. Among them, Sir Modred was a model of treachery, Sir Lancelot of bravery and of frailty in love, Sir Gawain of courtesy, Sir Galahad of chastity, etc.

Künstlerroman

From German *Künstler* ("artist") and French *roman* ("novel"), *Künstlerroman* refers to a narrative which traces the development of the author (or that of an imagined character like the author) from childhood to maturity. (See BILDUNGSROMAN, a *synonym for this term.) Most such novels depict the struggles of a sensitive, artistic child to escape from the misunderstandings and *bourgeois attitudes of his family and youthful acquaintances.

lacuna
A missing part in a manuscript, a break of some sort. *Lacuna* also means "a gap" or "a blank space"; the plural, *lacunae,* refers to obliterations resulting from tears or fadings.

laissez faire
French for "allow to act." In English use, *laissez faire* means noninterference in the affairs of others and applies especially to freedom of action. In economic, political, and social affairs, this phrase refers to the doctrine that government should intervene as little as possible.

lament
An expression of grief or sorrow; a poem, such as a *dirge or an *elegy, that indicates mourning. The laments of King David for Saul and Jonathan (in the Old Testament) are deeply emotional and painful. A modern example of a lament is Shelley's *A Lament,* the first stanza of which is

> O World! O Life! O Time!
> On whose last steps I climb,
> Trembling at that where I had stood before;
> When will return the glory of your prime?
> No more—Oh, never more!

lampoon
A sharp *satire, in prose or verse, directed against an in-

dividual or an institution. A lampoon severely ridicules the character, intentions, or behavior of a person or a society. Lampoons appeared often in the seventeenth and eighteenth centuries but are less common today because of *libel laws. Pope's *Epistle to Dr. Arbuthnot* is a series of lampoons in which the author defends himself against "the vicious or the ungenerous" persons who had attacked "my person, morals, and family."

laureate
Crowned with laurel as a mark of honor and esteem. (The foliage of laurel—a small evergreen tree or shrub—for centuries has been considered an *emblem of victory or distinction.) *Laureate* is applied to anyone who has been honored for achieving distinction in a particular field. See POET LAUREATE.

lay
A short lyric or narrative poem intended to be sung. *Lay* (also spelled *lai* and *ley*) comes from a German word meaning "song," but its meaning has been expanded to include historical narrative poems (ballads) such as Sir Walter Scott's *The Lay of the Last Minstrel* and Macaulay's *The Lays of Ancient Rome*. See BALLAD.

legend
A tradition or story handed down from earlier times and popularly accepted as true. *Legend* originally denoted a story about a saint but is now applied to any fictitious tale concerning a real person, event, or place. A legend is likely to be less concerned with the supernatural than a *myth, but *legend* and *myth* are related terms. (Also, see FABLE.) A well-known legend forms the basis of Washington Irving's short story *The Legend of Sleepy Hollow*.

Legend is also a name for brief explanatory comments accompanying photographs, maps, paintings, etc. See CAPTION.

legitimate theater
Professionally produced stage plays as distinguished from television, motion pictures, burlesque, ballet, puppetry, and vaudeville. The term derives from the fact that when the British Parliament in the eighteenth century authorized only three "legal theaters," other producers evaded the law by calling their offerings *pantomimes or concerts. See BURLESQUE, BURLETTA, PUPPETRY, VAUDEVILLE.

leitmotiv

A term from German, literally meaning "leading motive." It refers to the *theme or *motif associated throughout a musical drama with a particular situation, person, or idea. *Leitmotiv* (also spelled *leitmotif*) is often applied to the dominant *impression, *controlling image, or recurring *theme of a literary selection, as, for instance, the "practicality" of Franklin's *Autobiography* or the "revolutionary spirit" of Thomas Paine.

leonine verse

A kind of verse in which the last word rhymes with the last word before the *caesura (pause, break). W. S. Gilbert's "Oh, a private *buffoon* is a light-hearted *loon*" is an example of leonine rhyme, or verse. The name is derived from that of a French poet, Leoninus, who wrote numerous lines containing this kind of rhyme. See INTERNAL RHYME.

Lesbian

A term referring to Lesbos, a Greek island in the Aegean Sea (now called Mytilene). The word in the sense of "highly sensual" or "erotic" was derived from the reputed character and literature of the inhabitants of Lesbos. More specifically, *lesbian* refers to a female homosexual. See SAPPHIC.

letters

(1) A general term given to literature (see BELLES LETTRES); (2) the profession of literature ("a man of letters"); (3) communications in writing, such as notes and *epistles exchanged between friends, business firms, etc. (See AUTOBIOGRAPHY, EPISTLE, EPISTOLARY.) The correspondence of Charles Dickens, Charles Lamb, Robert Louis Stevenson, Oliver Wendell Holmes, Abraham Lincoln, and Winston Churchill is genuine literature, a *genre which is revealing, entertaining, and often creative and moving.

lexicography

The writing and compiling of *dictionaries. The term, derived from Greek, involves intricate processes of preparing word lists and presenting them as "entries" consisting of pronunciations, spellings, derivations, meanings, illustrative quotations, etc. (See DICTIONARY.) Samuel Johnson, himself a noted lexicographer, defined his role as that of "a writer of dictionaries, a harmless drudge," but he also wrote, "I am not so lost in lexicography as to forget that words are the daughters of earth and that things are the sons of heaven" —Johnson's way of echoing an earlier writer (George Herbert), who said, "Words are women, deeds are men." See LEXICON.

lexicon
(1) A wordbook or dictionary; (2) the vocabulary of a particular language, activity, social class, etc. The first of these meanings is explained in the entry for *dictionary;* the second is illustrated in these lines from Edward Bulwer Lytton's play *Richelieu:*

> In the lexicon of youth, which fate reserves
> For a bright manhood, there is no such word
> As "fail."

libel
Written or printed words or pictures that defame or that maliciously or damagingly misrepresent. See CALUMNY, SLANDER.

libido
Usually applied to the sexual instinct, *libido* refers to all the instinctual energies and desires that are derived from the *id (spirit, self). A libidinous person is lustful, lewd.

libretto
The text (words) of an *opera or similar musical *composition, such as a cantata or oratorio. Libretto, derived from an Italian word meaning "little book," often takes the form of a *pamphlet or booklet containing the *story, *tale, or *plot of the musical work.

light verse
Verse designed to entertain, amuse, or please. Light verse is ordinarily distinguished by its *wit and the subtlety and perfection of its *form rather than by depth or genuine significance. Light verse includes *doggerel, *epigrams, *limericks, *nonsense verse, *parodies, and *vers de société. Among noted contemporary American writers of light verse are Ogden Nash and Richard Armour.

limerick
A form of *light verse, a *stanza of five lines rhyming *aabba.* Limerick takes its name from a county in Ireland and social gatherings there at which *nonsense verse was

160

set out in facetious jingles. The tendency of limericks to become naughty is commented upon in this limerick by Morris Bishop:

> The limerick's furtive and mean;
> You must keep him in close quarantine,
> Or he sneaks to the slums
> And promptly becomes
> Disorderly, drunk, and obscene.

limited edition
An edition of a book limited to a specific number of copies. Copies of a limited edition are usually numbered. See EDITION.

line drawing
A drawing done in line (pen, pencil, brush, crayon) providing gradations in tone through changes in width and compactness.

line of verse
A phrase referring to a single line of metrical language. Strictly speaking, a verse is a line; *verse* means "a turning" and is properly applied to the method by which one line "turns" into another. (See VERSE.) In English, lines of poetry (verses) are measured in feet. See FOOT, METER, METRICS, PROSODY.

litany
(1) A form of prayer consisting of a series of *invocations with identical responses in succession; (2) the supplications (appeals) in the Book of Common Prayer of the Church of England; (3) a recitation that is ceremonial and repetitive. *Litany* is also applied to any prolonged, monotonous statement or account.

literal, figurative
The former means "word for word" and "exact." *Figurative* means "not literal," "metaphorical," "in a manner of speaking." See FIGURATIVE, LITERAL.

literary ballad
Another name for ART BALLAD, which see. A literary ballad is of known authorship and has some claim to literary distinction. See BALLAD, POPULAR BALLAD.

literary epic
An extended narrative poem, exalted in style and heroic in theme, that is modeled to some extent upon early epics of

unknown authorship. (See EPIC.) The literary epic is more artistically perfect than a popular, or *folk, epic but is not necessarily more vigorous or appealing. See ART EPIC.

literature

Writings in which expression and *form, in connection with ideas and concerns of universal and apparently permanent interest, are essential features. (See BELLES LETTRES, CLASSIC, LETTERS.) *Literature* is frequently, but unwisely, applied to any kind of printed material, such as circulars, leaflets, and handbills. The term is correctly reserved for prose and verse of acknowledged excellence, the value of which lies in its intense, personal, and superb expression of life in its varied meanings.

> In the civilization of today it is undeniable that, over all the arts, literature dominates, serves beyond all.
>
> Walt Whitman

> Literature is an investment of genius which pays dividends to all subsequent times.
>
> John Burroughs

> Life comes before literature, as the material comes before the work. The hills are full of marble before the world blooms with statues.
>
> Phillips Brooks

litotes

A form of *understatement in which something is affirmed by stating the negative of its opposite. *Litotes,* from a Greek word meaning "small" or "plain," is an antonym of *hyperbole and a near synonym for *meiosis. To say that a person is "no amateur" affirms the speaker's belief that he is a professional. In *Paradise Lost,* when Milton writes that his poem "with no middle flight intends to soar," he is saying that he expects his work to reach the highest levels imaginable.

littérateur

A literary man, one who devotes himself to the study or writing of literature. *Littérateur* is often applied to an amateur or *dilettante rather than to a dedicated, professional student, creator, or critic of *literature.

little magazine

A term applied to literary *journals of small circulation. The typical little magazine is underfinanced, short-lived, of small *format, and experimental in its approach to prose and poetry. Little magazines flourished in the United States, England, and France in the 1920s, but most of them ceased publication before the outbreak of World War II. Despite spotty records, these periodicals at one time or another provided first publication for Sherwood Anderson, Hart Crane, E. E. Cummings, T. S. Eliot, William Faulkner, Ernest Hemingway, Ezra Pound, Gertrude Stein, and Thornton Wilder.

little theater

Noncommercial drama, usually experimental and directed to the tastes and interests of limited audiences. Such semiprofessional or frankly amateurish productions, normally supported by community resources (talent and money), seek artistic rather than financial success. Writers who to some degree were products of the little theater movement in various countries include George Bernard Shaw and John Galsworthy (England), J. M. Synge and William Butler Yeats (Ireland), Ivan Turgenev (Russia), Eugene O'Neill, Paul Green, Thornton Wilder, and Clifford Odets (United States).

liturgical drama

Plays performed as part of church services. (*Liturgical* refers to public worship.) *Liturgical drama* applies particularly to the Mass (Holy Eucharist) and its forms of worship. The term is also applied to *mystery plays and *morality plays performed in *medieval times. See QUEM QUAERITIS.

liturgy

Ritualistic worship in the Christian Church. *Liturgy* applies to the *form, order, and manner of religious services, especially those dealing with the sacrament of Holy Communion.

local color

A term applied to writing which develops and promotes the mannerisms, dress, speech, and customs of a particular region. (See COLOR.) Writers who are local colorists try to be informative about the peculiarities of a given region and emphasize *verisimilitude of details about *dialect, local geographical features, and the like. See REGIONALISM.

Details of Yorkshire life are emphasized in novels by the Brontës; Thomas Hardy's novels contain much of the local color of Wessex; Bret Harte, Mark Twain, Joel Chandler Harris, Sarah Orne Jewett, and Robert Frost concentrated on special American regions in their efforts to deal with life in its larger aspects and wider applications.

locale

The *setting (scene) of a novel, play, or motion picture. See REGIONALISM.

localism

A manner of speaking, pronunciation, usage, or inflection that is peculiar to one locality. A localism may be a word or phrase that is used and understood in a particular section or region but that may not be in national use. (See PROVINCIALISM, REGIONALISM.) Localisms, which can also include *dialect, appear in every language; in American English they can be illustrated by such terms as *down-Easter* (native of New England, especially of Maine); *corn pone* (corn bread); *maverick* (an unbranded animal); *rustler* (cattle thief).

logic

The art, science, or technique of reasoning; a systematic investigation of the truth or falsity of an idea or argument. *Logic* is usually considered to mean "sound judgment" and "the making of correct inferences." (See DEDUCTION, INDUCTION, PREMISE, SYLLOGISM.) Logic may be called the "rule" or "standard" by which one evaluates the statements of others and by which one judges the soundness of one's own thinking.

Offenses against "straight and clear thinking" that violate "correct reasoning" have occurred often in literature and presumably will continue to do so. Among these faults may be mentioned (1) hasty generalizations, (2) begging the question, (3) non sequitur, (4) post hoc, (5) *bias, and (6) faulty *analogy.

Logic is an important study in itself, ranging from consideration of careless phrasing to the *canons and *criteria of philosophical, scientific, and literary methods first set forth by Aristotle in the fourth century B.C. and constantly revised and refined ever since. Two quotations from *literature will throw light upon the problem of *logic:*

He was in logic a great critic,

Profoundly skilled in analytic.
He could distinguish and divide
A hair 'twixt south and southwest side;
On either which he would dispute,
Confute, change hands, and still confute.

Samuel Butler, *Hudibras*

"Contrariwise," continued Tweedledee, "if it was so,
it might be; and if it were so, it would be; but as it isn't,
it ain't. That's logic."

Lewis Carroll, *Through the Looking-Glass*

logorrhea
Incoherent, repetitious speech. Logorrhea, derived from
Greek words meaning "flow " and "discharge" of words, is
an acute kind of prolixity and verbosity. In the first two
scenes of act 2 of *Hamlet*, Polonius is afflicted with logorrhea: he speaks at length, forgets what he has been saying,
starts a definition, cannot finish it, and generally talks ver-
bosely with many wanderings of thought.

long measure
Four lines of iambic *tetrameter which form a *stanza of a
*hymn. In hymnbooks, this phrase is abbreviated to L.M.
See BALLAD STANZA, COMMON MEASURE.

loose sentence
A sentence that is grammatically complete at one or more
points before its end. Most sentences, whether written or
spoken, are loose because they do not end with completion
of main statements but continue with additional words,
phrases, or clauses. See PERIODIC SENTENCE.

lost generation
The generation of men and women who came of age during or just after World War I (1914–1918). The term derives
from Gertrude Stein's comment to Ernest Hemingway,
"You are all a lost generation." Hemingway, himself a member of the lost generation, used the phrase as a *motto and
*theme for his novel *The Sun Also Rises* (1926). Members of
this lost generation, who found themselves without emotional or cultural stability in a time of social unheaval, included
F. Scott Fitzgerald, Louis Bromfield, Hart Crane, and John
Dos Passos. See BEAT GENERATION.

lullaby

A song used to lull a child to sleep. A lullaby is a cradlesong. Tennyson's song from *The Princess* is a lullaby:

> Sweet and low, sweet and low,
> Wind of the western sea,
> Low, low, breathe and blow,
> Wind of the western sea!
> Over the rolling waters go,
> Come from the dying moon, and blow,
> Blow him again to me;
> While my little one, while my pretty one, sleeps.

lyric

(1) A poem having the form and musical quality of a song; (2) a short, subjective poem with a songlike outburst of the author's innermost thoughts and feelings; (3) an adjective meaning "spontaneous," "rapturous," "undisciplined." *Lyric* is derived from Greek, Latin, and Middle English names for a musical instrument (the lyre) dating back to ancient Greece. As a noun or adjective, *lyric* is applied to any poem expressing personal emotion, to any short poem that does not primarily tell a story, and to *prose or *verse that is characterized by a direct, spontaneous outpouring of intense feeling.

lyrics

The words of a *song. See LIBRETTO.

macaronic

Composed of a mixture of languages. Macaronic verse mingles two or more languages in humorous, *burlesque style. For instance, an unknown writer altered the Mother Goose rhyme "Sing a song of sixpence, pocketful of rye" into this macaronic (mixture like a dish of macaroni) *doggerel:
> Cane carmen sixpence, pera plena rye,
> De multis atris avibus coctis in a pie.

madrigal

(1) A part song without instrumental accompaniment, usually for five or more voices and making much use of *contrapuntal effects; (2) a lyric poem, usually short and frequently concerning love, suitable for being set to music. Italian in origin, the madrigal was both fashionable and popular from the sixteenth century on in Italy, France, and England.

This song from Shakespeare's *Measure for Measure* is a madrigal:
> Take, oh, take those lips away,
> That so sweetly were forsworn;
> And those eyes, the break of day,
> Lights that do mislead the morn:
> But my kisses bring again, bring again;
> Seals of love, but sealed in vain, sealed
>   in vain.

magazine
A publication issued periodically, usually with a paper cover and containing *articles, *essays, *stories, or *poems by different writers. *Magazine* comes from a French word (*magasin*) meaning "store" or "storehouse" and has the general meaning of *miscellany or collection. See JOURNAL, LITTLE MAGAZINE, PERIODICAL, PULP MAGAZINE, SLICK MAGAZINE.

malapropism
The act or habit of using words ridiculously. A malapropism results from ignorance or from confusion of words similar in sound. Mrs. Malaprop, a character in Richard B. Sheridan's play *The Rivals,* made such remarks as "I would have her instructed in geometry that she might know something of the contagious countries" and "If I reprehend anything in this world, it is the use of my oracular tongue."

malediction
A *curse; an imprecation; a damning; *slander. *Malediction,* derived from Latin words meaning "speaking evilly," is illustrated under the entries for CURSE, DOGGEREL (Shakespeare's epitaph), and IMPRECATION.

manuscript
A *letter, *document, or book written by hand; writing as distinguished from print. *Manuscript* comes from Latin words meaning "written by hand," but the term is now applied to an author's *copy of a work, whether in longhand or typewritten, that is used as the basis for typesetting.

märchen
A German word for *folktale and *fairy tale. *Märchen,* both singular and plural, applies to the collection of stories by Jacob and Wilhelm Grimm. See FOLKLORE.

marginalia
Notes and comments written on the border (margin) of a page by the author or by an editor or reader. See RUBRIC.

Marinism
A style of writing named for a seventeenth-century Italian poet, Giovanni Marino. Marinism is a florid, bombastic style marked by extravagant *metaphors, *antithesis, and *con-

ceits. An example of Marinism, which is related to *Euphuism and *Gongorism, is contained in these lines by Richard Crashaw, a seventeenth-century English poet, in which he compares a woman's tear-filled eyes to
> Two walking baths, two weeping motions,
> Portable and compendious oceans.

Marxist
A follower of, and believer in, the theories of Karl Marx (1818–1883), a German philosopher, economist, and socialist. A Marxist subscribes to Marxism, a system of thought which expounds the doctrine that throughout history the state has exploited the masses, that class struggle has always been the principal means for effecting historical changes, that the capitalist system contains the seeds of its own decay, and that, after a period of dictatorship by the proletariat, a socialist order and classless society will emerge. Marxists and Marxism have played important roles in world literature since the Russian Revolution of 1917.

masculine ending
A line of verse in which the final syllable is stressed (accented), as in these lines from Ben Jonson's *Fancy:*
> And Fancy, I tell you, has dreams that have wings,
> And dreams that have honey,
> and dreams that have stings.

A closely related term is *masculine rhyme,* correspondence of sound limited to a single stressed syllable, as in the preceding quotation and in the words *disdain* and *complain, marsh* and *harsh.* See FEMININE ENDING, FEMININE RHYME.

masque
A form of entertainment in sixteenth- and seventeenth-century England consisting of dancing and *pantomime and, later, of added *song and *dialogue. As a kind of semidramatic, elaborate, and aristocratic *spectacle, the masque flourished in the hands of such writers as Ben Jonson and such stage designers as Inigo Jones. Shakespeare's *Tempest* contains a masque (act 4) in which *pastoral and mythological figures entertain Ferdinand and Miranda. The best-known of all masques is John Milton's *Comus* (1634). See ANTIMASQUE.

mass media
Forms of communication that reach large numbers of people.

(*Media* is the plural of *medium,* meaning "agency," "means," "instrument.") Mass media include television, films, newspapers, radio, and *slick magazines.

maxim

An expression of a general and practical truth. A maxim is an *adage, an *aphorism, an *apothegm. Maxims prefixed to Benjamin Franklin's *Poor Richard's Almanac* include such comments as "He that goes a borrowing goes a sorrowing," "It is hard for an empty sack to stand upright," and "He that riseth late must trot all day."

medieval

An adjective applying to the *Middle Ages, which is precisely the meaning of *medieval* in Latin (*medius,* "middle," and *aevum,* "age"). Scholars have never agreed about the exact period referred to as medieval or as the Middle Ages, but loosely both terms apply to the time in European history between classical antiquity (the late fifth century) and the *Renaissance (about 1350). More exactly, *medieval* refers to the later part of this period (after 1100) and may extend to 1500. See CHIVALRY, DARK AGES, FEUDALISM.

Medieval has come to mean "antiquated," "outmoded," or "old-fashioned" and is often used in these meanings in modern literature.

meiosis

The use of *understatement, a synonym for *litotes. *Meiosis,* from a Greek word meaning "leveling" or "lessening," is used to give the idea that something is less in importance or size than it really is. This rhetorical device is ordinarily used for humorous or satiric effects. When John Dryden referred to honor as "an empty bubble," he was making an ironic *understatement about one of mankind's most cherished ideals.

melodrama

A form of play that intensifies sentiment, exaggerates emotion, and relates sensational and thrilling action. Melodramas, from Greek words for *song* and *drama,* were originally romantic plays with music, singing, and dancing, but they evolved in the eighteenth century into productions with elaborate but oversimplified and coincidental *plots, touches of *bathos, and happy endings. Until recent years, touring companies of actors

170

presented melodramas all over the United States, plays such as *Ten Nights in a Barroom*. The sensational elements of melodrama are present in *Gothic novels and in current films, *Western stories, and television crime plays.

memoir

A biographical or autobiographical *sketch; a record of facts and events connected with a subject, period, or individual; a commentary on one's life, times, and experiences. *Memoir,* usually spelled *memoirs,* is derived from the Latin word for "memory" or "remembering." An author's memoirs usually focus attention on personalities and events known to, or experienced by, the writer. For example, several of the books published by such recent world figures as Winston Churchill and Dwight D. Eisenhower are memoirs. See AUTOBIOGRAPHY, BIOGRAPHY.

Menippean

Cynical, distrustful, contemptuous. *Menippean* is derived from the name of a Syrian writer, Menippus, who lived in the third century B.C. and whom Lucian, a later Greek satirist, called the "the greatest snarler and snapper of all the old dogs." (The word *cynic* is derived from a Greek term meaning "doglike," that is, snarling, "like a cur.") See CYNICISM.

mesostich

From Greek words meaning "middle" and "line of poetry," *mesostich* is a composition in which certain middle letters in successive lines form a word when put together. See ACROSTIC.

metaphor

A figure of speech in which a word or phrase is applied to a person, idea, or object to which it is not literally applicable. A metaphor is an implied *analogy which imaginatively identifies one thing with another. A metaphor is one of the *tropes, a device by which an author turns, or twists, the meaning of a word. For example, Martin Luther wrote "A mighty fortress is our God, / A bulwark never failing"; *mighty fortress* and *bulwark* are metaphors. Wordsworth wrote metaphorically when he said of England that "she is a fen of stagnant waters." In *Song of Myself,* Walt Whitman wrote that *grass* seemed to be "the beautiful uncut hair of graves." See ANALOGY, CONNOTATION, DEAD METAPHOR, FIGURATIVE LANGUAGE, MIXED METAPHOR, SIMILE, TROPE.

metaphysics

Investigation of, and speculation about, objects, ideas, and realms beyond what can be known from direct observation and experience. Metaphysics is a branch of philosophy that deals with first principles, such as *cosmic affairs, eternity, and ontology.

Metaphysical poetry is a term applied to writing that is highly intellectual and philosophical, that makes extensive use of ingenious *conceits (imaginative *images), and that usually combines intense emotion with mental ingenuity. The outstanding metaphysical poet in English literature was John Donne; among leading American poets of this school may be mentioned Edward Taylor and T. S. Eliot. For examples of metaphysical poetry, see CONCEIT.

metathesis

The transposition of letters, *syllables, or sounds. Metathesis is one of the processes that change language; for instance, Modern English *bird* was *brid* in *Old English, *drugath* in Old English is now *drought*, etc.

meter

The term *meter* is a poetic measure that refers to the pattern of stressed and unstressed *syllables in a *line, or *verse, of a *poem. The number of syllables in a line may be fixed and the number of stressed syllables may vary, or the stresses may be fixed and the number of unstressed syllables may vary. The number of stresses and syllables is fixed in the most frequent forms of meter in English verse, although actually this basic pattern occasionally varies so as to avoid sounding like a metronome. In some modern poetry, regular meter is largely forsaken, and *cadence is employed to approximate the flow of speech.

These meters are most commonly used in English poetry: iambic (˘ -), trochaic (- ˘), anapestic (˘ ˘ -), dactylic (- ˘ ˘). Every such metrical unit, or group of syllables, is called a *foot; the number of feet in a line of poetry determines its name; for example, a verse of three feet is called *trimeter and one of five feet is called *pentameter.

These lines are from Longfellow's *The Jewish Cemetery at Newport:*

> Gone are the living, but the dead remain,
> And not neglected; for a hand unseen,
> Scattering its bounty, like a summer rain,
> Still keeps their graves and their
> remembrance green.

It is impossible to read this stanza without hearing its rhythm. The meter is iambic pentameter, the most common meter in English and American verse.

> Gōne āre / thĕ lĭv/ĭng, būt / thĕ dēad / rĕmaīn,
> Ănd nōt / nĕglēct/ĕd; fŏr / ă hānd / ŭnseēn . . .

Here are the meters (metrical patterns) of several other poems:

Iambic pentameter

> Thĕ cūr/fĕw tōlls / thĕ knēll / ŏf pārt/ĭng dāy,
> Thĕ lōw/ĭng hērd / wĭnd slōw/lў o'ēr / thĕ lēa,

> Gray, *Elegy Written in a Country
> Churchyard*

(Note that in the second line, the prevailing meter is iambic, but not every foot is.)

Iambic tetrameter and iambic trimeter

> Yĕt thīs / ĭncōn/stăncу / ĭs sŭch
> Ăs yōu / tōo shāll / ădōre;
> Ĭ coūld / nŏt lŏve / thĕe, Dēar, / sŏ mŭch
> Lŏved Ī / nŏt Hōn/ŏr mōre.

> Lovelace, *To Lucasta, on Going to
> the Wars*

Trochaic tetrameter

> Whў sŏ / pāle ănd / wān, fŏnd / lōvĕr?
> Prīthĕe, / whў sŏ/ pāle?
> Wĭll, whĕn / lōokĭng / wĕll căn't / mōve hĕr,
> Lōokĭng/ ĭll / prĕvāil?

> Suckling, *Why So Pale and Wan?*

(The second and fourth lines indicate a variation in prevailing kind of foot and line length that is characteristic of much poetry.)

Dactylic tetrameter

> Jŭst fŏr ă/ handfŭl ŏf / sĭlvĕr hĕ/ lĕft ŭs,
> Jŭst fŏr ă/ rĭband tŏ / stĭck ĭn hĭs / cōat...
> Browning, *The Lost Leader*

(The prevailing foot is dactylic, but in each line the last foot is altered without destroying rhythmic effect.)

Anapestic tetrameter

> Nŏt ă wōrd / tŏ ĕach ōth/ĕr; wĕ kēpt /
> thĕ grĕat pāce
> Nĕck bŏ nĕck, / strĭde bŏ strĭde, /
> nĕvĕr chang/ĭng ŏur plāce...

> Browning, *How They Brought the Good
> News from Ghent to Aix*

method acting

A theory and technique of performing in which the actor identifies as closely as possible with the character to be presented and renders that role in an individualized, relatively quiet, and natural manner.

metonymy

A figure of speech in which the name of one object or idea is used for another to which it is related or of which it is a part. Thus, "the crown" or "scepter" may refer to a ruling monarch, "the bottle" may mean milk or strong drink, "the fleet" may stand for sailors, etc. "The tailor sews a fine seam" means that he does good tailoring. The Biblical verse "In the sweat of thy face shalt thou eat bread" illustrates metonymy: "sweat of thy face" means hard work and "bread" means food. In John Milton's line "When I consider how my light is spent," *light* stands for sight, vision, ability to see. See SYNECDOCHE.

metrical romance

An *adventure story in verse. The term is applied to such works as *Sir Gawain and the Green Knight,* Chaucer's *The Knight's Tale* (in *The Canterbury Tales*), and Sir Walter Scott's *The Lady of the Lake.*

metrics

The science of *meter. *Metrics,* the systematic study and

investigation of the patterns of *rhythm in poetry, is a synonym for *prosody. See METER, SCANSION.

Middle Ages

The period in European history from about the end of the Roman Empire (476) to the beginnings of the Renaissance (about 1350). For further comment, see MEDIEVAL.

Middle English

The English language as spoken and written after the Norman Conquest (1066) and preceding the *Renaissance in England. The dates commonly given are 1100 and 1500, but these are only approximate.

For an illustration of Middle English, here is the Lord's Prayer approximately as it appeared in John Wycliffe's translation in the fourteenth century:

> Oure fadir that art in heuenes, halwid be thi name; thi kyngdom cumme to; be thi wille don as in heuen and in erthe; ȝif to vs this day ouer breed oure other substaunce; and forȝeue to vs oure dettis as we forȝeue to oure dettours; and leede vs nat in to temptacioun, but delyuere vs fro yuel. Amen.

miles gloriosus

A Latin term meaning "a boastful soldier." The braggart warrior was a *stock character in Greek and Roman comedy (Plautus wrote a play entitled *Miles Gloriosus* in the second century B.C.) and has remained a dramatic figure ever since. The best-known miles gloriosus in literature is Shakespeare's Sir John Falstaff (*Henry IV,* Parts 1 and 2). Sergeant Bilko of television fame carries on the *tradition of the bragging coward, and so does an officer in George Bernard Shaw's *Arms and the Man.*

milieu

Environment, condition, medium. *Milieu,* a term from French, also means surroundings, sphere, element, and background. The milieu of an author is the physical setting of his life and the intellectual climate of his times. The milieu of Shakespeare was the theatrical world of Elizabethan London. The milieu of William Faulkner was rural and small-town Mississippi. See AMBIENCE, SETTING.

Miltonic

A reference to John Milton, English poet (1608–1674), considered to rank with Shakespeare and Chaucer among the greatest poets of all time in English literature. The adjective is sometimes applied to authors who serve their government (as Milton did); to writers with strong ethical and moral beliefs; to defenders of free speech and haters of *censorship; to authors whose style is dignified and lofty (Milton has been called "the God-gifted organ-voice of England").

A Miltonic sonnet is a fourteen-line poetic form (see SON-NET) which has the same *rhyme scheme for the *octave (first eight lines) as the *Petrarchan sonnet (*abbaabba*) but does not pause after the octave and does not follow a fixed rhyme scheme in the *sestet (final six lines). *On His Blindness* ("When I consider how my light is spent . . . / They also serve who only stand and wait") is a Miltonic sonnet.

mime

(1) A form of popular *comedy developed in Italy in the fifth century B.C. which presented events of everyday life through dances, gestures, and *dialogue; (2)*pantomime, the art of portraying a character or mood by the use of gestures, facial expressions, and bodily movements. The term *mime* is now most often used as a verb meaning to imitate or copy in action or speech and as a noun meaning an actor, a professional entertainer, who is clever in mimicking or imitating others. Charlie Chaplin was a mime in silent movies for many years. See DUMB SHOW, MIMESIS, PANTOMIME.

mimesis

A Greek word for "imitation." In the *Poetics,* Aristotle first stated the principles of mimesis by commenting that *tragedy is an imitation of *action, not mere mimicry but the selection, arrangement, and presentation of acts that reveal the relation of art and life. Hamlet's speech to the players (*Hamlet,* act 3, scene 2) reveals the principles of mimesis:

> . . . the purpose of playing, whose end, both of the first and now, was and is, to hold, as 'twere, the mirror up to nature; to show virtue her own feature, scorn her own image, and the very age and body of the time his form and pressure.

mimetic

An adjective that refers to mimicry. A mimetic literary selection is one that places primary emphasis upon the creation of imagined actions and *dialogue in such ways as to make unmistakable their reality, their actuality. See BELIEF, MIMESIS, NATURALISM, REALISM, VERISIMILITUDE.

minnesinger

A "singer of love." *Minnesinger,* derived from German words for *love (Minne)* and *sing,* refers specifically to a group of *medieval German lyric poets. See MINSTREL, TROUBADOUR.

minstrel

(1) A musician, singer, or poet; (2) a professional entertainer of the *Middle Ages who was attached to one great household or who wandered about the countryside; (3) an itinerant comedian with blackened face. See GLEEMAN, JONGLEUR, TROUBADOUR, VAUDEVILLE.

miracle play

A *medieval dramatic form dealing with Biblical stories or the lives of saints. Miracle plays were usually presented in a series, or *cycle, such as dramas dealing with the Virgin Mary, the fall of man, the creation of the world, etc. In France, a religious drama that dealt with a religious or moral but non-Biblical theme was known as a mystery play, but elsewhere *miracle* and *mystery* have been synonymous terms. *Sister Beatrice,* by the Belgian writer Maurice Maeterlinck (1862–1947), is a modern example of the miracle play. See MORALITY PLAY, MYSTERY PLAY.

miscellany

A group of various unselected items; a medley. In literature, *miscellany* refers to a collection of literary compositions by several authors, dealing with various topics and assembled in a book. The first such volume was a medley of *Elizabethan *songs and *sonnets published in England in 1557 and known as *Tottel's Miscellany.* An *anthology and a *chrestomathy are forms of miscellany.

mise-en-scène

The stage setting of a play. A French term, *mise-en-scène* refers to the scenery and stage properties of an acted play, to the arrangement of actors and the handling of technical equipment. With a literal meaning of "putting in the scene," *mise-en-scène* is used to refer to the surroundings or environment of any event. See AMBIENCE, MILIEU, SETTING.

mixed metaphor

A use in the same expression of two or more *metaphors (implied analogies, comparisons) that are incongruous or illogical, as referring to someone as "a well-oiled cog in the beehive of industry" or to an administration that "will put the ship of state on its feet." Effective writers rarely mix metaphors; when they do, the mixing is usually deliberate and effective. For example, in *Lycidas,* Milton referred to corrupt clergymen as "Blind mouths! that scarce themselves know how to hold / A sheephook."

mock epic

A long, humorous poem in which a slight or trivial subject is treated in a lofty, exalted, and heroic manner. A mock epic is a mockery, an imitation, a *burlesque of *epic presentation and subject matter. Chaucer's *The Nun's Priest's Tale* (from *The Canterbury Tales*) is a mock epic. Jonathan Swift's *The Battle of the Books,* a prose satire, and Pope's *The Rape of the Lock* are mock epics. From the last-named, these lines narrating the emotions of a girl from whose head a lock of hair is snipped illustrate a mock epic approach:

> Then flashed the living lightning from her eyes,
> And screams of horror rend the affrighted skies.

mock heroic

A term closely related to mock epic, *mock heroic* refers to the *style* of a kind of *satire that treats "ordinary" characters and events in the ceremonious manner and lofty language usually reserved for major happenings and elevated personages. *Mock heroic* refers more to *style than to *form (see MOCK EPIC); for instance, Joseph Fielding's *Tom Thumb* is a play written in a mock heroic manner. Mock heroic passages occur in Byron's poem *Don Juan.* Oscar Wilde's drama *The Importance of Being Earnest* contains *dialogue in which characters discuss with great solemnity numerous trivial occurrences.

monody

(1) A poem in which one person laments the death of another (see DIRGE, ELEGY, THRENODY); (2) an *ode sung by

an actor in Greek tragedy. *Monody* comes from a Greek term meaning "singing alone." In an introduction to *Lycidas,* Milton wrote, "In this monody, the author bewails a learned friend, unfortunately drowned...." Matthew Arnold referred to his *lament entitled *Thyrsis* as "a monody, to commemorate the author's friend, Arthur Hugh Clough, who died at Florence, 1861."

monologue
From Greek terms meaning "one word" or "one speech," *monologue* refers to a specch by one person. (See DIALOGUE.) In *drama, *monologue* refers to a form of entertainment by a single speaker or to an extended part of the text of a play uttered by an actor. (See SOLILOQUY.) A device used to reveal the flow of thoughts through a character's mind in plays or novels is called *interior monologue. (See STREAM OF CONSCIOUSNESS.) In everyday life, *monologue* is sometimes used disparagingly to refer to the remarks of someone who talks glibly and incessantly. See LOGORRHEA.

monometer
A one-foot line of verse. Monometer, rare in verse in English, is illustrated in this sad fifteen-line poem by Robert Herrick, written in *iambic *feet (see METER):
Thus I / Passe by / And die: / As One / Unknown /
And gone: / I'm made / A shade, / and laid / I'the grave: /
There have / My Cave. / Where tell / I dwell, / Farewell.
Also, see AMPHIMACER.

montage
A combination of elements that forms a unified whole, a single *image. (See COLLAGE.) *Montage* is used in literature as a device to establish a *theme or create an *atmosphere through a series of rapidly presented impressions or observations. In *U.S.A.,* John Dos Passos used what he referred to as "newsreels," but they are actually montages. The device of montage, frequently used by writers of *impressionism, appears in the *interior monologue of novels and plays and in motion-picture and television productions.

mood
A word coming from *Old English *mod* that meant "heart," "spirit," and "courage," *mood* refers to a disposition of mind, a feeling, an emotional state. The *mood* of a literary work re-

fers to its predominating *atmosphere or *tone. (Comment on *mood* appears also under the entries for CONTROLLING IMAGE and DOMINANT IMPRESSION.) Every major work of literature has a prevailing mood, but many also shift in mood to achieve *counterpoint, to provide *comic relief, or to reflect changing circumstances in *plot.

morality play

An *allegory in dramatic form current from the fourteenth to the sixteenth century. Most morality plays employed personified *abstractions of vices and virtues (Shame, Lust, Mercy, Conscience). A morality play, unlike *miracle and *mystery plays, did not necessarily use Biblical or strictly religious material and was more concerned with morality than spirituality. The best-known of all morality plays is *Everyman* (fifteenth century). The *theme of this drama is the summoning of Everyman (everyone) by Death. On his passage to Death, Everyman discovers that, of all his supposed friends, only Good Deeds will go with him. Other characters in the play are Fellowship, Kindred, Knowledge, Strength, and Beauty.

morpheme

A term in linguistics for the smallest meaningful unit in a language. A morpheme may be a word (*it*), a prefix or suffix (*ad-, -ism*), or an *accent (*PER-mit, per-MIT*).

motif

A recurring *theme, idea, or subject in a literary work (or musical *composition). A motif is closely related to *dominant impression, the unifying thread in a work. The abduction of a princess or queen by a fairy lover is a motif in some medieval *romances and *fairy tales. The dullness and drabness of life are a motif in James Joyce's *Dubliners*. In Thomas Wolfe's novels, the motif is that of a lost boy, a searcher for something (for a father, a belief, a way of life) to which he can cling.

motivation

Reasons and explanations for action through the presentation of convincing and impelling causes for that action. Motivation consists of the psychological impulses and drives which impel a character in literature to act as he does. The motives supplied to characters by novelists and dramatists are combinations of temperament and circumstance that realistically account for what they do, do not do, say, and do not say. When suitable motivation of characters is supplied by the imaginative ability and understanding of an author, a reader *knows* and fully accepts the emotional and circumstantial forces that made their deeds inevitable. Readers can accept the fact that Othello smothers Desdemona when he thinks her unfaithful; motivation for this act has been supplied by revealing the intensity of his pride and jealousy. See BELIEF, CHARACTERIZATION.

motto

An especially appropriate word or saying attached to or inscribed on an activity, institution, or undertaking; a *maxim adopted as an expression of a guiding principle or basic aim.

Then conquer we must, for our cause it is just,
And this be our motto: "In God is our trust!"

The Star-Spangled Banner, stanza 4

mummery

(1) A dramatic performance or ceremony performed by persons wearing masks or fantastic disguises; (2) any activity regarded as false, absurd, or pretentious. Mummery, an integral part of festivities engaged in in certain localities at New Year's, the beginning of Lent, Christmas, etc., is a farcical presentation, a kind of *pantomime. See MASQUE.

✓muse

(1) The genius or powers characteristic of a literary artist; (2) the goddess regarded as inspiring a poet or other writer. *Muse,* especially when capitalized, refers to one of a number of goddesses in classical mythology, specifically the nine daughters of Zeus who presided over various arts: epic poetry, lyric poetry, history, music, dance, tragedy, religious music, comedy, and astronomy. Homer began the *Iliad* by appealing to a muse; in book 7 of *Paradise Lost* Milton requests a muse to "descend from heaven"; the *prologue to Shakespeare's *Henry V* begins "O for a Muse of fire that would ascend / The brightest heaven of invention." See AFFLATUS.

musical comedy

A play with music. A typical musical comedy is based on a slight *plot, presents songs and dances in solo and group performance, and is lighthearted, whimsical, or satiric. Such a production is a combination of light *opera, *vaudeville, and *burlesque. Notable musical comedies include *The Merry Widow, Show Boat, Oklahoma!, South Pacific,* and *My Fair Lady.*

mystery play

A dramatic form, especially popular during the *Middle Ages, which dealt with Biblical stories, such as the "mystery" of the life, death, and resurrection of Jesus Christ. Mystery plays were so called for another reason: the French word *mystère* means "craft," and many "mysteries" were performed by members of craft guilds, such as the shipwrights' guild, the stationers' guild, etc. Although some scholars make a distinction, the terms *mystery play* and *miracle play* are now used interchangeably. See MIRACLE PLAY, MORALITY PLAY.

mystery story

A mystery is anything that is kept secret or that remains unknown or unexplained. A mystery story is a form of *narration in which the methods, details, and motives of a crime are entertaining and baffling. More exactly, the term *mystery story* can be applied to a DETECTIVE STORY (which see), to a *Gothic tale or novel (terror, frightening events), and to a novel of *suspense (excited uncertainty). Most speakers mean detective story when they refer to a mystery, since any tale of *adventure involving a criminal act that is not immediately explained is a mystery story. In this sense, Stevenson's *Treasure Island* is a mystery story, although of a kind different from Dashiell Hammett's *The Thin Man* or Raymond Chandler's *The Long Goodbye.*

mysticism

(1) Obscure thought or speculation; (2) the beliefs and ideas of persons who claim to have immediate intuition and insight into mysteries beyond normal understanding. Mysticism takes many forms in the mental, spiritual, and emotional lives of authors, but varied aspects of it are traceable in the works of William Blake, Samuel Taylor Coleridge, Herman Melville, and Walt Whitman. In the opinion of many students of literature, *transcendentalism is a form of mysticism.

myth

(1) A legendary or traditional story, usually one concerning a superhuman being and dealing with events that have no natu-

ral explanation; (2) an unproved belief that is accepted uncritically; (3) an invented idea or story.

A myth usually attempts to explain a phenomenon or strange occurrence without regard to scientific fact or so-called common sense. The myth, appealing to emotion rather than to reason, dates from ancient times when rational explanations were neither available nor apparently wanted. A myth is less "historical" than a *legend and less concerned with *didacticism than a *fable, but all three forms are fictitious stories, many of which have persisted through *oral transmission.

mythopoesis

The making of *myths. A mythopoeic writer consciously makes a mythic *frame or background for his work. For instance, in *The Plumed Serpent,* D. H. Lawrence used ancient myths of Mexico to explain the primal behavior and blood consciousness that ruined the lives of sophisticated Europeans. In a sense, Melville's *Moby Dick* is a created myth, because its action is a symbol of primeval conflict. William Butler Yeats, T. S. Eliot, and William Faulkner were mythopoeic writers in some of their work.

narcissism

Excessive admiration of oneself. *Narcissism* is derived from Narcissus, a youth in classical mythology who became infatuated with his own image reflected in a pool. (Eventually, Narcissus wasted away and was transformed into the flower of the same name.) Self-love and inflated *ego (egoism) are evidenced by numerous characters in history, among them Nero, Julius Caesar, and Alexander the Great, and by such strictly literary creations as Becky Sharp in Thackeray's *Vanity Fair* and Heathcliff in Emily Brontë's *Wuthering Heights. Narcissism,* in psychiatry, refers to sexual excitement stemming from admiration of one's own body.

narration

A *form of discourse the principal purpose of which is to relate an event or series of events. *Narration,* from a Latin word meaning "tell," is also called "narrative," which may be used as an adjective or noun. Narration (or narrative) appears in history, news stories, *biography, *autobiography, and the like but is usually applied to such *forms of writing as the *anecdote, *conte, *exemplum, *fable, *fabliau, *fairy tale, *incident, legend, *novel, *novelette, *short story, and *tale. The primary and basic appeal of narration is to the emotions of the reader or hearer. See FICTION, PLOT.

narrative hook

A device used at the beginning of a work of fiction intend-ed to arouse the interest of readers and make them eager to read further. Beginning *in medias res is a kind of narrative hook. Other forms are the use of *paradox, of a startling quotation, the mention of a murder or accident, or indeed any statement that will excite curiosity which de-mands satisfaction. Notice how many intriguing questions are raised in the reader's mind by this beginning of William Faulkner's story *A Rose for Emily:*

> When Miss Emily Grierson died, our whole town went to her funeral: the men through a sort of respectful affection for a fallen monument, the women mostly out of curiosity to see the inside of her house, which no one save an old man-servant—a combined gardener and cook—had seen in at least ten years.

naturalism

In literature, an attempt to achieve fidelity to nature by reject-ing idealized portrayals of life. *Naturalism* may be further de-fined as a technique or manner of presenting an objective view of man with complete accuracy and frankness. Naturalistic writers hold that man's existence is shaped by heredity and environment, over which he has no control and about which he can exercise little if any choice. Novels and plays in this move-ment, emphasizing the animal nature of man, portray charac-ters engrossed in a brutal struggle for survival. Émile Zola, founder of the French school of naturalism, held that a novelist should dissect and analyze his subjects with dispassionate, scien-tific accuracy and minuteness.

Among adherents of naturalism in American literature, in at least some of their works, were Theodore Dreiser, Ernest Hemingway, Eugene O'Neill, and William Faulkner. See REALISM.

near rhyme

Corresponding sounds which are not true or exact. For instance, Pope employed near rhyme with *restored* and *word.*

negative capability

A term used by John Keats as a name for the impersonality and objectivity of a writer. Negative capability, which has about the same meaning as *aesthetic distance, applies to the "innate universality" which Keats attributed to Shakespeare, that capacity which the latter had for "being in uncertainties, mysteries, doubts, without any irritable reaching after fact and reason." *Negative capability* is used by some critics to describe qualities in a writer which enable him to keep his own personality entirely apart from what he is relating or discussing.

nemesis

In classical mythology, Nemesis was the goddess of divine retribution (punishment). Spelled with a small letter, *nemesis* applies to (1) a rival or opponent who cannot be overcome or handled; (2) any situation or condition which one cannot change or triumph over; (3) an agent, or an act, of punishment. *Nemesis,* roughly synonymous with *fate, is generally used in literature to suggest that everyone gets his share of good and bad fortune and that, sooner or later, justice will prevail. For instance, in *Macbeth,* Macduff is the nemesis of Macbeth and Lady Macbeth.

neoclassicism

A style of writing developed in the seventeenth and eighteenth centuries that rigidly adhered to *canons of *form derived from classical antiquity. Neoclassicism ("new" *classicism) was notable for emotional restraint, elegance and exactness of *diction, strict observance of the three *unities, common sense, *rationalism, and *logic. The "modern" writers cited under the entry CLASSICISM were neoclassicists. In architecture, *neoclassicism* refers to the use of Greek orders and decorative details, geometric compositions, plain wall surfaces, etc.

neologism

A new word or phrase, a *coinage. *Neologism* also applies to a new doctrine, such as a fresh interpretation of the *Bible or of some other work of literature. See ACRONYM, COINAGE, PORTMANTEAU WORD.

Neoplatonism

A philosophical system originating in the third century A.D., based on *Platonism, Oriental *mysticism, and traces of

Christianity. Both *Neoplatonism* and *Platonism* are rather vague terms; generally, they apply to concern with aspirations of the human spirit (see HUMANISM), with the placing of mind over matter, with optimistic but somewhat mysterious approaches to the fundamental problems of man and the universe. Among Neoplatonic literary selections may be mentioned Wordsworth's *Ode on Intimations of Immortality from Recollections of Early Childhood.*

New Criticism

A form of criticism (evaluation) that relies on close and detailed analysis of the language, imagery, and emotional or intellectual meanings of a literary work. New Criticism emphasizes concentrated study and subsequent interpretation of a selection as a selection rather than as a biographical or historical study or as a statement of philosphy, ethics, or sociology. In New Criticism, analysis of the text itself results in reputed discovery of layers of meaning. This approach, first developed at Vanderbilt University, has among its followers such American authors as Allen Tate, Robert Penn Warren, Yvor Winters, and Kenneth Burke. See CRITICISM, EXPLICATION.

nihilism

A term derived from a Latin word meaning "nothing," "a thing of no value," *nihilism* means (1) total rejection of established laws and institutions; (2) anarchy, terrorism, or other revolutionary activity; (3) total and absolute destructiveness. In philosophy, *nihilism* refers to an extreme form of skepticism that involves denial of any possible objective basis for truth. *Existentialism may be considered a form of nihilism to the degree that it considers traditional values and beliefs unfounded and all human existence aimless, senseless, and useless.

nihil obstat

A Latin term meaning "nothing stands in the way." In the Roman Catholic Church, *nihil obstat* refers to permission to publish a book (after certification that it contains nothing contrary to Catholic faith or morals). See IMPRIMATUR.

Nobel prize

An award named after Alfred B. Nobel (1833–1896), Swedish engineer and chemist, who left a large sum of money (nine million dollars) the interest from which is annually distributed to persons considered to have contributed outstandingly to mankind. Nobel prizes are awarded in peace, physics, chemistry, medicine or physiology, economics, and literature. English and American winners of the Nobel prize for literature have included Rudyard Kipling, William Butler Yeats, George Bernard Shaw, Sinclair Lewis, John Galsworthy, Eugene O'Neill, Pearl Buck, T. S. Eliot, William Faulkner, Bertrand Russell, Winston Churchill, Ernest Hemingway, and John Steinbeck.

nocturne

A lyric poem that expresses thoughtful feelings considered appropriate to evening and nighttime. *Nocturne* applies in music to a *composition with a *mood of twilight or evening. Gray's *Elegy Written in a Country Churchyard* has a nocturnal feeling. Carl Sandburg's *Nocturne in a Deserted Brickyard* provides an illustration:

> Stuff of the moon
> Runs on the lapping sand
> Out to the longest shadows...
> Fluxions of yellow and dusk on the waters
> Make a wide dreaming pansy of an old pond
> in the night.

noh

Classic drama of Japan. Noh, often spelled nō, was developed in the fourteenth century from ritual dances associated with ancient Shinto worship. Noh plays are formal, restrained, and subtle. See KABUKI.

nonce word

A term coined and used for a particular occasion. *Nonce* means "the present," "now," and so a nonce word is a *coinage, a *neologism, newly designed to fit a specific situation. Lewis Carroll's jabberwocky is a nonce word. The coinages in James Joyce's *Ulysses* and *Finnegans Wake* are nonce words.

nonfiction

As opposed to *fiction and distinguished from *drama and *poetry, nonfiction is that branch of literature presenting ideas and opinions based upon facts and reality. Considered as nonfiction are such types of writing as *autobiography, *biography, the *essay, and history. However, most fiction and drama and some poetry contain nonfictional elements; most nonfiction reveals some imaginative (invented) passages.

nonsense verse

A form of light verse which is entertaining because of its rhythmic appeal and absurd or farfetched ideas. See DOGGEREL, JINGLE, LIGHT VERSE, LIMERICK, MACARONIC, NURSERY RHYME. Also, see JABBERWOCKY; this *stanza from Lewis Carroll's *Jabberwocky* will serve to illustrate nonsense verse:
> "And hast thou slain the Jabberwock?
> Come to my arms, my beamish boy!
> O frabjous day! Callooh! Callay!"
> He chortled in his joy.

noumenon

In the philosophy of Immanuel Kant (1724–1804; German thinker), *noumenon* refers to anything which can be the object only of mental intuition and not the result of using one's senses. Sometimes referred to as "the object of pure reason," *noumenon* is in contrast to *phenomenon* (a fact, circumstance, or occurrence that can be observed). These lines from Wordsworth's *The Excursion* are noumenal:
> ... One in whom persuasion and belief
> Had ripened into faith, and faith become
> A passionate intuition.

novel

A lengthy fictitious prose narrative portraying characters and presenting an organized series of events and settings. A work of *fiction with fewer than 30,000 to 40,000 words is usually considered a *short story, *novelette, or *tale, but the novel has no actual maximum length. Every novel is an account of life; every novel involves *conflict, *characters, *action, *settings, *plot, and *theme. See EPISTOLARY, HISTORICAL NOVEL, PROBLEM NOVEL, POINT OF VIEW, ROMANCE.

novelette

A short *novel. Among short novels are Voltaire's *Candide*, Fitzgerald's *The Great Gatsby*, John Buchan's *The Thirty-nine Steps*, Bram Stoker's *Dracula*, Stevenson's *Dr. Jekyll and Mr. Hyde*, George Eliot's *The Lifted Veil*, Joseph Conrad's

The Secret Sharer, Virginia Woolf's *Between the Acts,* Melville's *Billy Budd,* and Hemingway's *The Old Man and the Sea.*

novella

An Italian term meaning "a story," *novella* refers to a relatively short prose narrative, comparable in length to a long *short story or a *novelette. Boccaccio's *The Decameron* is a collection of 100 novelle (plural form), pithy tales of varying length that focus upon one dominant event rather than a series of actions. Among celebrated European writers of novelle may be mentioned Goethe and Thomas Mann.

nursery rhyme

A simple poem or song for infants and young children. See LULLABY.

objective correlative

A chain of events, or a situation, which makes objective a particular (subjective) emotion. *Objective correlative,* a term first used by T. S. Eliot in a critical study of *Hamlet,* implies an impersonal means of communicating feeling. Eliot wrote, "When the external facts, which must terminate in sensory experience, are given, the emotion is immediately evoked." Eliot held that the emotions which dominated Hamlet are not justified by the facts in the play. The term *objective correlative* is widely and somewhat vaguely used by adherents of the *New Criticism. See AESTHETIC DISTANCE, NEGATIVE CAPABILITY, OBJECTIVITY.

objectivity

(1) A dealing with outward things; (2) reality as it is, or seems to be, apart from one's thoughts and feelings; (3) intentness on objects external to the mind. In literature, objectivity is a quality of impersonality, of freedom from personal sentiments, beliefs, and emotions. Some of the work of Henry Fielding, Anthony Trollope, and Ernest Hemingway, for example, treats events as external rather than as affected by the reflections and *point of view of the author. See AESTHETIC DISTANCE, NEGATIVE CAPABILITY, OBJECTIVE CORRELATIVE.

obligatory scene

An *episode which is so fully expected by the audience that a dramatist is "obliged" to provide it. In *Ghosts*, by Henrik Ibsen, the audience, aware that Regina and Oswald are half sister and brother, witnesses their growing sexual interest in each other. The episode in which they "discover" their true relationship is an obligatory scene.

occasional verse

*Poetry (or *doggerel) written for a special occasion, usually to commemorate a social, historical, or literary event. When occasional verse is witty or satiric, it is sometimes called vers de société. Among well-known literary selections written for special occasions are Spenser's *Epithalamion* (celebrating his marriage); Milton's *Lycidas* (on the death of Edward King, the author's friend); Tennyson's *Ode on the Death of the Duke of Wellington;* Kipling's *Recessional* (for Queen Victoria's Diamond Jubilee, 1897). See POET LAUREATE.

octameter

A verse (line) of poetry consisting of eight feet. (See FOOT, METER.) Octameter, also spelled *octometer,* is rare in poetry; each of these lines from Tennyson's *Locksley Hall* consists of eight feet (trochaic octameter):

> In the spring a livelier iris changes on the
> burnished dove;
> In the spring a young man's fancy lightly
> turns to thoughts of love.

octastich

A group of eight lines of poetry. *Octastich* is made up of *octa* (an element in loan words from Greek and Latin meaning "eight") and *stich* ("row, line, verse"). See OCTAVE, OTTAVA RIMA.

✓octave

Like *octastich, an octave refers to a *stanza of eight lines, but especially to the first eight lines in an *Italian sonnet. Usually, but not always, the octave of a sonnet asks a question answered in the *sestet (six following lines) or states a condition or generalization which is "resolved" in the sestet. See SONNET.

octavo

The size of a book (about 6 by 9 inches) determined by folding the printed sheets to form eight leaves (sixteen pages). The term *octavo*, which also applies to a book of this size, is usually abbreviated to 8vo. See FOLIO.

ode

Originally, an ode was a poem meant to be sung, but its meaning has been altered to apply to a lyric poem with a dignified *theme that is phrased in a formal, elevated *style. (See COWLEYAN ODE, HORATIAN, PINDARIC.) Among well-known odes are Shelley's *To a Skylark,* Dryden's *Alexander's Feast,* Gray's *The Bard* and *The Progress of Poesy,* James Russell Lowell's *Ode Recited at the Harvard Commemoration,* and Allen Tate's *Ode on the Confederate Dead.*

Oedipus complex

Sexual desire of a son for his mother. As a psychiatric term, *Oedipus complex* refers to the unresolved desire of a child for sexual gratification through a parent of the opposite sex. This condition involves identification with, and later hatred of, the parent of the same sex, who is considered by the child as a rival. Actually, in *Freudianism, when the boy is sexually attracted to his mother, there is an Oedipus complex; when the girl desires her father, an Electra complex results. (Electra incited her brother to kill their mother in revenge for the latter's murder of their father.)

Oedipus complex is derived from the story of Oedipus, a figure in Greek *legend, who was once a king of Thebes. As prophesied, he unknowingly killed his father and married his mother. Both the Oedipus complex and the Electra complex have been used in modern fiction and drama, notably in the work of Eugene O'Neill and Tennessee Williams.

Old English

A term referring to the English language as it was spoken and written from about A.D. 450 to about 1150. (See ANGLO-SAXON.) Contrary to what might be expected from primitive and nomadic tribes such as the Angles, Saxons, and Jutes, Old English had a vocabulary of some 50,000 words and was capable of conveying sophisticated ideas. For instance, a native Old English word, *God,* was combined with *spell* ("talk," "message") into *Godspell* or, in modern

English, *gospel.* Old English *godsunu* has become modern *godson.* Old English now appears at least as foreign as Latin or French, but many words are recognizable, such as *hete* ("hate"), *heofon* ("heaven"), *sawol* ("soul"), *fyr* ("fire"), and *weorc* ("work").

Olympian

Majestic, aloof, incomparably superior. *Olympian* refers to Mount Olympus, a mountain in Greece and the mythical home of the greater Greek gods. Such writers as Shakespeare and Milton have been referred to as Olympian because of their transcendent genius. In *The Master: Lincoln,* Edwin Arlington Robinson paid this tribute to Abraham Lincoln:

> The saddest among kings of earth,
> Bowed with a galling crown, this man
> Met rancor with a cryptic mirth,
> Laconic—and Olympian.

omniscience

Infinite knowledge; complete awareness or understanding; ability to see everything. Omniscience is exercised by those authors who tell a story from an omniscient *point of view. With this technique, a writer is capable of seeing, knowing, and telling whatever he wishes. The author, assuming omniscience for himself, is free to move his characters in time and place, to describe the physical action and private thoughts of characters, to comment upon what happens and to make clear the *theme of his story in whatever ways he chooses. Most of the world's novels and plays considered greatest are told from an omniscient point of view.

one-acter

A play consisting of one act. A one-acter, like a *short story, demands concentration on one *theme as well as *economy in *style, *setting, and plotting. Sir James M. Barrie, George Bernard Shaw, John Galsworthy (England); Gerhart Hauptmann (Germany); Johan August Strindberg (Sweden); and Eugene O'Neill and Paul Green (United States) have written many successful one-act plays.

onomastics

A study of the origin and history of proper names. From a Greek term meaning "names," onomastics is concerned with the *folklore of names, their current application, spellings, pronunciations, and meanings. An example of onomastics is George Stewart's *Names on the Land* (1945, 1957), a historical account of place naming in the United States.

onomatopoeia

The formation and use of words that suggest by their sounds the object or idea being named: *bowwow, bang, buzz, cackle, clatter, hiss, murmur, sizzle, twitter, zoom.* Onomatopoeia is also a figure of speech, the use of "imitative" words for rhetorical effect. In the hands of an accomplished writer, onomatopoeia is a powerful device by which sound is made, in Alexander Pope's words, "an echo to the sense," as he illustrated in *An Essay on Criticism:*

Soft is the strain when Zephyr gently blows,
And the smooth stream in smoother numbers flows;
But when loud surges lash the sounding shore,
The hoarse, rough verse should like
the torrent roar:
When Ajax strives some rock's vast weight to throw,
The line too labors, and the words move slow.

opera

A *drama set to music. From Latin and Italian words meaning "work," an opera is an extended dramatic *composition in which parts are sung to instrumental accompaniment. Many operas include arias, choruses, recitatives (declamatory passages), and ballet. Although opera is musical drama, it is more serious, artistic, and dignified than *musical comedy, *mummery, and *vaudeville.

opéra bouffe

A French term for "comic opera," "a farcical musical drama," an "operatic *extravaganza." This form, apparently developed from *vaudeville music, was a forerunner of the comic operas of Gilbert and Sullivan.

operetta

A short, amusing, lighthearted *opera. An operetta, a diminutive (smaller form) of opera, emphasizes music and *spectacle and contains some spoken dialogue as incidental. Except for minor differences in staging, an operetta and an opéra bouffe are identical.

195

opprobrium

Disgrace or reproach brought about by conduct considered shameful. *Opprobrium* is a *synonym for *infamy* and *strong condemnation*. Daniel Webster suffered opprobrium when he championed the Compromise of 1850 in his Seventh of March speech. Whittier heaped opprobrium upon Webster in his poem *Ichabod:*

> All else is gone; from those great eyes
> The soul has fled:
> When faith is lost, when honor dies,
> The man is dead!

oral transmission

The spreading or passing on of material by word of mouth. The term is applied especially to the *ballad, the *epic, and *folklore, some of which, in the opinion of some scholars, were originally made known to audiences only by recitation and singing and were handed down to succeeding generations through memory rather than in written form. The theory of oral transmission is that traditional material (not only the *forms just mentioned but also *folktales, *fables, *proverbs, old wives' tales, and *songs) were first the property of the so-called common people who repeated (or sang) such items, consciously or unconsciously altered them, and taught them to their children from one generation to the next.

oration

A formal speech delivered on a special occasion. An oration, characterized by elevated *style and *diction and by studied delivery, is an eloquent address suitable for an anniversary celebration, political controversy, a funeral, and academic exercises. The most famous oration in literature may be Mark Antony's speech in *Julius Caesar* (act 3, scene 2): "Friends, Romans, countrymen, lend me your ears ...." Other orations are Demosthenes's *Philippic against the ruler of Macedon; Cicero's *diatribes against Catiline; Daniel Webster's Seventh of March speech (see OPPROBRIUM); Abraham Lincoln's Gettysburg Address.

organization

Forming coordinated and interdependent parts into a whole; giving organic character and *structure to a literary selection. The organization of all *fiction is largely determined by *plot. The organization of *drama depends upon its division into *acts and *scenes. The organization of *poetry is affected by its *meter, *rhyme scheme, arrangement in *stanzas, etc. The patterns of organization in essays, biography, articles, etc., include chronology (time sequence), space (see POINT OF VIEW), similarity or contrast, analysis, and *logic.

Every effective work of literature possesses and reveals some kind of order and organization, but the organic form of any selection apparently has developed from a conception in the thought, personality, and feelings of its author as opposed to dependence upon a fixed and mechanical structure dictated by *convention. For this reason, no two novels or lyric poems or short stories or plays ever reveal precisely the same organization.

originality

In literature, *originality* applies to the ability to think and express oneself in an independent way. Originality is a matter of creative ability, of individuality, of providing a unique approach to a given subject. Only a few geniuses in literature have conceived wholly fresh ideas and completely novel ways of conveying them, but every author worth reading has revealed some capacity for independent thought, individual insight, and constructive imagination. Goethe has provided an illuminating comment on originality:

> The most original authors of modern times are such not because they create anything new but only because they are able to say things in a manner as if they had never been said before.

ottava rima

A *stanza of eight iambic pentameter lines rhyming *abababcc.* Ottava rima has been used by many authors, including Spenser, Milton, Keats, and Byron. This is ottava rima, the second stanza of W. B. Yeats's *Sailing to Byzantium:*

> An aged man is but a paltry thing,
> A tattered coat upon a stick, unless
> Soul clap its hands and sing, and louder sing
> For every tatter in its mortal dress,
> Nor is there singing school but studying
> Monuments of its own magnificence;
> And therefore I have sailed the seas and come
> To the holy city of Byzantium.

197

outline

(1) A general sketch, report, or account that indicates only the main features of a selection, book, or project; (2) the arrangement of clusters of related ideas in a sequence that will reveal the *order and *organization of a written *composition or a speech. Every literary work of any distinction is so ordered and organized that an outline can be made of its contents and structure.

oxymoron

A figure of speech in which two contradictory words or phrases are combined to produce a rhetorical effect by means of a concise paradox. For example, *sophomore* comes from two Greek words meaning "wise" and "foolish." The phrase *eloquent silence* is an oxymoron. These lines from Tennyson's *Lancelot and Elaine* contain several oxymora:

> The shackles of an old love straighten'd him,
> His honour rooted in dishonour stood,
> And faith unfaithful kept him falsely true.

See ANTITHESIS.

P

pace

Rate of movement; tempo. A literary selection, such as a *novel, is said to have a slow pace if it contains *digressions, if it has substantial amounts of *exposition and *description, and if its *incidents do not follow in rapid succession. An *adventure story, *fairy tale, *ballad, or *detective story is likely to move at a fast pace. With rare exceptions, every outstanding work of narrative literature varies its pace to accommodate differing *moods and *actions.

paean

(1) A song of joy, praise, or triumph; (2) a *hymn of thanksgiving. Paean, derived from the name of a legendary Greek physician to *Olympian gods, originally referred to a song of healing or to an *incantation of some sort, but later the term was applied to songs before battle or on other momentous occasions. Sophocles's *Antigone* contains numerous paeans, notably the cry of exultation beginning "Wonders are many, and none is more wonderful than man."

paeon

A *foot consisting of one long (stressed) syllable and three short (unstressed) ones in any order of appearance. Such a foot is unsuited to English, but Gerard Manley Hopkins used paeons of various kinds in his poem *The Windhover*. In this poem, Hopkins's reference to a falcon as "dapple-dawn-drawn" is a paeon in which an accented syllable is followed by three unaccented syllables.

pageant

(1) An elaborate public *spectacle designed to celebrate a historical event; (2) a costumed procession or tableau; (3) a scaffold or stage on which plays were performed in the *Middle Ages; (4) anything comparable to a spectacle or procession in splendor, colorful variety, and grandeur. In modern times, *pageant* is applied to any elaborate outdoor performance, march, or procession. See MUMMERY, SPECTACLE.

paleography

The study of ancient writings. Derived from Greek words meaning "old" and "writing," paleography is a method of determining the date, origin, and authenticity of *manuscripts through a study of writing materials, styles of handwriting, inks, etc.

palindrome

A word, sentence, or verse reading the same backward as forward: "civic"; "Madam, I'm Adam"; "Able was I ere I saw Elba." (See ACRONYM, ANAGRAM.) A palindrome is a word stunt not calculated to contribute to literature, but early in the eighteenth century an obscure English poet did write a revealing line: "Lewd did I live & evil I did dwel'."

palinode

A piece of writing that retracts something written earlier; a *recantation. A famous palinode is Chaucer's *Legend of Good Women,* in which the author "takes back" what he had earlier said about the unfaithfulness of women in poems such as *Troilus and Criseyde.*

panegyric

An *oration, dignified speech, or written *composition praising someone or some achievement. A panegyric is a formal and elaborate commendation. (See ENCOMIUM, EULOGY.) The term *panegyric* has come to mean excessive flattery, such as that in a blurb for a literary work or in the nominating speeches of politicians.

pantheism

The doctrine and belief that God is the entire universe or, put another way, that every part of the universe is a manifestation of God. *Pantheism* refers to any philosophical or religious concept that identifies God and the universe. Goethe, Wordsworth, and Emerson wrote several poems about pantheism; the following lines from Wordsworth's *Lines Composed a Few Miles Above Tintern Abbey* provide a poetic definition and explanation:

> ... And I have felt
> A presence that disturbs me with the joy
> Of elevated thoughts; a sense sublime
> Of something far more deeply interfused,
> Whose dwelling is the light of setting suns,
> And the round ocean and the living air,
> And the blue sky, and in the mind of man;
> A motion and a spirit, that impels
> All thinking things, all objects of all thought,
> And rolls through all things.

pantomime

(1) A play or entertainment in which performers express ideas and actions by movements only; (2) the art and technique of conveying emotions or feelings by mute gestures. The name *pantomime* was originally given to ancient Roman actors in a *dumb show but later was attached to a performance itself, such as that in which a harlequin appears. Pantomime appears in silent motion pictures, in Christmas entertainments and other *pageants, in *puppetry, and in stage plays when, at intervals, no *dialogue is spoken. See CHARADE, COMMEDIA DELL'ARTE, MIME.

parable

A story designed to convey some religious principle, moral lesson, or general truth. A parable always teaches by comparison with actual events (the situation that called forth the parable for illustration). In this sense, a parable is an *allegory and thus differs from some *apologues and *fables. Well-known examples of parables are those of the Biblical prodigal son and the good Samaritan.

paradox

(1) A statement apparently self-contradictory or absurd but really containing a possible truth; (2) a self-contradictory, false *proposition; (3) an opinion or statement contrary to generally accepted ideas. Shakespeare employed a paradox when he wrote, "Cowards die many times before their deaths." Wordsworth's comment "The child is father of the man" is a paradox. See EPIGRAM, HYPALLAGE, OXYMORON.

paragoge

The addition of a sound or group of sounds at the end of a word. Paragoge is illustrated in *righto* (for *right*), *boughten* (for *bought*), *lovèd* (for *loved*).

paraphrase

Restatement of a passage giving the meaning in another form; rewording. From Greek terms meaning "beside" and "speech," paraphrase usually involves expanding the original text so as to make it clear. Many modern critics object to paraphrasing, but the activity is essential for everyone who wishes to absorb what he reads. Here, for example, is a paraphrase of Keats's *sonnet *On First Looking into Chapman's Homer:*

> I have read widely in the great classics of literature and have noted many examples of superb poetry. I had often been told of the work of Homer and the poetry which he had created, but I never really understood or appreciated its beauty and power until I read Chapman's translation. Then I felt as awed as some astronomer who unexpectedly discovers a new planet, or as surprised and speechless as Cortez [Balboa] and his followers were when they saw the Pacific Ocean for the first time, from Panama.

Parnassus

A mountain in central Greece, famed as the home of Apollo and the Muses. *Parnassus* is sometimes used to refer to the world of poetry and poets and to any center of artistic activity. It was to the Parnassian world of literature that Dr. Johnson referred in *The Rambler:* "Parnassus has its flowers of transient fragrance, as well as its oaks of towering height, and its laurels of eternal verdure."

parody

Any humorous, satirical, or *burlesque imitation of a person, event, or serious work of literature. Parody is designed to ridicule in nonsensical fashion or to criticize by clever duplication. (See BURLESQUE, CARICATURE, LAMPOON, TRAVESTY.) Here is a parody of Walt Whitman by a minor American poet, Bayard Taylor:

> Everywhere, everywhere, following me;
> Taking me by the buttonhole, pulling off my boots,
> hustling me with the elbows;

Sitting down with me to clams and the
   chowder-kettle;
Plunging naked at my side into the sleek,
   irascible surges;
Soothing me with the strain that I neither
   permit nor prohibit;
Flocking this way and that, reverent, eager,
   orotund, irrepressible;
Denser than sycamore leaves when the
   north-winds are scouring Paumanok;
What can I do to restrain them? Nothing,
   verily nothing.

paronomasia

An *archaism for *pun; the use of a word in different
senses or of words similar in sound to achieve *humor or a
double meaning. In John Donne's *Hymn to God the Father,*
paronomasia occurs in the use of *Son (sun)* and *done
(Donne):*
   ... Swear by Thyself that at my death Thy Son
   Shall shine as he shines now and heretofore;
   And, having done that, thou hast done;
   I fear no more.

parrhesia

Boldness of speech; freedom of expression. Parrhesia, a kind of
blunt frankness, is common in modern literature, especially in
the use of plain talk for the physiological and sexual activities
of men and women. See EUPHEMISM.

passion play

A dramatic presentation of the sufferings of Christ on the Cross
or his anguish subsequent to the Last Supper. In Europe during
*medieval times, many *mystery plays were called passion
plays. A *drama dealing with the life, trial, crucifixion, and
resurrection of Christ has been presented at intervals since the
seventeenth century at Oberammergau, Germany.

pastoral

(1) A poem or other artistic *composition dealing with the life
of shepherds or with simple rural existence; (2) a picture or
work of art representing the life of shepherds; (3) simplicity,
charm, and serenity such as those attributed to country life.
Pastoral, from the Latin word *pastor* ("shepherd"), applies to

any literary *convention that places kindly rural people in nature-centered activities. Milton's *Lycidas,* Spenser's *The Shepheardes Calender,* and Arnold's *Thyrsis* have pastoral qualities. (See BUCOLIC, ECLOGUE, GEORGIC.) A *pastorale* is a piece of music (*opera, cantata) suggestive of country life. Pastoral *drama, pastoral *elegies, and pastoral *romances are different kinds of *compositions, each with rural settings and characters.

pathetic fallacy
Crediting inanimate objects with the emotions and traits of human beings. The phrase was coined by John Ruskin (1819–1900), an English author, who quoted the following lines from a nineteenth-century English poem and then wrote:
> They rowed her in across the rolling foam—
> The cruel, crawling foam.
>> The foam is not cruel, neither does it crawl. The state of mind which attributes to it these characters of a living creature is one in which the reason is unhinged by grief. All violent feelings have the same effect. They produce in us a falseness in all our impressions of external things, which I would generally characterize as the "pathetic fallacy."

Poetry and prose are filled with examples of what may be called false emotionalism and impassioned *metaphors: cruel sea, smiling skies, laughing waters, etc. Sense-making or not, the pathetic fallacy can produce beautiful effects, as in Coleridge's lines: "The one red leaf, the last of its clan / That dances as often as dance it can." See BATHOS, PATHOS.

pathos
From a Greek word meaning "suffering," *pathos* refers to that ability or power in literature (and other arts) to call forth feelings of pity, compassion, and sadness. In *King Lear,* Cordelia's plight involves pathos, and she is therefore a pathetic figure, as Ophelia in *Hamlet* and Little Nell in Dickens's *The Old Curiosity Shop* are. See BATHOS, EMPATHY, PATHETIC FALLACY.

patter song
A comic song depending upon rapid delivery. Patter songs, which appear often in Gilbert and Sullivan *operettas, depend upon clever wording and tricky musical phrasing, as in these lines from *H.M.S. Pinafore:*
> And so do his sisters, and his cousins,
> and his aunts!

His sisters and his cousins,
Whom he reckons up by dozens,
And his aunts!

pedantry
Display of learning; slavish attention to rules and details; rigid adherence to book knowledge at the expense of common sense. *Pedantry* or *pedantic* is applied to writing that contains many *allusions, foreign phrases, quotations, and the like. In Shakespeare's *Love's Labour's Lost,* Holofernes, the village schoolmaster, is an incurable pedant who prides himself on the precision of his pronunciation and the excellence of his Latin. See PRECIOSITY.

Pegasus
In classical mythology, Pegasus was a winged horse reputedly sprung from Medusa's body at her death. The name has long been associated with poetry and poetic inspiration, perhaps because Pegasus is supposed to have opened the inspiring fountain of the *Muses with a stroke of its hoof. A well-known *anthology is entitled *The Winged Horse Anthology.* Poets have sometimes called on Pegasus as a *symbol and *source of poetic aid instead of on the Muses. See DIVINE AFFLATUS.

penny dreadful
A sensational novel of crime, adventure, or violence. The term is an *archaism even in England for cheap and morbid *melodrama. See DIME NOVEL, PULP MAGAZINE.

pentameter
A line of five metrical feet. (See METER.) Pentameter, from Greek words meaning "five" and "measure," is more widely used in poetry in English than any other length of line.

pentastich
A *stanza consisting of five lines. *Pentastich* is a *synonym of *cinquain. This song from Tennyson's *The Princess* is a pentastich:

Dear as remembered kisses after death,
And sweet as those by hopeless fancy feigned
On lips that are for others; deep as love,
Deep as first love, and wild with all regret;
O Death in Life, the days that are no more!

perfect rhyme

The identity of sound in words pronounced the same or in which stressed vowels and following consonants are the same: *Pain, pane; rein, reign; bough, bow; line, fine.* See RHYME.

periodical

A publication issued at regularly recurring intervals. *Periodical* derives its name from *periodic* (recurring at intervals) and is applied to *magazines and *journals but not ordinarily to newspapers.

periodic sentence

A sentence that is not grammatically complete until the end, or nearly the end, of the sentence is reached. Writers often produce an effect of *suspense by holding back the termination of a main clause, as in this sentence by Bret Harte:

> And pulseless and cold, with a Derringer by his side and a bullet in his heart, though still calm as in life, beneath the snow lay he who was at once the strongest and yet the weakest of the outcasts of Poker Flat.

peripety

A sudden turn of events. *Peripety,* also spelled *peripeteia,* as in the original Greek, is a reversal of fortune for the *protagonist in *drama or *fiction. Aristotle gives as an example of peripety the scene in Sophocles's *Oedipus Rex* in which the First Messenger, believing he will free Oedipus from fear, does the exact opposite: the parents who have died, the messenger reports, were really Oedipus's foster parents. See ACTION, CATASTROPHE, CLIMAX, CRISIS.

persiflage

Light, bantering talk; flippancy; raillery. A term from French, *persiflage* refers to the kind of jesting that appears in much of the dialogue in plays by such writers as Oscar Wilde and Noel Coward. For example, these comments in Wilde's *Lady Windermere's Fan* are persiflage:

> Nowadays we are all of us so hard up that the only pleasant things to pay are compliments. They're the only things we *can* pay.

> In this world there are only two tragedies. One is not getting what one wants, and the other is getting it.

persona

An invented person; a character in *drama or *fiction. *Persona,* a Latin word meaning "mask," is used in *Jungian psychology to refer to one's "public personality"—the façade or mask presented to the world but not representative of inner feelings and emotions. (See DRAMATIS PERSONAE.) In literary criticism, *persona* is sometimes used to refer to a person figuring in, for example, a poem, someone who may or may not represent the author himself.

personal essay

An informal *composition employing an intimate *style and an urbane, relaxed, conversational manner to deal with subject matter that at least in part is *autobiographical. See ESSAY, FAMILIAR ESSAY, INFORMAL ESSAY.

personification

A figure of speech in which *abstractions, animals, ideas, and inanimate objects are endowed with human form, character, traits, or sensibilities. In personification, an entirely imaginary creature or person also may be conceived of as representing an idea or object. A kind of *metaphor, personification is a frequent resource in poetry and occasionally appears in other types of writing as well. An exquisite example of personification appears in Keats's *Ode on a Grecian Urn,* in which a vase is referred to as a woodland recorder of events:

> Sylvan historian, who canst thus express
> A flowery tale more sweetly than our rhyme.

See ALLEGORY, APOSTROPHE, PATHETIC FALLACY, PROSO-POPOEIA.

persuasion

A form of *argumentation that is designed to convince, arouse, attain a specific goal. Persuasion attempts to prevail on listeners or readers to do something, to react positively, and to bring such conviction that the recipient will think, believe, and be moved to respond actively. Persuasion may make use of the other *forms of discourse, but it usually combines an appeal to emotions with an appeal to the intellect. A common form of persuasion is the *oration (such as Winston Churchill's speeches to the British people during World War II) and the pamphlet (such as the tracts which John Milton wrote advocating that divorce be granted on grounds of incompatibility).

Petrarchan
A reference to Petrarch (1304–1374), an Italian scholar and poet. *Petrarchan* is specifically applied to a form of the *sonnet divided into an *octave and *sestet. (See ITALIAN SONNET.) A Petrarchan *conceit is an exceptionally elaborate and exaggerated comparison. (See CONCEIT.) Petrarchism, a style introduced by the poet in his sonnets, is notable for its formal perfection, grammatical complexity, and elaborate *figurative language.

Philippic
A speech filled with angry accusations, denunciations, and *invective. *Philippic* is a term derived from the orations of Demosthenes (a fourth-century-B.C. Athenian statesman and orator) that attacked King Philip II of Macedon (an ancient country in the Balkan Peninsula) as an enemy of Greece. See ORATION.

Philistine
A person indifferent to culture and refinement; a commonplace, conventional individual. *Philistine* was the name of one of the inhabitants of ancient Philistia, a country at constant war with the Israelites. Philistines were considered barbaric (see BARBARISM), rude, warlike, and uncouth. In an essay (*Sweetness and Light*) Matthew Arnold a century ago called persons hostile to culture and devoted to material prosperity Philistines. The word *Philistinism* now means an obsession with wealth and a contempt for "art, beauty, culture, or spiritual things."

phoneme
A basic unit of sound. A phoneme may be illustrated by the difference in sound and meaning of *pit* and *bit.* In linguistics, a phoneme is any one of a small set of units by which *morphemes, words, and sentences are represented. See ALLOPHONE.

phonetics
The study and science of speech sounds: their production, transmission, and reception. Phonetics also involves the analysis, transcription, and classification of the sounds of speech.

phonics
A method of teaching reading and pronunciation based upon

the phonetic (sound) interpretation of spelling. (See PHONEME, PHONETICS.) *Phonics,* an obsolete term for *phonetics,* is considered a singular (not plural) noun.

picaresque

A term applied to fiction in which adventures of a rogue are narrated in humorous or satiric scenes. *Picaresque,* from a Spanish word meaning "knave" or "rascal," applies to *novels and *tales that depict in realistic detail the everyday lives of common people. A typical picaresque novel presents the life story of a rogue who makes his way more through his cunning than through hard work. *Gil Blas* is the best-known picaresque story in French; Defoe's *Moll Flanders* is the most famous in English.

Pindaric

A reference to Pindar, a fifth-century-B.C. Greek poet. Specifically, *Pindaric* refers to a form of *ode consisting of several divisions, each of which is composed of a *strophe and *antistrophe of identical form and a contrasting *epode. A Pindaric ode is also called "regular." (See COWLEYAN ODE, ODE.) A well-known Pindaric ode is John Dryden's *Alexander's Feast.*

pirated edition

An unauthorized *edition of a literary work. A pirated edition is usually a work stolen from one country and published in another. Every pirated work today is an infringement of *copyright, but before the establishment of international copyright conventions, publications often appeared in foreign countries without permission; for example, numerous eighteenth- and nineteenth-century English novels appeared in the United States in pirated editions.

pitch

Variations from high to low in the sounds of an utterance. Depending upon the relative rapidity of the vibrations by which it is produced, *pitch* refers to the degree of height or depth of a vocal or musical tone.

plagiarism

Literary theft. Plagiarism is taking or closely imitating the language and thoughts of another author and representing them as one's own. Plagiarism, from a Latin word meaning "kidnapper," ranges from inept *paraphrasing to outright theft. "Borrowing," wrote John Milton, "if it be not bettered by the borrower, among good authors is accounted plagiarie" [plagiarism].

platonic

Entirely spiritual, free from sensual desire. The phrase *platonic love* refers to affection without sexual desire. Platonic criticism seeks the values of a literary work in its extrinsic (external) qualities rather than in the work itself. See ARISTOTELIAN.

Platonism

The doctrines and teachings of Plato (427–347 B.C.), Greek philosopher, whose primary concern was with aspirations of the human spirit, with man's possibilities and destinies. In the *Dialogues,* Plato repeatedly urged mankind to seek and express ideas of justice, love, courage, friendship, and virtuous living. Platonism contends that physical objects are short-lived representations of unchanging ideas and that ideas alone provide true knowledge. Platonism also implies the immortality of the soul, which through a series of incarnations (rebirths), has the power and ability to recall ideas and *images from one life to the next.

Platonism has had great appeal for many writers through the centuries, including Spenser (*Hymn in Honor of Beauty*), Ralph Waldo Emerson (essays and poems), and William Wordsworth *(Ode on Intimations of Immortality from Recollections of Early Childhood).*

play

A literary *composition in dramatic form intended to be presented on a stage by actors who assume identities, speak *dialogue, and perform *actions devised by an author. See DRAMA.

play-within-a-play

A segment of dramatized action (a miniature *drama) that is presented within the framework of a larger and longer *play. The principal *plots of such plays as Shakespeare's *The Taming of the Shrew* and Francis Beaumont's *The Knight of the Burning Pestle* are set within the framework of a play-within-a-play. A well-known example of this *form is the performance arranged for King Claudius in act 3, scene 2, of *Hamlet*. See FRAME STORY.

plot

A plan or scheme to accomplish a purpose. In literature, *plot* refers to the arrangement of events to achieve an intended effect. A plot is a series of carefully devised and interrelated *actions that progresses through a struggle of opposing forces (*conflict) to a *climax and a *denouement. A plot is different from a *story or story line (the order of events as they occur). This distinction has been made clear by E. M. Forster, the English novelist:

> We have defined a story as a narrative of events arranged in their time sequence. A plot is also a narrative of events, the emphasis falling on a causality [see CAUSE AND EFFECT]. "The king died and then the queen died" is a story. "The king died, and then the queen died of grief" is a plot.

plurisignation

The result of using words with multiple meanings and thus producing differing lines of thought and understanding. (See AMBIGUITY.) Plurisignation, from Latin words meaning "several distinguishing marks," is a standard means of achieving *irony. See DOUBLE ENTENDRE, OXYMORON, PARADOX.

poem

A *composition in *verse that is characterized by a highly developed artistic *form, the use of *rhythm, and the employment of heightened language to express an imaginative interpretation of a situation or idea. See POETRY, VERSE.

poesy

An *archaism for *poetry. *Poesy* refers to the techniques and art of poetic *composition in general. In *The Defence of Poesy* (1595), Sir Philip Sidney defended poetry (and all imaginative literature) against its attackers.

poetaster

An inferior poet. A poetaster is a versifier, a dabbler, a *dilettante in verse. The suffix -*aster* is a Latin term denoting anything that merely apes the true thing or that imperfectly resembles it.

poetic diction

Words selected for their supposedly poetic quality; *diction somewhat different from that of ordinary speech and *prose. In his *Poetics,* Aristotle wrote that poets should use *metaphors, unusual words, and various stylistic ornaments. Just what is—or should be—considered poetic diction has been argued for centuries, but since early in the nineteenth century, such words as *whilom, oft, perchance, thrice, eftsoons,* etc., have appeared less and less frequently. Wordsworth once announced his intention of "fitting to metrical arrangement a selection of the *real language* of men in a state of vivid sensation." Poets of the twentieth century have generally denied differences between the language of poetry and that of prose or speech; current tendencies are to permit in poetry the widest possible range in vocabulary.

poetic justice

An ideal distribution of rewards and punishments. The phrase was first used in the seventeenth century to express the notion that in literature (as not always in life) the good should be rewarded and the evil punished. The word *poetic* does not imply that the concept refers only to poetry; rather it refers to the Greek term from which *poetic* was derived: "a maker," that is, any writer of verse or prose. As generally understood, poetic justice applies to the logical and thoroughly motivated outcome of a play, novel, or narrative poem, even though evil seems temporarily rewarded and good meets with defeat or disaster. In *The Dunciad,* Pope wrote:

> Poetic Justice, with her lifted scale,
> Where, in nice balance, truth with gold she
>   weighs,
> And solid pudding against empty praise.

poetic license

Liberty taken by a writer (poet, novelist, dramatist, essayist, etc.) to produce a desired effect by deviating from conventional *form, established rules, and even fact and *logic. For example, any writer (and especially a poet) may claim the "license" to depart from normal word order (see INVERSION), to employ *archaisms, to use—and overuse—*figurative language, to employ *cadence and *rhythm to degrees not found in ordinary speech, etc. The greatest poets do not permit liberty to become license and rarely indulge in breaches of idiom, grammar, and pronunciation (for the sake of *rhyme).

poetic prose

Ordinary spoken and written language (*prose) that makes use of *cadence, *rhythm, *figurative language, or other devices ordinarily associated with *poetry. (See POLYPHONIC PROSE.) Novelists, essayists, and short-story writers occasionally use a short passage of poetic prose to achieve a special effect. Such *composition is somewhat rarer now than it was in earlier centuries, but it occasionally appears in current or recent literature. Note, for example, the cadence and rhythm, the *diction, and the word repetition in this opening paragraph from Ernest Hemingway's *In Another Country:*

> In the fall the war was always there, but we did not go to it any more. It was cold in the fall in Milan and the dark came very early. Then the electric lights came on, and it was pleasant along the streets looking in the windows. There was much game hanging outside the shops, and the snow powdered in the fur of the foxes and the wind blew their tails. The deer hung stiff and heavy and empty, and small birds blew in the wind and the wind turned their feathers. It was a cold fall and the wind came down from the mountains.

poetics

(1) Literary *criticism dealing with *poetry; (2) a treatise (treatment) of poetry; (3) the study of *prosody (meter, versification). *Poetics* is an *archaism, a disused term for the art and *technique of poetry. (See POESY.) However, Aristotle's *Poetics,* possibly the most influential work ever written on poetry, has remained a *bible for critics and writers for more than twenty centuries.

poet laureate

A poet appointed for life as an officer of the royal household in Great Britain. A poet laureate was formerly expected to compose verse for state occasions, but for a century now the title has been largely a mark of distinction for a writer recognized as eminent or representative. (See LAUREATE.) The first poet laureate officially recognized in England was Ben Jonson (1573–1637), but the specific title was first given to John Dryden

(1631–1700). Among poets laureate have been Wordsworth, Tennyson, Alfred Austin, Robert Bridges, and John Masefield.

poetry

(1) Literary work in metrical form or patterned language; (2) the art of rhythmical *composition, written or spoken, designed to produce pleasure through beautiful, elevated, imaginative, or profound thoughts. Poetry cannot really be defined because it involves many differing aspects of subject matter, form, and effect; here are a few of many thousands of attempts to explain what poetry is and does:

> Poetry is the record of the best and happiest moments of the best and happiest minds.
>
> Shelley

> Poetry...a criticism of life under the conditions fixed for such a criticism by the laws of poetic truth and beauty.
>
> Matthew Arnold

> Poetry is the imaginative expression of strong feeling, usually rhythmical...the spontaneous overflow of powerful feelings recollected in tranquillity.
>
> Wordsworth

> ...the poetry of words [is] the rhythmical creation of beauty. Its sole arbiter is taste....Unless incidentally, it has no concern whatever cither with duty or with truth.
>
> Poe

> Poetry is language that tells us, through a more or less emotional reaction, something that cannot be said.
>
> Edwin Arlington Robinson

> ...the rhythmic, inevitably narrative, movement from an overclothed blindness to a naked vision.
>
> Dylan Thomas

All poetry may be called verse, but not all *verse is poetry. Like poetry, verse is patterned language. These lines consist of words arranged in a pattern:

> Here lies the body of Jonathan Blank:
> He dropped a match in a gasoline tank.

Such verse is metrical and rhythmical, but it is not poetry because it does not contain the high and genuine thought,

214

the imagination, and the deep emotion of true poetry. See DOGGEREL.

point of view

(1) A specified position or method of consideration and appraisal; (2) an attitude, judgment, or opinion. In literature, *point of view* has several special meanings: (1) *physical* point of view has to do with the position in time and space from which a writer approaches, views, and describes his material; (2) *mental* point of view involves an author's feeling and attitude toward his subject; (3) *personal* point of view concerns the relation through which a writer narrates or discusses a subject, whether first, second, or third person.

In *personal* point of view, several arrangements are possible. If a writer assumes the point of view of a character, he becomes an "author participant" and usually writes in the first person. This is the point of view of Defoe's Robinson Crusoe, who, as author, relates what happened to him and reveals his own feelings in his own words. If the writer adopts the point of view of a minor character, he becomes an "author observant" who sits on the sidelines and reports the story. In several of Conrad's stories (for example, *Heart of Darkness*), the narrator observes more than he participates. When an author selects an impersonal point of view and detaches himself completely, he becomes Godlike, an "author omniscient." He sees all, hears all, knows all: his all-seeing eye can focus wherever he pleases; he can see into the minds of characters, and even report everyone's innermost thoughts. Thackeray's *Vanity Fair* is written from an omniscient point of view. See OMNISCIENCE.

In lengthy works of fiction, writers sometimes employ combinations of these methods (points of view).

polyphonic prose

Prose which exhibits such devices of poetry as *alliteration, *assonance, *cadence, and *rhythm. *Polyphonic* is derived from Greek words meaning "many-voiced." See POETIC PROSE.

popular ballad

An uncomplicated, short, story-telling *poem intended for oral recitation or singing. (See BALLAD, FOLK BALLAD.) One scholar (F. B. Gummere) has said of the popular ballad that it is "impersonal in material, probably connected in its origins with the communal dance, but submitted to a process of oral tradition among people who are free from literary influences and fairly homogeneous in character." In certain sections of the United States, especially in the southern Appalachian Mountains, popular ballads that originated in England and Scotland are still known and sung. See ORAL TRANSMISSION.

portmanteau word

A term made by putting together parts of other words. (See COINAGE, NEOLOGISM.) *Portmanteau,* from French words meaning "to carry" and "cloak," is the English name of a trunk or suitcase that opens into two halves. Lewis Carroll, who applied the term *portmanteau word* to expressions he invented, had in mind "two meanings packed up into one word," as Humpty Dumpty explained to Alice in *Through the Looking-Glass.* Portmanteau words concocted by Lewis Carroll included *slithy* (*lithe* and *slimy*) and *frumious* (*fuming* and *furious*). In *Finnegans Wake,* James Joyce used numerous portmanteau words, such as *bisexcycle* and *ordinailed ungles.*

potboiler

A mediocre literary work produced solely for financial gain; a task performed to keep the pot boiling, that is, to eat. See GRUB STREET, HACK.

pragmatism

A philosophical movement emphasizing practical consequences and values. Pragmatism stresses utility and practicality. A major advocate of pragmatism (which in Greek meant "deed" or "business") was the American psychologist and philosopher William James, who wrote, "The 'whole meaning' of a conception expresses itself in practical consequences, consequences either in the shape of conduct to be recommended, or in that of experience to be expected." James, John Dewey, and many other pragmatists have held that living is more important than logical thinking and that thought should aim not so much at discovering final truths as at satisfying practical ends. Pragmatism has been influential in the development of *realism in modern literature throughout the world.

preamble

An introductory statement; a preface; an introduction. *Preamble,* from Latin words meaning "walking before," applies to any introductory portion of a written *document that states the reasons for, and explains the purpose of, what follows. The best-known preamble in the United States is that which sets forth the principles of American government: "We the people of the United States, in order to form a more perfect Union...."

preciosity

Excessive refinement in language, taste, or *style. Preciosity, a term applied to consciously fastidious work, is a kind of *fine writing; *Euphuism is also roughly synonymous. These lines from Pope's *The Rape of the Lock,* exhibit preciosity for the purpose of ridiculing it (see BURLESQUE, MOCK EPIC, MOCK HEROIC):

> From silver spouts the grateful liquors glide,
> While China's earth receives the smoking tide.

(Hot coffee is poured from silver pots into china cups.) See PURPLE PROSE.

précis

A short *summary of the essential ideas of a larger *composition. A précis (the form is both singular and plural) is the basic thought of a passage, reproduced in miniature and retaining something of the *mood and *tone of the original. (See ABRIDGMENT.) This statement by Henry Fielding is followed by a précis:

> But as for the bulk of mankind, they are clearly devoid of any degree of taste. It is a quality in which they advance very little beyond a state of infancy. The first thing a child is fond of in a book is a picture, the second is a story, and the third a jest. Here then is the true Pons Asinorum which very few readers ever get over. (69 words)

> Most people lack taste; they remain childlike. Readers, like children, rarely ever get over the "bridge of asses" constituted by pictures, stories, and jokes. (24 words)

prelude

A preliminary; in literature, a brief poem preparatory to a longer one. In music, a prelude is a short, independent *composition for instruments. James Russell Lowell's lengthy verse *parable *The Vision of Sir Launfal* is in two extended parts, each with a prelude. See EPILOGUE, PROLOGUE.

premise

A *proposition (statement) supporting, or helping to support, a conclusion. A premise is an assumption, a basis on which reasoning proceeds. (See LOGIC, SYLLOGISM.) For example, in writing *A Connecticut Yankee in King Arthur's Court,* Mark Twain started with the premise that knighthood and medieval chivalry are forms of childish *barbarism. His novel satirically exposes the abuses of *feudalism and reveals his own conclusions about democracy.

Pre-Raphaelite

One of a group of young English writers and artists who, about 1850, united to resist *conventions in literature and art and sought to revive the style and spirit of Italian artists before the time of Raphael (1483–1520). Pre-Raphaelite poetry, such as that of Dante Gabriel Rossetti and William Morris, exhibits sensuousness, archaic *diction, *symbolism, and elaborate attention to the physical details of nature.

primary source

A source is any place or thing from which something comes or is obtained. A primary source is one that is of first, direct, and immediate importance. In literary scholarship, a primary source refers to a person with firsthand knowledge, a manuscript written at the time or on the scene of the subject being studied, a recorded contemporary conversation, etc. For example, a primary source for a biographer of Thomas Jefferson would be written comments about him by such contemporaries as George Washington and Benjamin Franklin. See SECONDARY SOURCE.

primitivism

Belief that the qualities of early cultures are superior to those of contemporary civilization. The doctrine of primitivism flourished in eighteenth- and early nineteenth-century France and England. Rousseau attacked French life and society as artificial and corrupt and urged a return to nature; Wordsworth and William Blake in England exhibited strong traces of primitivism in their poetry. A concept of the noble savage produced an idealized American Indian, depicted many times in the *Leatherstocking Tales* of James Fenimore Cooper. Elements of primitivism, related to the natural goodness of man and the "essential" evils of civilization, have persisted up to the present. See REALISM, ROMANTICISM.

problem novel, play

In all narrative literary works, a problem deals with the choices of action open to characters involved or to society at large. Thus a problem novel or problem play depicts characters in a state of *conflict, a statement true of every worthwhile piece of fiction or drama. In a narrower sense, a problem novel or play suggests a thesis. *Uncle Tom's Cabin* is a problem novel not only because of conflicts faced by its characters but also because its purpose was to reveal the injustices of slavery. Arthur Miller's *Death of a Salesman* deals with problems faced by Willy Loman, his wife, and his sons, but it is a problem play in that it is concerned with what the author considers false values in society. Other problem novels and plays which both develop conflict and reveal a thesis are Remarque's *All Quiet on the Western Front,* Steinbeck's *The Grapes of Wrath,* Galsworthy's *Justice,* and Clifford Odets's *Waiting for Lefty.* See PROPAGANDA, THEME, THESIS.

profile

A term generally referring to an outlined view, especially the human face viewed from one side. In literature, profile is a form of writing which combines biographical material with character interpretation. A profile offers a silhouette, a partial view, rather than a rounded portrait of a subject and bears somewhat the relation to a full-length *biography that a *short story does to a *novel.

prolepsis

A figure of speech in which an expected event is referred to as though it had already occurred: Hamlet, wounded, exclaims, "Horatio, I am dead." Prolepsis is also a rhetorical device in *argumentation: anticipating and answering an opponent's objections. The term additionally may refer to the assigning of an event or person to a period earlier than the actual one and in this meaning is a synonym of *anachronism and prochronism.

proletarian

A reference to the proletariat, that is, unpropertied classes who must sell their labor to survive. *Proletarian* is derived from a Latin term naming a Roman citizen who contributed to the state only through bearing children (*proles*). A proletarian novel or play is one that portrays distressing social and economic conditions among working classes. See PROPAGANDA; SOCIOLOGICAL NOVEL, PLAY; THESIS.

prologue

The opening section of a longer work. In ancient Greek trage-dy, a prologue was the part of a *play that set forth the subject of the *drama before the *chorus entered. The term is now used to refer to the preface or introductory part of a *novel, long *poem, or play. In his Prologue to *The Canter-bury Tales,* Chaucer provides a background and *setting for what is to follow as well as detailed *sketches of the charac-ters who are to appear. The first part of Shakespeare's *Henry IV* opens with an explanatory speech; the second part begins with a prologue called an induction. See EPILOGUE.

prop

An item of furniture, an ornament, or a decoration in a stage *setting; any object handled or used by an actor in a performance. *Prop,* an abbreviation of *property,* refers to any physical object used in a stage presentation other than the stage itself, costumes of the actors, and lighting effects.

propaganda

Information, ideas, or rumors spread to help or harm a person, group, movement, belief, institution, or nation. The term *propaganda* originally referred to a committee of cardinals es-tablished early in the seventeenth century by the Roman Cath-olic Church with supervision over the training of priests for work in foreign missions. *Propaganda* is now applied to any literary work, scheme, or association for influencing opinion in political, social, religious, ethical, economic, or other matters. A propaganda (or propagandistic) *play or *novel seeks to ad-vance particular doctrines or principles, such as, for instance, the novels of Upton Sinclair in their advocacy of socialism. Propaganda is attacked by most critics and general readers because it is an attempt to influence opinions and actions delib-erately, but by this definition all education and most literature are propagandistic. See PROBLEM NOVEL, PLAY; SOCIOLOGICAL NOVEL, PLAY; THESIS.

proposition

(1) A plan, scheme, or suggestion; (2) a statement of the subject of an argument (see ARGUMENTATION, PERSUASION); (3) a state-ment in which something is affirmed or denied, that is, a *prem-ise. The first of these three definitions is illustrated in this remark by Celia in Shakespeare's *As You Like It:* "It is as easy to count atomies [specks in a sunbeam] as to resolve the proposi-

tions of a lover." The second definition is explained in Francis Bacon's remark in his essay *Of Cunning:* "It is a good point ... for a man to shape the answer he would have in his own words and propositions." The beginning of Abraham Lincoln's Gettysburg Address illustrates the third definition: "Fourscore and seven years ago our fathers brought forth on this continent a new nation, conceived in liberty, and dedicated to the proposition that all men are created equal."

proscenium
That part of the stage in a modern theater which lies between the orchestra and the curtain. A proscenium arch is a decorative structure that separates a stage from an auditorium. *Proscenium* is often used as a *synonym for the stage itself.

prose
The ordinary form of spoken and written language. The term *prose* applies to all expression in language that does not have a regular rhythmic pattern. Coleridge offered a helpful definition: "I wish our clever young poets would remember my homely definitions of prose and poetry: that is, prose—words in their best order; poetry—the best words in their best order." A surprised character in Molière's *Bourgeois Gentleman* remarks, "Good Heavens! For more than forty years I have been speaking prose without knowing it." See POETIC PROSE, POLYPHONIC PROSE.

prosody
The science and study of *versification. The term *prosody,* from Greek words meaning "modulation of voice" and "song sung to music," involves such topics as *accent, *meter, *rhyme, *rhythm, and *stanza form. See SCANSION.

prosopopoeia
Representation of an imaginary, absent, or dead person as acting or speaking. *Prosopopoeia* is a *synonym for *personification.

protagonist
The leading character of a *drama, *novel, or other literary work. *Protagonist* in Greek meant "first combatant"; such a person is not always the *hero of a work, but he is always the principal and central character. The rival of a protago-

nist is an *antagonist. In Maugham's *Of Human Bondage,* Philip Carey, the clubfooted orphan, is the protagonist; in Hemingway's *The Old Man and the Sea,* Santiago, an old Cuban fisherman, is the protagonist. See AGON, DEUTERAGONIST, TRITAGONIST.

prototype
The original or model on which something is formed or based; someone or something that serves to illustrate the typical qualities of a class. *Prototype,* from a Greek word meaning "original," is closely related to *archetype. For instance, Ananias, a liar mentioned in the Bible (Acts 5), is a prototype of all persons who tell lies; the bragging soldier (*miles gloriosus) of ancient drama was the prototype of all cowardly braggarts in literature, including Shakespeare's Falstaff.

proverb
A short saying, usually of unknown or ancient origin, that expresses some useful thought or commonplace truth. In the Bible, a proverb is a profound saying or maxim that requires interpretation. Proverbs are usually expressed in simple, homely language that is sometimes allegorical or symbolic: "A stitch in time saves nine." (See ADAGE, APHORISM, APOTHEGM, GNOMIC, MAXIM, SAW, SAYING.) A student of proverbs goes by the awesome name of paroemiologist.

provincialism
(1) A word, expression, or pronunciation peculiar to a section or province. See LOCALISM. (2) Narrowness of mind or ignorance resulting from sheltered life without exposure to cultural or intellectual activity. Most of the characters in Thomas Hardy's novels employ provincialisms in their speech and reflect provincialism in their lives. See LOCAL COLOR, REGIONALISM.

psyche
(1) The spirit, mind, or soul of man; (2) the mental (psychological) structure of a person, viewed as a moving force in his life. *Psyche,* which in Greek means "breath," in classical mythology was considered a *personification of the soul in the form of a beautiful girl who was loved by Eros (Cupid). (A classic account of this love story appears in Walter Pater's *Marius the Epicurean,* a philosophical *romance.) In literature, psyche is generally understood to be the animating principle or directing force in one's behavior.

psychedelic

An adjective applied to a mental state of calm and tranquillity. *Psychedelic* also refers to pleasurable sense perceptions and hallucinations. A psychedelic drug, such as mescaline or LSD, is one that fosters a trancelike state.

psychoanalysis

(1) A technical procedure for investigating unconscious mental processes; (2) a systematic *structure of theories concerning the relation of conscious and unconscious emotional processes. *Psychoanalysis* applies to professional (medical) investigation, diagnosis, and treatment, but the implications of this method are apparent in scores of plays, novels, and short stories. Stevenson's *Dr. Jekyll and Mr. Hyde,* Hawthorne's *Ethan Brand,* and Poe's *The Fall of the House of Usher* are three of scores of short stories alone that have been termed psychoanalytical in form and development.

psychological novel

A narrative that focuses on the emotional lives of its characters and explores their varied levels of mental activity. A psychological novel concentrates less on *what* happens than on the *why* and *wherefore* of *action. Such a narrative emphasizes "interior" characterization and the motives that result in "external" action. In a sense, a psychological novel is an interpretation of "inner" or "invisible" lives. Thus, the stories in Chaucer's *Canterbury Tales* are psychological, and so are the great tragedies of Shakespeare. Dickens, Thackeray, Henry James, Hardy, and Conrad wrote psychological novels as well, but the term is more often applied to twentieth-century works that use such devices as *interior monologue and *stream of consciousness techniques.

pulp magazine

A *periodical containing lurid or sensational stories or articles, printed on low-quality paper made of wood pulp. See CONFESSION, SLICK MAGAZINE, WESTERN STORY.

pun

A play on words; the humorous use of a word emphasizing different meanings or applications. (See EQUIVOQUE, PARONOMASIA.) The pun has often been called "the lowest form of wit"; one English writer (John Dennis) remarked that the maker of a bad pun would not hesitate "to pick a pocket," and Charles Lamb scornfully wrote, "A pun is a pistol let off at the ear, not a feather to tickle the intellect." Puns, however, have appeared in literature since the time of Homer (eighth century B.C.). An effective pun appears in these lines by a nineteenth-century versifier, Anita Owen:

> O dreamy eyes,
> They tell sweet lies of Paradise;
> And in those eyes the lovelight lies
> And lies—and lies—and lies!

puppetry

The art of making artificial figures perform on a miniature stage; *mummery. Puppetry, derived from a Latin word for *doll,* involves the manipulation of small figures representing persons or animals through the use of rods, wires, strings, or fingers. A puppet show is a dramatic performance, such as a Punch-and-Judy show, in which characters are made to act while the manipulator (or someone else) speaks words.

Puritanism

The principles and practices of Puritans, a class of English Protestants within the Church of England who, in the sixteenth century, began demands for reform in doctrine and worship. In the seventeenth century, Puritanism became a powerful political party. (See CALVINISM.) The Puritans who came to the New World on the *Mayflower* wished to set up a form of government in which their ideas of "purified" religion could prevail. *Puritanism* has come to imply strictness in moral and religious matters. A puritanical person is considered rigidly austere. Although Puritanism is a pejorative term, what James Russell Lowell said should be remembered: "Puritanism, believing itself quick with the seed of religious liberty, laid, without knowing it, the egg of democracy."

purple prose

Writing filled with exaggerated literary devices and marked by ornate diction and structure. Purple prose (so called because *purple* implies *regal* or *princely*) makes excessive use of parallelism, imagery, figurative language, *poetic diction, *cadence, and polysyllabication. Such writing is sometimes referred to as "purple patch," because it stands out from the passages around it. See FINE WRITING, PRECIOSITY.

pyrrhic

(1) A metrical foot of two short (unaccented) syllables. Common in classical poetry (Greek and Latin), the pyrrhic foot is unusual in English verse; in fact, a pyrrhic may be considered a double *anacrusis. See DIBRACH. (2) An ancient Greek warlike dance in which the motions of combat were imitated. The war dances of North American Indians were pyrrhic in nature. (3) An adjective applying to a victory won at too great a cost. (Pyrrhus, king of Epirus, won a notable battle with the Romans in the third century B.C. but lost so many of his men that he allegedly said, "One more such victory and we are lost.")

quadrivium

During the *Middle Ages, the four subjects leading to a Master of Arts degree: arithmetic, astronomy, geometry, and music. (See SEVEN LIBERAL ARTS.) *Quadrivium* is a Latin word meaning "place where four ways meet," that is, a crossroads.

quantitative verse

Metrical language whose underlying *rhythm is determined by the duration of sound in utterance. Quantitative verse makes use of the quantity of time allowed or required for the pronunciation of a word and is common in Greek, Latin, Hebraic, and Japanese poetry. English verse is "qualitative" in that it largely relies on *accent, *rhythm, and *meter. However, English poetry does have some quantitative values: see, for example, the quotation from Coleridge under the entry FOOT.

quarto

A book size of about 9½ by 12 inches, determined by folding printed sheets twice to form four leaves (eight pages). *Quarto* is often abbreviated as 4to. See FOLIO, OCTAVO.

quatorzain

A poem of fourteen lines. A quatorzain does not follow all

the forms prescribed by a *sonnet pattern. Every well-known *rondel in English is a quatorzain.

quatrain

A *stanza or *poem of four lines. The quatrain is the most common stanzaic form of poetry written in English. This quatrain, with a typical *rhyme scheme of *abab,* is by William Savage Landor:

> I strove with none; for none was worth
> my strife,
> Nature I loved, and, next to Nature, Art;
> I warmed both hands before the fire of life;
> It sinks, and I am ready to depart.

quem quaeritis

A Latin term meaning "whom do you seek?" The expression is applied to the earliest known form of liturgical drama; it is based on the visit to Christ's tomb by three women who discovered that the tomb was empty. An angel, guarding the sepulcher, asked, "Whom do you seek?" When told that Christ had risen, the women departed joyfully. See LITURGICAL DRAMA, MYSTERY PLAY.

quintain

A *stanza of five lines. (See CINQUAIN, PENTASTICH, TANKA.) Poe's *To Helen* consists of three quintains, of which this is the second:

> On desperate seas long wont to roam,
> Thy hyacinth hair, thy classic face,
> Thy Naiad airs have brought me home
> To the glory that was Greece
> And the grandeur that was Rome.

R

ratiocination

The process of logical reasoning. Ratiocination is a systematic method of thinking with order and precision, proceeding from careful examination of data to exactly phrased conclusions. (See DEDUCTION, INDUCTION.) The word was given literary significance by Edgar Allan Poe, who wrote several stories that he called ratiocinative, among them *The Purloined Letter, The Gold Bug,* and *The Mystery of Marie Roget. Ratiocination* signifies a kind of writing which solves, through logical thought processes, some sort of enigma. See DETECTIVE STORY.

rationalism

Acceptance of reason (intellect) as the supreme authority in matters of belief, conduct, and opinion. Rationalism is a doctrine in philosophy which holds that reason alone is a *source of knowledge, entirely independent of experience. It is also a theological doctrine that the human mind, unaided by divine revelations, is an adequate or sole guide to religious truths. This concept of the supremacy of the intellect made rationalism an ally of *neoclassicism and an opponent of *Calvinism, *mysticism, and *Puritanism. See DEISM, HUMANISM, PRIMITIVISM.

realism

(1) A theory of writing in which the familiar, ordinary aspects of life are depicted in a matter-of-fact, straightforward manner

designed to reflect life as it actually is; (2) treatment of subject matter in a way that presents careful descriptions of everyday life, often the lives of so-called middle or lower classes.

Realism, which refers to both the content and technique of literary creation, has been evident in literature from its very beginnings. For example, the English novelist and essayist C. S. Lewis has referred to

> ... the dragon "sniffing along the stone" in *Beowulf;* Layamon's Arthur, who, on hearing that he was king, sat very quiet and "one time he was red and one time he was pale"; the pinnacles in *Gawain* that looked as if they were "pared out of paper"; Jonah going into the whale's mouth "like a mote at a minster door"; ... Falstaff on his death-bed "plucking" at the sheet...

Although realism has always suggested accuracy of speech and detail, thorough background information, and a concern for *verisimilitude, the term took an added meaning during the nineteenth and early twentieth centuries on the Continent and in England and the United States: emphasis on photographic details, probing analysis of "things as they really are," the frustrations of characters in atmospheres of depravity, decay, or sordidness. *Realism* has been, and remains, a somewhat elusive, vague term, but it is fair to say that varied aspects of "realistic" subject matter and treatment have appeared in numerous plays, poems, and short stories of modern times and in novels by such writers as Daniel Defoe, Henry Fielding, Thackeray, Dickens, Balzac, Zola, Tolstoi, Mark Twain, William Dean Howells, John Galsworthy, Sinclair Lewis, and John O'Hara. See DETERMINISM, MIMETIC, NATURALISM, PRAGMATISM, VERISIMILITUDE.

Reason, Age of
See AGE OF REASON, ENLIGHTENMENT.

recantation
Withdrawal or disavowal of earlier opinions or actions. From Latin words meaning "to sing back," "to sing again," a recantation is a repudiation, a formal "taking back" of a previous deed or statement. (See PALINODE.) Late in life, Boccaccio agreed to "direct the mind toward eternal things" and wrote a recantation of such "delights of the temporal" as his bawdy work *The Decameron.*

recto

A Latin word meaning "right." The term is used to refer to a right-hand page of a book and to the front of a leaf (as opposed to *verso). In a book with numbered pages, recto pages always have the odd numbers.

redaction

Editing or revising a work for publication. Redaction also may involve digesting a longer work. (See ABRIDGMENT.) Sir Thomas Malory's *Morte d'Arthur,* a compilation, *translation, and *abridgment of *Arthurian romances, is a redaction.

reformation

The act of amending or improving what is unsatisfactory, wrong, or corrupt. Spelled with an uppercase letter, *Reformation* applies to the sixteenth-century religious movement which had for its object reform within the Roman Catholic Church and led to the establishment of Protestant churches. The Reformation was a dual movement: it was a Protestant revolution and also a reformation within the Catholic Church which led to the reduction of abuses, establishment of schools, and firmer discipline for the clergy. In *The Magic Mountain,* Thomas Mann wrote, "The invention of printing and the Reformation are and remain the two outstanding services of central Europe to the cause of humanity." In his first inaugural address, Thomas Jefferson listed the principles which had guided the steps of the newly created United States "through an age of revolution and reformation."

refrain

A phrase or verse (line) recurring at intervals in a *poem or *song, usually at the end of a *stanza. A refrain may help to establish the *meter of a poem, indicate its *tone, or reestablish its *atmosphere. A refrain may also be a nonsense line (such as "With a hay, and a ho, and a hey nonino" in Shakespeare's *As You Like It*) or a word or phrase that takes on added significance each time it appears (like the word "Nevermore" in Poe's poem *The Raven*). See INCREMENTAL REPETITION, REPETEND.

regionalism

(1) Representation in literature of a particular section or area; (2) fidelity in writing to a specific geographical region,

accurately representing its speech, manners, customs, folk-lore, beliefs, dress, and history. See LOCAL COLOR.

Regionalism is an element in nearly all literature, since most selections involve a *locale or *setting; the term, however, is usually applied to writings in which locale is thought of as a subject interesting in itself. The Wessex novels of Thomas Hardy are regional literature. The poetry of Robinson Jeffers is filled with *allusions to California and the Pacific; Yevgeny Alexandrovich Yevtushenko's poems deal exclusively with his home area in Russia and the emotions of his neighbors; Dylan Thomas's poetry is loaded with references to his native Wales. Such novelists as Willa Cather, Ellen Glasgow, Thomas Wolfe, and William Faulkner have exhibited regionalism in much of their work. For most literary craftsmen, the impetus, ideas, and imagery of their writing spring from the land and the people closest to them.

Renaissance

The activity, spirit, and time of the revival of art, learning, and literature in Europe extending over a period of 300 years (about 1350 to 1650). *Renaissance,* also spelled *Renascence,* means "rebirth," but the Renaissance was less a rebirth than an epoch which marked a transition from the medieval to the modern world. In literature, the period was notable for a revival of interest in the *humanities and a rediscovery of *classic works of Greek and Roman origin. The Renaissance, however, was a many-pronged era that included vigorous new trends in art, science, religion, and politics. Also, the Renaissance ushered in the growth of cities and commerce, as well as increased travel throughout Europe and resolute and determined colonization in the New World. Intellectually and socially, the period witnessed increased emphasis on the importance of human lives as contrasted with the subordination of individuals during feudal times. See ELIZ-ABETHAN, FEUDALISM, HUMANISM.

repartee

Conversation full of quick, witty replies. Repartee, a term from French, appears often in the plays of Wilde, Shaw, Noel Coward, and William Saroyan and in *fiction by such writers as Raymond Chandler, James Thurber, and Peter De Vries. See PERSIFLAGE, STICHOMYTHIA.

repertoire
A store or stock of items available. In literature, *repertoire* refers to the list (or inventory) of plays which a company of actors is prepared to perform. Both *repertoire* and *repertory* are terms sometimes applied to the collected works of an author and to the kinds of personal experience and collected data which a writer can use, upon demand, in his work.

repetend
A word or phrase repeated at irregular intervals in a poem. A repetend resembles a *refrain except that it may only partially repeat and may appear anywhere in a selection. The following lines from Poe's *Ulalume* contain several repetends:
> The skies they were ashen and sober;
> The leaves they were crispèd and sere—
> The leaves they were withering and sere.

The repetend is only one of several devices in poetry based on repetition; others are *alliteration, *anaphora, *assonance, *consonance, *meter, refrain, and *rhythm.

requiem
Any chant, *dirge, *hymn, or musical service for the dead. *Requiem,* which means "rest," is the first word in the Roman Catholic Requiem mass, a service dedicated to asking repose for the souls of the dead. At the funeral of Ophelia (in *Hamlet*), the priest, who suspects that she was a suicide, exclaims:
> We should profane the service of the dead
> To sing sage requiem and such rest to her
> As to peace-parted souls.

Stevenson's *Requiem* is a buoyant poem containing these lines:
> Under the wide and starry sky,
> Dig the grave and let me lie.
> Glad did I live and gladly die,
> And I laid me down with a will.

resolution
(1) The events following the *climax of a *play or *story (see ACT, FALLING ACTION); (2) determination, resolve, or purpose such as, for instance, the plan announced by Wordsworth and Coleridge in their Preface to the *Lyrical Ballads* to revolt against what they considered the artificial literature of their day; (3) a formal expression of opinion by an organization, club, legislature, etc., such as the Declaration of Independence.

restoration

The act of renewal, revival, or reestablishment, such as the return of something to a former, original, or unimpaired state: the restoration of colonial Williamsburg. In literature, the *Restoration* refers to the return of Charles II to the English throne in 1660; the Restoration age in English literature is commonly considered the years from 1660 to the revolution in 1688, when Parliament regained power.

résumé

A summing up; a *summary. (See ABRIDGMENT, ABSTRACT, EPITOME.) *Résumé,* a French term meaning "resumed," is also applied to a brief account of personal, educational, and professional experience and qualifications, such as that of an applicant for work.

revenge tragedy

A form of *drama popular in *Elizabethan England. The typical revenge (exacting punishment, "getting even") tragedy emphasized bloodshed, violence, and lurid incidents involving incest, adultery, ghosts, suicide, dead bodies, etc. The *theme of a revenge tragedy usually involved the revenge of a son for his father (*Hamlet*) or a father for his son (Thomas Kyd's *The Spanish Tragedy*).

revue

A form of theatrical entertainment. A revue, a French term for *review,* consists of a variety of dances, choruses, songs, and skits. A typical revue parodies or satirizes current fads, recent events, and persons in the public eye; it normally has no real *plot but is lavish in its stage settings, scenery, costuming, etc.

rhetoric

The theory and principles concerned with effective use of language, both written and oral. To the ancient Greeks, rhetoric was essential for *argumentation and oratory (the Greek word *rhetor* means "orator"), and it eventually became one of the *seven liberal arts. (See TRIVIUM.) According to *Aristotelian theory, rhetoric was a way of organizing material for the presentation of truth, but Socrates (and many later thinkers) have considered it a superficial art, that of "making great matters small and small things great." In modern times, *rhetoric* has come to mean the art or science of literary uses of language. It is concerned with the effectiveness and general appeal of communication and with methods of achieving literary quality and vigor. Rhetoric is only loosely connected with specific details of mechanics, grammar, etc. See ARGUMENTATION, EFFECTIVE-NESS, PERSUASION.

rhetorical question

A question asked solely to produce an effect or to make a statement but not expected to receive an answer. The purpose of such a question, to which the answer is obvious, is usually to make a deeper impression upon the hearer (or reader) than a direct statement would. James Russell Lowell's line in *The Vision of Sir Launfal* is a rhetorical question: "And what is so rare as a day in June?" Shakespeare uses a series of rhetorical questions in this speech by Shylock in *The Merchant of Venice:*

> Hath not a Jew eyes? Hath not a Jew hands, organs, dimensions, senses, affections, passions; fed with the same food, hurt with the same weapons, subject to the same diseases, heal'd by the same means, warm'd and cooled by the same winter and summer, as a Christian is? If you prick us, do we not bleed? If you tickle us, do we not laugh? If you poison us, do we not die? And if you wrong us, shall we not revenge?

rhyme

Similarity or identity of sound in words. Two words rhyme (or rime) when their accented vowels and all succeeding sounds are identical: *rain, stain; skating, dating; emotion, demotion; fascinate, deracinate.* Rhyme is more than an ornament in *poetry. It provides pleasing sense impressions; it helps to establish stanzaic form; it is an aid in memorizing; it contributes to the *unity of a poem. For comment on the many different kinds of rhyme in poetry, see DOUBLE RHYME, END RHYME, EYE RHYME, FEMININE RHYME, HALF RHYME, HEAD ' RHYME, IMPERFECT RHYME, INTERNAL RHYME, LEONINE VERSE, MASCULINE ENDING, PERFECT RHYME, RHYME ROYAL.

rhyme royal

A form of verse (also spelled *rime royal*) consisting of seven-line *stanzas of iambic *pentameter in a fixed *rhyme scheme (*ababbcc*). Its introducer, Geoffrey Chaucer (1340–

1400), used this form in many of his poems. This stanza from Wordsworth's *Resolution and Independence* is in rhyme royal:

There was a roaring in the wind all night:
The rain came heavily and fell in floods;
But now the sun is rising calm and bright.
The birds are singing in the distant woods;
Over his own sweet voice the stockdove broods;
The jay makes answer as the magpie chatters;
And the air is filled with pleasant noise of waters.

rhyme scheme

The pattern of rhymes used in a *poem, usually marked by letters to indicate correspondences. The four-line *stanza, or *quatrain, is usually written so that the first line rhymes with the third and the second with the fourth; this rhyme scheme is noted as *abab*. In an *English sonnet, the fourteen lines have a rhyme scheme of *abab, cdcd, efef, gg*.

rhythm

Uniform recurrence (repetition) of beat or *accent; the measured flow of words in *verse or *prose. Rhythm in verse is most often established by a combination of accent and number of syllables. (See METER.) In prose, rhythm is marked by variety of movement; among contributors to prose rhythm are *balanced sentences, variety in sentence structure and length, transitional devices, and *euphony. (See CADENCE, POLYPHONIC PROSE.) An example of rhythmic prose is provided under the entry POETIC PROSE. Also, see SPRUNG RHYTHM.

rising action

That part of a *plot involving *complication and *conflict and leading up to a *climax, or turning point, in a play (or novel). In much classical and Elizabethan drama, rising action largely occurred in the first two acts of a five-act production. See ACT.

Robin Hood theme

A pattern, or *formula, of action in which poor or disadvantaged persons achieve success through the aid of some benefactor or outside agency. The expression derives its name from the legendary English outlaw who robbed the rich to give to the poor and who was a model of generosity, courage, and justice. The Robin Hood theme is a variant version of the Cinderella story, in which a drudge is helped by a good fairy to win a prince and thus "live happily ever after."

rodomontade
A French term meaning "boasting," "bragging." The word is derived from the name of a boastful king in Ariosto's *Orlando Furioso,* an Italian *epic. (See BRAGGADOCIO.) Falstaff's description of his fight with highwaymen (Shakespeare's *Henry IV,* Part 1, act 2, scene 2) is rodomontade.

roman à clef
A French phrase for a *novel that represents actual historical characters and events in the form of fiction. With the literal meaning of "novels with a key," romans à clef include such titles as Aldous Huxley's *Point Counter Point,* Ernest Hemingway's *The Sun Also Rises,* Somerset Maugham's *Cakes and Ale,* and Robert Penn Warren's *All the King's Men.*

roman à thèse
A French term for a novel with a *thesis. See PROBLEM NOVEL, PLAY; PROPAGANDA.

romance
A term originally referring to a *medieval narrative in prose or verse dealing with heroic persons and events. *Romance* now applies to any fictional account of heroic achievements, colorful scenes, passionate love, or supernatural experiences. A romance is sometimes considered a fanciful or extravagant story or daydream. Sir Walter Scott was a notable writer of romances of a traditional sort, but the term is currently applied most often to "romantic fiction" or to a love affair.

romanticism
The term *romanticism* cannot be precisely applied to a specific state of mind, *point of view, or literary technique. As a movement, it arose so gradually in so many different aspects in so many parts of Europe that a satisfactory definition is impossible. In France, Victor Hugo (1802–1885) emphasized as a controlling idea in romanticism the "liberalism of literature," the freeing of an artist from restraints and rules imposed by classicists and the encouragement of

revolutionary political ideas. In Germany, Heinrich Heine (1797–1856) thought the dominant aspect of romanticism was its revival of the past (medievalism) in letters, art, and life. A later English writer (Walter Pater, 1839–1894) suggested that the adding of strangeness to beauty constituted the romantic spirit of the age. Other writers have insisted that the so-called romantic mood is a desire to escape from reality, especially unpleasant reality. This widespread movement of the eighteenth and nineteenth centuries exhibited each of these characteristics.

Specifically, romanticism may be called a literary attitude in which imagination is considered more important than formal rules and reason (*classicism) and than a sense of fact (*realism).

Romanticism as applied to the social, political, and literary revolution that swept through Western Europe and culminated in England from 1798 to 1832 had psychological implications and suggests changes in attitude toward the human experience from which literature is derived. Among these changes were increasing emphasis on the individual as opposed to social *convention and *tradition; emphasis on mystery and the supernatural—strangeness and wonder as opposed to common sense, the infinite as opposed to the finite; emphasis on the imaginative and emotional as opposed to the rational—an appeal to the heart rather than the head.

In effect, romanticism is a literary and philosophical theory which tends to place the individual at the center of life and experience and represents a shift from *objectivity to *subjectivity. These concepts of romanticism have contributed significantly to the establishment of the modern democratic world.

Romany

(1) A gypsy, a nomadic person whose ancestors migrated from India and settled in various parts of Asia, Europe, and North America; (2) the language of gypsies, a *dialect form of Indic. As an adjective, *Romany* refers to the customs, habits, and traditions of gypsies, about whom George Borrow, a nineteenth-century English traveler and author, wrote extensively.

rondeau

A short poem, the name of which is derived from a French word meaning "little circle." A rondeau typically consists of fifteen (or thirteen or ten) lines using only two rhymes. Austin Dobson's *With Pipe and Flute* is a rondeau:

> With pipe and flute the rustic Pan
> Of old made music sweet for man;
> And wonder hushed the warbling bird,
> And closer drew the calm-eyed herd,
> The rolling river slowlier ran.
>
> Ah! would,—ah! would, a little span,
> Some air of Arcady could fan
> This age of ours, too seldom stirred
> With pipe and flute!
>
> But now for gold we plot and plan;
> And from Beersheba unto Dan
> Apollo's self might pass unheard,
> Or find the night-jar's note preferred—
> Not so it fared when time began
> With pipe and flute!

rondel

A short poem resembling the *rondeau. A rondel is usually a group of *stanzas totaling fourteen lines running on two rhymes; the first two lines are repeated at the middle of the poem and again at the end. The rondel differs from the rondeau only in number of lines and the use of complete, not partial, lines for the *refrain.

round character

A person in a literary selection who is so fully described as to be recognizable, understandable, and individually different from all others appearing in the same selection. E. M. Forster said, "The test of a round character is whether it is capable of surprising in a convincing way," by which he meant that such a person is not a *stock character or a mere *type. See CHARACTER, CHARACTERIZATION, FLAT CHARACTER, FOIL.

roundel

A poem in the *pattern of a *rondeau but consisting of eleven lines. Like the rondeau and the *rondel, the roundel uses only two rhymes and a twice-repeated refrain.

roundelay

A term used as a label for such fixed forms as the *rondeau, *rondel, and *roundel. *Roundelay* may mean the musical background (setting) for a poem in fixed form and also a round dance itself.

Round Table

The famous table, made round to avoid quarrels as to precedence, about which King Arthur and his knights gathered. (See ARTHURIAN, KNIGHTS OF THE ROUND TABLE.) *Round table* also refers to a discussion, or conference, in which each person has equal status and equal time to present his views.

Rubaiyat

From an Arabic word, *rubaiyat* means *quatrain (four-line *stanza). The term is nearly always used in a title, *The Rubaiyat of Omar Khayyam,* a translation by Edward Fitzgerald of lines by the eleventh-century Persian poet and astronomer. Two of the best-known quatrains from *The Rubaiyat* are these:

> A Book of Verses underneath the Bough,
> A Jug of Wine, a Loaf of Bread—and Thou
> Beside me singing in the Wilderness—
> Oh, Wilderness were Paradise enow!

> The Moving Finger writes; and having writ,
> Moves on; nor all your Piety nor Wit
> Shall lure it back to cancel half a Line,
> Nor all your Tears wash out a Word of it.

rubric

A title, heading, or direction (in a *manuscript or book) that is written or printed in red or otherwise distinguished from the remainder of the text. *Rubric,* from Latin for *red,* also applies to a direction for religious services inserted in a liturgical book. See MARGINALIA.

rune

(1) An *aphorism, *poem, or *saying with mystical meaning; a riddle.   (2) One of the characters of an ancient Germanic alphabet. The Norse god Odin was said to have lost his sanity because of a rune sent him by a maiden rejecting his love. The *Anglo-Saxon poet Cynewulf (ninth century) inserted runic characters into some of his verses.

run-on line

A verse (one line) of poetry having a thought that carries over to the next line without a pause. There is no grammatical or sense break until the end of the fourth line in this *quatrain from Tennyson's *In Memoriam:*

> And gathering freshlier overhead
> Rocked the full-foliaged elms, and swung
> The heavy-folded rose, and flung
> The lilies to and fro, and said . . .

See END-STOPPED LINE, ENJAMBEMENT.

S

saga

A lengthy narrative or *legend about heroic events. *Saga,* derived from an Icelandic word meaning *saw (saying), applies particularly to any Scandinavian story of medieval times dealing with the adventures of persons of lofty rank. *Saga* now refers to any traditional legend, *myth, or *tale involving extraordinary, marvelous, or detailed experiences and achievements; Longfellow adapted material from Icelandic sources for his *Saga of King Olaf;* Galsworthy's "saga novel" is entitled *The Forsyte Saga.*

Sapphic

A term referring to Sappho, a Greek poetess born on the island of Lesbos (Mytilene) in the seventh century B.C. (See LESBIAN.) *Sapphics* is a name applied to four-line *stanzas in a *meter used by Sappho and imitated by the English poet Swinburne in a volume entitled *Sapphics.* A Sapphic verse (line) consists of eleven syllables (see HENDECASYLLABIC) as in this excerpt from a stanza by Swinburne: "Softly touched mine eyelids and lips; and I too." A Sapphic ode is virtually the same as a *Horatian ode.

sarcasm

A form of *irony; bitter and often harsh derision. Sarcasm consists of sneering or cutting remarks; it is always personal, always jeering, and always intended to hurt. Byron's comment on Robert Southey, another English poet, is filled with sarcastic remarks, such as

> He first sank to the bottom—like his work,
> But soon rose to the surface—like himself;
> For all corrupted things are buoyed like corks,
> By their own rottenness. . . .

Sassenach
A term for "Englishman," Irish in origin, that is usually used disparagingly by *Gaelic persons residing in the British Isles. See ANGLO-SAXON.

satire
The ridiculing of folly, stupidity, or vice; the use of *irony, *sarcasm, or ridicule for exposing or denouncing the frailties and faults of mankind. Satire is a literary manner, or *technique, that blends *humor and *wit with a critical attitude toward human activities and institutions. *Satire* is a general term, one usually considered to involve both moral judgment and a desire to help improve a custom, belief, or tradition. (See BURLESQUE, CARICATURE, INVECTIVE, LAMPOON, PARODY.) *Horatian satire is gentle, chiding, and corrective; *Juvenalian satire is savage and bitter; modern satire is genial (Mark Twain), witty (George Bernard Shaw), or fun-provoking (E. B. White, James Thurber). Outstanding satirists of the past and present are Aristophanes, Juvenal, Horace, Molière, Dryden, Pope, Swift, Thackeray, Evelyn Waugh, Aldous Huxley, Sinclair Lewis, John P. Marquand, Philip Roth, and John Cheever.

saw
A wise *saying, a homely but sententious remark ("Beauty's but skin deep"). (See MAXIM, PROVERB.) In *As You Like It,* when describing the seven ages of man, Shakespeare referred to the justice

> In fair round belly with good capon lined,
> With eyes severe and beard of formal cut,
> Full of wise saws and modern instances [examples].

saying
A general term for any expression or utterance, especially one that reveals a general truth. Among kinds of sayings are the *adage, *aphorism, *apothegm, *epigram, *maxim, *motto, and *proverb.

scansion

The metrical analysis of poetry; the division of a line of poetry into feet by indicating *accents and counting *syllables. Scansion is a method of studying the mechanical elements by means of which the poet has secured rhythmical effects. Scansion involves consideration of the *foot, length of line (*meter), and *rhyme scheme of a group of poetic verses. Scansion of the first five lines of Keats's *Endymion* is as follows:

A thing / of beau/ty is / a joy / forever: *a*
Its love/liness / increas/es; it / will never   *a*
Pass in/to noth/ingness; / but still / will keep   *b*
A bow/er qui/et for / us, and / a sleep   *b*
Full of / sweet dreams, / and health, /
    and qui/et breathing.   *c*

scenario

An *outline of the *plot of a dramatic work, providing particulars about *characters, *settings, and *situations. *Scenario* is most often used as a name for a detailed script of a motion picture: a treatment setting forth action in the sequence it is to follow, detailed descriptions of scenes and characters, actual words (text) to be spoken or shown on the screen, etc. The *plot of a film or television production is sometimes loosely called its scenario.

scene

(1) The place where some act or event occurs; (2) an *incident or *situation in real life; (3) a division of an *act of a *play; (4) a unit of dramatic action in which a single point is made or one effect obtained.

scholiast

An ancient commentator on the classics. A scholiast wrote *marginalia explaining the grammar and meaning of passages in *medieval manuscripts that were based on Greek and Latin texts.

science fiction

Narrative which draws imaginatively on scientific knowledge, theory, and speculation in its *plot, *theme, and *setting. Science fiction is a form of *fantasy in which hypotheses form the basis, by logical *extrapolation, of space travel, adventures on other planets, etc. The form has been in existence since at least the second century: Lucian, a Greek writer, created a *hero who traveled to the moon. Jules Verne (*Twenty Thousand Leagues under the Sea*) wrote science fiction more than a century ago.

scop
An *Anglo-Saxon poet. A scop was a sort of *bard to the court, although he may have wandered about the countryside like a *gleeman. A scop drew his stories from *traditions and *legends of early Germanic peoples and from Biblical accounts.

Scotticism
A word or *idiom peculiar to, or characteristic of, the *dialect of English spoken in Scotland. The poems of Robert Burns, for example, are filled with Scotticisms: *frae* ("from"), *haet* ("hate"), *wale* ("choose"), etc.

secondary source
A *source of information that is not primary or original; facts or opinions that are not firsthand and direct. (See PRIMARY SOURCE.) A secondary source of information about a writer would be an encyclopedia article concerning him; a primary source would be facts in a *Who's Who* sketch prepared (or approved) by the author himself.

semantics
The study of meaning; a branch of linguistics that deals with the meanings of words and with historical changes in those meanings. Semantics may also be thought of as the relations between signs (words, *symbols) and the mental and physical actions called forth by their meanings. See GENERAL SEMANTICS.

seminal
Highly original and thus influencing the development of future events. The work of a seminal writer, such as Bacon, Shakespeare, Wordsworth, or Mark Twain, possesses the "seeds" of growth and causes changes and developments in the thoughts and attitudes of others, readers and authors alike.

Senecan
A reference to Lucius Seneca, a first-century Roman philosopher and writer of tragedies. Seneca's plays, modeled on those of Euripides, had a profound effect upon *Renais-

sance playwrights in their subject matter and use of dramatic *conventions. Senecan tragedy invariably appeared in five *acts, dealt with powerfully conflicting emotions, resulted in *catastrophe, and employed much *bombast. See REVENGE TRAGEDY.

sensibility
Capacity for feeling or sensation; responsiveness to sensory stimuli. *Sensibility* implies quickness and acuteness of apprehension or feeling and, in general, indicates emotionalism rather than *rationalism. As a *synonym for "keen consciousness" or "appreciation," *sensibility* is closely related to *empathy. (See SYMPATHY.) Laurence Sterne's *Tristram Shandy* is a novel of sensibility; Jane Austen's *Sense and Sensibility* (1811) is a narrative contrasting rationalism and this form of emotionalism. Aldous Huxley has written:

> Experience is not a matter of actually having swum the Hellespont, or danced with dervishes, or slept in a dosshouse. It is a matter of sensibility and intuition, of seeing and hearing the significant things, of paying attention at the right moments, of understanding. . . .

sensual, sensuous
Sensual refers, usually unfavorably, to enjoyments and delights derived from the senses and ordinarily implies coarseness, grossness, and lewdness. Falstaff, for instance, took a sensual delight in eating and drinking. *Sensuous* refers, often favorably, to what is experienced through the senses; for example, one enjoys such a sensuous poem as Keats's *The Eve of St. Agnes.*

sententia
A wise saying; a philosophical statement. *Sententia* is a *synonym for *maxim. Sententiae (plural) are usually formal and judicial; use of them results in a sententious style—one containing pithy sayings and moralizing comments.

sentimentalism
Excessive indulgence in sentiment or emotionalism; predominance of feeling over reason and intellect. Sentimentalism in literature is "emotion run wild," with emphasis on feeling rather than on events and circumstances which produced the feeling. Sentimentalism produces a reaction of sentimentality: a quick, too-ready reaction to emotion. Dickens carefully aroused

for readers sensations of pity in *The Old Curiosity Shop*, but as Little Nell uncomplainingly fades away into death, sentimentality takes over rather than a more sensible reaction toward the forces that have undermined the orphan's chances for happiness.

septenary

An adjective referring to the number seven. As a noun, *septenary* means a period of seven years, the number seven, and a line of poetry containing seven feet. See FOURTEENER, HEPTAMETER.

sequel

(1) A literary work that continues the narrative of a preceding work; (2) a result or consequence; (3) a subsequent course of affairs. *Sequel,* from a Latin word meaning "follow," is used in each of these meanings in literature. Galsworthy's *To Let* (1921) is a sequel to *In Chancery* (1920); these novels are sequels to *The Man of Property* (1906), and the three combined form *The Forsyte Saga.* For comment on *sequel* as "following action" or "consequence," see ACTION, CAUSE AND EFFECT, PLOT.

serenade

A performance of vocal or instrumental music as a tribute to someone or to some institution. A serenade is usually a song sung by a gallant under his lady's window (the word is derived from an Italian term meaning "evening song"). Shelley's *Indian Serenade* is a poem imitating such a song. A once well-known serenade is that of a minor American poet, Bayard Taylor, called *Bedouin Song,* a part of which is:
> My steps are nightly driven,
> By the fever in my breast
> To hear from thy lattice breathed
> The word that shall give me rest.
> Open the door of thy heart,
> And open thy chamber door,
> And my kisses shall teach thy lips
> The love that shall fade no more
> Till the sun grows cold,
> And the stars are old,
> And the leaves of the Judgment Book unfold.

sestet

The last six lines of an *Italian sonnet; any *poem or *stanza of six lines. *Sestet,* also spelled *sextet,* may also refer to a group of six vocalists or instrumentalists. See OCTAVE, PETRARCHAN.

sestina

A poem of six six-line *stanzas and an *envoi of three lines. The sestina is a complicated, difficult verse form involving repetition in each stanza of words arranged in different order from their appearance in preceding stanzas. The form has been used by Dante, Petrarch, Sir Philip Sidney, Swinburne, Kipling, Ezra Pound, and W. H. Auden.

setting

The environment or surroundings of anything. The term is usually applied in literature to the *locale or period in which the *action of a play, novel, motion picture, etc., takes place. In theatrical jargon, *setting* may also refer to scenery or properties (see PROP). The setting of *Macbeth* is Scotland in the eleventh century; more specifically, the *incidents in the play occur in seven different settings—Forres, Inverness, Dunsinane, the forests (witches' scenes), Duncan's camp, Fife, and England. See LOCAL COLOR, LOCALE, REGIONALISM.

seven deadly sins

According to *medieval theology, the seven deadly (capital, cardinal) sins were pride, anger (wrath), envy, sloth (laziness), lust (lechery), covetousness (avarice), and gluttony. Each of these sins resulted in spiritual death; each could be atoned for only through complete and perfect repentance. These sins were often presented in *allegory and *personification in medieval and *Renaissance times. Dante treated each of them in his poetry; Chaucer's *The Parson's Tale* and Spenser's *The Faerie Queene* deal with these flaws. See SEVEN VIRTUES.

seven liberal arts

The seven subjects (or disciplines) studied in *medieval universities. The three studies of the four-year course leading to a baccalaureate degree were the trivium: grammar (really Latin grammar), *logic, and *rhetoric (especially speaking, oratory). The four subjects following in a three-year curriculum leading to an advanced degree were the quadrivium: arithmetic, geometry, astronomy, and music. See QUADRIVIUM, TRIVIUM.

seven virtues

In the teachings of scholasticism, the seven virtues were courage (fortitude), prudence, justice, temperance, faith, hope, and charity (love for one's fellows). These virtues were frequently allegorized and personified (see ALLEGORY, PERSONIFICATION) as, for example, in Spenser's *The Faerie Queene.* Seven was a mystic or magic number to the ancients, as witness the seven ages of the world, seven blessings of heaven, seven heresies, seven gifts of the spirit, seven gods of luck, seven names of God, seven sorrows of Mary, etc.

Shakespearean sonnet

A poem of fourteen lines arranged in three *quatrains and a *couplet. This *stanza was developed by earlier poets (Wyatt and Surrey) during the first half of the sixteenth century; it is referred to also as an *English sonnet, but the Shakespearean sonnet is so named for its greatest practitioner, who wrote 154 such poems. The following sonnet illustrates the form and reveals the poet's belief in the power of poetry to outlive mankind:

Shall I compare thee to a summer's day?
Thou art more lovely and more temperate:
Rough winds do shake the darling buds of May,
And summer's lease hath all too short a date:
Sometime too hot the eye of heaven shines,
And often is his gold complexion dimmed;
And every fair from fair sometime declines,
By chance, or nature's changing course untrimmed;
But thy eternal summer shall not fade,
Nor lose possession of that fair thou owest
Nor shall Death brag thou wander'st in his shade,
When in eternal lines to time thou growest:
So long as men can breathe or eyes can see,
So long lives this, and this gives life to thee.

short measure

A *stanza used for *hymns, consisting of four lines, rhyming *abab* or *abcb*. Short measure (or short meter) is so called because three of the lines in the *quatrain consist of three feet (iambic trimeter). This is a short measure (often abbreviated as S.M.) from a hymn by Isaac Watts:

> There is a dreadful Hell,
> And everlasting pains;
> There sinners must with devils dwell
> In darkness, fire, and chains.

See COMMON MEASURE, LONG MEASURE.

short short story

A brief piece of prose *fiction, more condensed than a *short story. Such a selection may vary in length from 500 to 1,500 words, a length in which *conflict, *characterization, and *setting must be handled deftly and economically. (See ECONOMY.) A short short story contains every ingredient of a *short story but with heightened *focus and brevity. See VIGNETTE.

short story

A relatively short narrative (under 10,000 words) which is designed to produce a single dominant effect and which contains the elements of *drama. A short story concentrates on a single *character in a single *situation at a single moment. Even if these conditions are not met, a short story still exhibits *unity as its guiding principle. An effective short story consists of a character (or group of characters) presented against a background, or *setting, involved, through mental or physical *action, in a *situation. Dramatic *conflict—the collision of opposing forces—is at the heart of every short story.

Short stories have existed in one form or another throughout history. More than 2,000 years ago, the Old Testament revealed narratives about King David, Joseph, Jonah, and Ruth which were essentially short stories. The *fabliau and the *exemplum were *medieval forms of such narratives. Edgar Allan Poe is considered the father of the modern short story. The *genre has flourished throughout the world for more than a century in the works of Maupassant, Mérimée, Zola, Turgenev, Chekhov, Hawthorne, Stevenson, Hardy, and hundreds of twentieth-century craftsmen.

sigmatism

Defective pronunciation, or overuse, of sibilants. *Sigmatism,* from the Greek word for *s, sigma,* has long been a problem for poets because *s, z, j, sh, zh,* and *ch* necessarily appear often in English words and frequently sound harsh or hissing. Joseph Addison commented on "the hissing so much noticed by foreigners," and Tennyson referred to his own restricted use of sibilants as "kicking the geese out of the boat." Poe deliberately used sigmatism to achieve a sensory effect in these lines:

> Now each visitor shall confess
> The sad valley's restlessness.
> Nothing there is motionless—
> Nothing save the airs that brood
> Over the magic solitude.

simile
A *figure of speech in which two things, essentially different but thought to be alike in one or more respects, are compared. In a simile the point of likeness is expressed by *like, as,* or *as if.* (See EPIC SIMILE, METAPHOR.) Similes, which make imaginative comparisons for purposes of explanation or ornament, are essential in all poetry and occur frequently in prose as well. Two similes appear in this quatrain from Robert Burns:

> O, my luve is like a red, red rose
> That's newly sprung in June;
> O, my luve is like the melodie
> That's sweetly played in tune.

similitude
Likeness, resemblance. *Similitude* also has the meaning of semblance: Bunyan referred to his *Pilgrim's Progress* as being "delivered under the similitude of a dream." Sometimes, *similitude* is used as a *synonym for *simile. See VERISIMILITUDE.

situation
A location or position; a state of affairs. In literature, *situation* is a term used to refer to the group of circumstances in which a *character finds himself and to the *setting and conditions under which a work of *fiction begins its *action. (See PLOT.) The opening situation in *Macbeth* is that of a nobleman (Macbeth) who is expecting a visit from his ruler to the castle in Inverness, Scotland. The situation in Flaubert's *Madame Bovary* is that of a young woman living a life of tedium in a small village as the wife of a mediocre physician.

250

skald

An ancient Scandinavian poet. A skald (also spelled *scald*) played about the same role as an Anglo-Saxon *scop did.

Skeltonics

Rough, unstressed, and rollicking verses named for their originator, John Skelton (1460–1529), an English poet. Skeltonics resemble *doggerel, have an irregular rhyme scheme, and are composed of lines of varying length. This excerpt from a poem by Skelton will illustrate:

> Merry Margaret, as midsummer flower,
> Gentle as falcon or hawk of the tower,
> With solace and gladness,
> Much mirth and no madness,
> All good and no badness;
> So joyously,
> So maidenly,
> So womanly,
> Her demeaning...

sketch

(1) A short, descriptive *essay; (2) a short play or brief dramatic performance; (3) any simply constructed *composition that presents a single *character, single *scene, or single *incident. (See CHARACTER SKETCH, VAUDEVILLE.) A sketch may also be a rough design, plan, or first draft of a literary work or a brief, hasty outline of an *article, *essay, or book. Dickens's *Sketches by Boz* ("Boz" was a *pseudonym sometimes used by Dickens) is a series of comments on life and manners, published at random in various *periodicals.

slander

A malicious, false, and defamatory statement or report. (See LIBEL.) Legally, slander is defamation or *calumny by oral utterance rather than in writing, drawings, or pictures. The nineteenth-century English critic John Ruskin slandered some of the paintings of James McNeill Whistler, but he was sued for libel by Whistler only when he wrote and published statements such as: "I have seen, and heard, much of *Cockney impudence before now; but never expected to hear a coxcomb ask two hundred guineas for flinging a pot of paint in the public's face." (Whistler was awarded damages of one farthing, a now-withdrawn English coin, then worth less than one cent.)

slant rhyme

A *synonym for approximate rhyme, usually the substitution of *assonance for real *rhyme. The words *giver* and *never* are an example of slant rhyme.

slapstick

Broad comedy characterized by violent and boisterous *action; *farce combined with horseplay in a comic form. The term derives its name from a stick, or lath, used by harlequins in *commedia dell'arte and *pantomime. Such a slapstick would make a noise when it was used to strike a fellow actor. So-called comic *sketches in *vaudeville involving pie-in-the-face acts, dunkings, and pratfalls are examples of slapstick *farce.

slice of life

Accurate transcription into *fiction or *drama of a segment of actual experience. (See TRANCHE DE VIE.) In the slice of life technique, a novelist or dramatist opens a door for the reader, permits him to see and hear characters, and then closes the door without comment or observation. This method is related to that of *stream of consciousness but with a difference noted by Edith Wharton in *The Writing of Fiction:*

> The stream of consciousness differs from the slice of life in noting down mental as well as physical reactions but resembles it in setting them down just as they come, with a deliberate disregard of their relevance in the particular case, or rather with the assumption that their very unsorted abundance constitutes in itself the author's subject.

The unselective presentation of life—life the way it is, without neat and specific beginning and ending, with extreme *realism—has been an important technique for such writers of *naturalism as Zola, Maupassant, Dreiser, James Joyce, Frank Norris, Eugene O'Neill, and James T. Farrell.

slick magazine

A popular, basically nonliterary *periodical. A slick magazine, or a slick, derives its name from the appearance of the coated (polished) stock on which it is printed. See MASS MEDIA, PULP MAGAZINE.

society

As used in literature, *society* means human beings generally or, less often, an organized group of persons living as members of a community. Society may also be considered as classes of people grouped according to worldly status. In ecology, *society* refers to an integrated group of social organisms of the same species held together by mutual dependence. Thomas Paine made clear what was, for him, a distinction between *society* (association, community) and *government:* "Society in every state is a blessing, but government, even in its best state, is but a necessary evil."

sociological novel, play

A narrative or dramatic work that deals primarily with social questions and problems, that focuses on environmental and cultural factors more than on personal and psychological characteristics. A sociological work centers principal attention on the *society in which characters live, its effects upon them, and the social forces that control *action. Such a work develops a thesis but is not necessarily an all-out effort in propaganda. In *Middlemarch,* George Eliot made a sociological examination in narrative form of a small town. *Muckraking produced several notable sociological works by writers such as Upton Sinclair and Lincoln Steffens. John Steinbeck, Albert Halper, Erskine Caldwell, and John Dos Passos have written sociological novels; Clifford Odets, Irwin Shaw, and Tennessee Williams have written sociological plays. See PROBLEM NOVEL, PLAY; PROLETARIAN; PROPAGANDA; THESIS.

sock

A lightweight shoe worn by ancient Greek and Roman actors in *comedy. See BUSKIN.

Socratic

A term referring to Socrates, a fifth-century-B.C. Athenian philosopher. Socratic irony is a *technique of pretending ignorance with a view toward later defeating one's conversational opponent. (See IRONY.) The Socratic method of discourse or *argumentation involves using questions to develop an idea. The intent of the queries is to get the answerer to form his own opinions or make admissions and concessions that will help to establish a *proposition. In *Paradise Regained,* Milton called Socrates the "wisest of men." Plutarch reported that Socrates considered himself neither an Athenian nor a Greek but a "citizen of the world."

solecism

An error, *impropriety, or inconsistency; a breach of etiquette or manners. Specifically, a solecism is an ungrammatical or substandard use (misuse) of language. The word is derived from the name of a city in Asia Minor where "incorrect" Greek was spoken. See BARBARISM, ILLITERACY, MALAPROPISM.

soliloquy

A speech delivered by a character in a *play (or other literary composition) while he is alone. A soliloquy is an utterance (discourse) by a person (usually an actor) who is talking to himself or is disregardful of, or oblivious to, any hearers present. *Soliloquy,* derived from a Latin word meaning "talking to oneself," is frequently used in *drama to disclose a character's innermost feelings or to provide information needed by the audience (readers). Shakespeare's most famous soliloquies appear in *Macbeth, Hamlet,* and *Othello.* The device has been used often by Eugene O'Neill, Thornton Wilder, Tennessee Williams, Edward Albee, and Samuel Beckett. See ASIDE, INTERIOR MONOLOGUE, MONOLOGUE, STREAM OF CONSCIOUSNESS.

song

A short, metrical composition intended for singing; a *lyric; a *ballad. Derived from words in Icelandic, German, and *Old English meaning "to sing," *song* is most often employed in literature to refer to a lyric poem adapted to expression in music. Shakespeare's plays contain some of the finest songs ever written. They are of various kinds: the *aubade, the *dirge, the *ballad, the *pastoral lyric, etc. Ben Jonson's *Song: to Celia* may be the best-known song in literature:

> Drink to me only with thine eyes,
> And I will pledge with mine;
> Or leave a kiss but in the cup,
> And I'll not look for wine.
> The thirst that from the soul doth rise
> Doth ask a drink divine;
> But might I of Jove's nectar sup,
> I would not change for thine.

I sent thee late a rosy wreath,
Not so much honoring thee
As giving it a hope, that there
It could not withered be.
But thou thereon didst only breathe,
And sent'st it back to me;
Since when it grows, and smells, I swear,
Not of itself, but thee.

sonnet

A poem of fourteen lines, usually in iambic *pentameter, with *rhymes arranged according to certain definite patterns (*rhyme schemes). A sonnet usually expresses a single, complete thought, idea, or sentiment. The sonnet (a word adapted from a Latin term for "sound") was developed in Italy early during the *Renaissance and was introduced into England by Thomas Wyatt and the Earl of Surrey (Henry Howard) in the sixteenth century. This *stanza has continued to flourish on both sides of the Atlantic ever since. Wordsworth's *Scorn Not the Sonnet* pays a tribute to this stanzaic form and mentions a few of the world's greatest sonneteers:

Scorn not the Sonnet; Critic, you have frowned,
Mindless of its just honors; with this key
Shakespeare unlocked his heart; the melody
Of this small lute gave ease to Petrarch's wound;
A thousand times this pipe did Tasso sound;
With it Camoëns soothed an exile's grief;
The Sonnet glittered a gay myrtle leaf
Amid the cypress with which Dante crowned
His visionary brow: a glow-worm lamp,
It cheered mild Spenser, called from Faeryland
To struggle through dark ways; and when a damp
Fell round the path of Milton, in his hand
The Thing became a trumpet; whence he blew
Soul-animating strains—alas, too few!

See ENGLISH SONNET, ITALIAN SONNET, OCTAVE, PETRARCHAN, SESTET, VOLTA.

sonnet sequence

A group of *sonnets composed by one person and having a unified *theme or subject. The sonnets of such a sequence, or succession, are usually love poems that reflect the progress (and setbacks) of an attachment and reveal the inward emotions of the writer. Among sonnet sequences are Shakespeare's 154 poems in this form, Sir Philip Sidney's *Astrophel and Stella,* Spenser's *Amoretti,* Elizabeth Barrett Browning's *Sonnets from the Portuguese,* and groups by Edna St. Vincent Millay and W. H. Auden.

Sophoclean
A reference to Sophocles, a fifth-century-B.C. Greek dramatist. The influence of Sophocles upon drama, especially upon plays of the *Renaissance period, was profound. A moving tribute to Sophocles has been paid by Edith Hamilton, a renowned scholar of the classics:

> In every way, Sophocles is the embodiment of what we know as Greek, so much so that all definitions of the Greek spirit and Greek art are first of all definitions of his spirit and his art. He has imposed himself upon the world as the quintessential Greek . . . he is direct, lucid, simple, reasonable . . . a great tragedian, a supremely gifted poet, and yet a detached observer of life.

source
In literature, *source* refers to any book, *manuscript, person, or statement supplying information for use by a writer. (See PRIMARY SOURCE, SECONDARY SOURCE.) The term *source* also designates the origin of literary works, artistic forms, or philosophical ideas. In this sense, the *Petrarchan sonnet is the source of the *English sonnet; dadaism is a source of *surrealism; the principal source of Shakespeare's *Macbeth* was Holinshed's *Chronicles of England, Scotland, and Ireland.*

spectacle
Anything presented to the sight or view, especially something striking, unusual, or impressive. In literature, *spectacle* usually refers to a display on a large scale. In a novel or narrative poem, description of a spectacle is sometimes called a set piece, a passage more or less extraneous to the *plot and introduced to supply *color, background, or glamour. In Thackeray's *Vanity Fair,* the lavish ball given on the eve of Napoleon's entry into Belgium is a spectacle.

Spenserian stanza
A stanzaic pattern consisting of eight lines in iambic *pentameter followed by a line of iambic *hexameter. The *rhyme scheme is *ababbcbcc.* This form derives its name from Ed-

mund Spenser (1522–1599), the English poet who created this pattern for *The Faerie Queene*. Others who have used the Spenserian stanza include Robert Burns (*The Cotter's Saturday Night*), Shelley (*Adonais*), Keats (*The Eve of St. Agnes*), and Byron (*Childe Harold*).

spondee

A *foot of two *syllables, both of which are accented (long): *fourteen, blue-green*. Spondees in English are usually composed of two words of one syllable each (*one, two*). In this line of iambic pentameter from Milton's *Paradise Lost,* the first three feet are spondaic:

> Rōcks, cāves, / lākes, fēns, / bōgs, dēns, /
> and shādes / of deāth . . .

See FOOT, METER, SCANSION.

spoonerism

The transposition of initial or other sounds of words. *Spoonerism* is derived from the name of an English clergyman and Oxford don, W. A. Spooner, noted for such accidental interchange of sounds. Examples attributed to Spooner: "beery wenches"(for "weary benches"); "you have deliberately tasted two worms" (for "wasted two terms"); and "you can leave Oxford by the town drain" (for "down train"). See METATHESIS.

sprung rhythm

A term coined by the nineteenth-century English poet Gerard Manley Hopkins to designate a system of *prosody with the *accent falling on the first *syllable of every *foot; a varying number of unaccented syllables may follow the accented one, but all feet are given equal time length in pronouncing. The result of such varying feet is unusual metrical irregularity, but Hopkins claimed that sprung rhythm is found in most speech and in prose and music. The device can be illustrated with lines from Hopkins's own poetry. The first line of *The Windhover* is in regular iambic *pentameter:

> Ĭ caught / this morn/ing morn/ing's min/ion, king-

The first line of *The Starlight Night* contains the same number

of feet and of accented syllables, but the rhythm (*meter) is
sprung:

Loŏk ắt thĕ / stārs! / Loōk, / loŏk up̆ ắt th̆e / skīes!

stage whisper
A loud whisper (hushed sound) on a stage, meant to be
heard by the audience but not by other characters on the
stage. See ASIDE.

stanza
The arrangement of lines of verse in a pattern. A stanza has a
fixed number of verses (lines), a prevailing kind of *meter, and
a consistent *rhyme scheme. Such a group of lines forms a
division of a poem or constitutes a selection in its entirety. The
more common forms of stanza (stanzaic patterns) are the *couplet, *tercet, *quatrain, *rhyme royal, *ottava rima, *Spenserian stanza, and *sonnet. Also, see BALLADE, BALLAD STANZA,
CHAUCERIAN STANZA, CINQUAIN, CLOSED COUPLET, COWLEYAN
ODE, HAIKU, HEROIC COUPLET, HORATIAN, LIMERICK, OCTAVE,
ODE, PINDARIC, RONDEAU, RONDEL, ROUNDEL, SESTET, SESTINA,
TANKA, VILLANELLE.

static character
A figure (*character) in a *novel, *play, or *short story who
changes little, or not at all, during the progress of action. See
CHARACTERIZATION, FLAT CHARACTER.

status symbol
An object, habit, custom, or possession by which the social or
economic state or condition of the possessor may be judged. A
status *symbol is usually something designed or acquired to
display or reflect a socioeconomic position higher than the
possessor has actually attained.

stave
A line of *verse; a *stanza; a group of lines for musical notation.

stichomythia
Originally, *stichomythia* referred to *dialogue in a Greek
*play in which characters engaged in one-line exchanges.
The term has been broadened in meaning to include all
*repartee and oral fencing matches between *characters in
plays or other *genres. Hamlet and his mother engage in
stichomythia in the scene during which Polonius is killed

(act 3, scene 4). The King and Queen engage in prolonged stichomythia in Shakespeare's *Richard III* (act 4, scene 4). A modern example appears in T. S. Eliot's *Murder in the Cathedral* when Thomas à Becket is addressed in four harsh lines:

First Knight: Absolve all those you have excommunicated.

Second Knight: Resign the powers you have arrogated.

Third Knight: Restore to the King the money you appropriated.

First Knight: Renew the obedience you have violated.

stock character

A familiar figure belonging by custom and *tradition to certain types of writing. The *hero and *villain of *melodrama are stock characters (that is, kept regularly on hand). The court *fool, the braggart soldier (*miles gloriosus), the wicked witch, the country bumpkin, the hard-nosed detective, the *confidant (confidante), and the nymphomaniac are stock characters in various forms of literature and pseudoliterature. See FLAT CHARACTER.

stock response

A reaction by readers or spectators which follows a standard, predictable pattern. An uncritical, unsophisticated response is cheering the *hero or hissing the *villain. Traditional *symbols representing mother love, filial devotion, the home, the flag, etc., receive stock responses of veneration. Terror is a stock response to the perils faced by a brave hero or frail heroine. Genuine literary artists strive to provide solid reasons for responses desired. See SENTIMENTALISM.

stock situation

A recurring pattern, *incident, or *situation in *fiction and *drama. Mistaken identity is a stock situation, and so are such patterns as "boy meets girl, boy loses girl, boy gets girl"; rags to riches; revenge; the love triangle; and man against the elements. Some stock situations are fundamental rather than contrived; they are *archetypal in that they reecho human views and predicaments. When such situations are treated as stereotypes, they constitute *formula writing.

stoicism

Repression of emotion, indifference to pain and pleasure. *Stoicism* is derived from the philosophy of a group of fourth-century-B.C. Greek philosophers, the Stoics, who believed that men should be free from passions, unmoved by grief or joy, and passively receptive in enduring setbacks to health, happiness, and prosperity. Stoicism is reflected in the work of Epictetus, a first-century Greek philosopher, and that of Marcus Aurelius, a second-century Roman emperor and writer. The *stock character of the "strong, silent man" exhibits stoicism, and to a degree, so do some of the characters in some of the *novels and *short stories of Rudyard Kipling, Jack London, and Ernest Hemingway.

story

A narrative, either true or fictitious, in *prose or *verse, designed to interest, amuse, or inform hearers or readers. (See BALLAD, EPIC, FICTION, NOVEL, PLOT, SHORT STORY, TALE. Also, see ACTION, ANECDOTE, CHRONICLE, FABLE, NOVELLA, ROMANCE.) This statement by Robert Louis Stevenson, himself a noted teller of stories, is informative:

> There are only three ways of writing a story: you may take a plot and fit *characters to it; or you may take a character and choose *incidents and *situations to develop it, or you may take a certain *atmosphere and get action and persons to express and realize it.

Also useful is this comment by Guy de Maupassant about the purpose and effect of a story, and indeed of all *fiction:

> The public is composed of numerous groups who cry to us [writers]: "Console me, amuse me, make me sad, make me sympathetic, make me dream, make me laugh, make me shudder, make me weep, make me think."

story-within-a-story

A narrative enclosed within another. Examples are the lengthy *incidents scattered through the adventures of Dickens's Mr. Pickwick and his friends (*The Pickwick Papers*) that create as much interest as the major narrative. Other examples appear in the form of *anecdotes and incidents related by Huck and Jim in Twain's *The Adventures of Huckleberry Finn*. See FRAME STORY.

stream of consciousness

A manner of writing in which a character's perceptions and thoughts are presented as occurring in random form. In this technique, ideas and sensations are revealed without regard for logical sequences, distinctions between various levels of reality (sleep, waking, etc.), or syntax. Stream of consciousness, a phrase coined by William James in his *Principles of Psychology* (1890), attempts to set forth the inner thoughts of a *character in the seemingly haphazard fashion of everyday thinking. This method of writing has been used by many authors, among them James Joyce, Virginia Woolf, Dorothy Richardson, and William Faulkner. See INTERIOR MONOLOGUE, SOLILOQUY.

stress

(1) Importance, significance; (2) physical, mental, or emotional tension or strain; (3) *accent or *emphasis on *syllables in a metrical pattern, or in words alone (see ARSIS, ICTUS.) Thus, (1) Stendhal, in *The Red and the Black,* places stress (significance) upon the conflicting elements in Julien Sorel's personality that brought about his downfall; (2) Martin Arrowsmith, in Sinclair Lewis's *Arrowsmith,* undergoes stress when he is deciding between professional, financial success and pure science; and (3) stress falls upon the first syllable of *gunner.*

strophe

The part of an ancient Greek choral *ode sung by the chorus when moving from right to left. (See ANTISTROPHE, EPODE.) In a *Pindaric ode, the strophe is the first of the three series of lines forming the divisions of each section. In modern poetry, *strophe* may refer to any separate section of a *poem that is not a true *stanza because it does not follow a regularly repeated pattern.

structure

The planned framework of a literary selection. (See ORGANIZATION, OUTLINE.) For instance, the structure of a *play is based upon its divisions into acts and scenes; the structure of an essay depends upon a list of topics and the *order of their presentation; the structure of a *Spenserian stanza is determined by its use of eight iambic pentameter lines followed by an *alexandrine, etc. In *New Criticism, *structure* is used to refer to that part of a poem subject to *paraphrase, that is, the *explicit statement of a selection as opposed to its *texture (*images, sound pattern, etc.)

Sturm und Drang

A German expression meaning "storm and stress." The phrase is now used to refer to a time of trouble, difficulty, and *stress in the life of an individual or nation. Historically, Sturm und Drang applied to an eighteenth-century revolutionary literary movement in Germany characterized by opposition to established forms of society, extreme nationalism, and impetuosity in *style and *diction. Goethe's *Faust* reveals the influence of this movement.

style

(1) The manner of putting thoughts into words; (2) a characteristic mode of construction and expression in writing and speaking; (3) the characteristics of a literary selection that concern form of expression rather than the thought conveyed.

Style, derived from a Latin word meaning "writing instrument," cannot be satisfactorily defined, but hundreds of experts have tried. Lord Chesterfield defined *style* as "the dress of thought." Alfred North Whitehead, a philosopher and mathematician, said, "Style is the ultimate morality of mind." Cardinal Newman wrote, "Style is a thinking out into language." Jonathan Swift suggested "Proper words in proper places make the true definition of style." Buffon, an eighteenth-century French writer and naturalist, said, "The style is the man himself."

If style is thought to consist of the mannerisms and methods of an individual writer, then one can refer to the *pompous* style of Dr. Johnson, the *whimsical* style of Charles Lamb, the *allusive* style of T. S. Eliot, the *clipped* style of Hemingway, etc. Most critics agree, however, that "what one says" and "how he says that something" are basic elements in style. Therefore, style may be thought of as the impress (influence) of a writer's personality upon his subject matter.

subjectivity

Concentration upon self; the personal, reflective involvement of a person with himself or of a writer with his material. (See OBJECTIVITY.) *Subjectivity* refers to writing in which the expression of personal feeling and experience is

primary. Samuel Butler's *The Way of All Flesh,* Somerset
Maugham's *Of Human Bondage,* and Thomas Wolfe's *You
Can't Go Home Again* are representative of many
semiautobiographical works. (See BILDUNGSROMAN.) *Autobiography is almost wholly subjective, as many *personal essays are. Many of the essays and *poems of Dylan Thomas
are centered upon the author's experiences and individualized reactions.

Subjectivity also refers to the thoughts and feelings of
literary characters. In *My Last Duchess,* for instance, the
central element is the speaker's revelation of himself. In
*biography and the psychograph, emphasis on the person-
ality of the subject being examined is almost constant. In
critical writing, the personal taste and individual literary
standards of the critic are fully involved. (See CRITICISM.) In
the sense of "privacy of thought" and individualism, subjectivity is a pervasive element in literature.

sublimity

Nobility, impressiveness, grandeur. *Sublimity* refers to qualities in a literary work that transport a reader, carry him out
of himself, and set his thoughts on a loftier plane. Presumably all purposeful writers seek to attain "the sublime" in
their work, but sublimity is commonly considered to have
been reached only by such masterpieces as Dante's *Divine
Comedy,* Shakespeare's plays, Milton's *Paradise Lost,* Goethe's *Faust,* and perhaps another score or so of literary
monuments.

subplot

A secondary, or minor, *plot in a play or other literary work
which may contrast with the principal plot, highlight it, or be
unrelated. See COUNTERPLOT.

summary

A brief but *comprehensive statement or recapitulation of
previously noted facts or ideas; a statement or restatement of
main points. See ABRIDGMENT, BRIEF, DIGEST, EPITOME,
SYNOPSIS.

superego

A term largely used in *psychoanalysis to refer to man's
*psyche, or psychic apparatus. Man's superego is that mental
and emotional force which reconciles his *ego drives and his

social and ethical ideas and ideals. Illness results when the superego fails to mediate between man's drives and his responsibilities to *society. In literary, and less scientific, circles than psychiatry, *superego* is an approximate *synonym for "conscience," "ethics," or "acceptance of moral law." Macbeth and Iago acted as they did because their superegos failed them. In Dickens's *A Tale of Two Cities,* Sydney Carton's superego enabled him to perform a deed which gave real meaning to his life. See EGO, EGOISM; ID.

supernaturalism

That which is above and beyond what is natural; events not explainable by known laws and observations. (See PRETERNATURAL.) Speculating about the unknown and inexplicable has been a preoccupation of mankind through all recorded history; the development of *myths, *legends, and *epics is an indication of this obsession. Explorations of the occult and of infinity, *mysticism, and numerology are other manifestations of the consuming desire of man to know what lies beyond the finite mind. Imaginative and inventive *fiction and *poetry have built upon this appeal and have fostered it since the beginnings of literature.

surprise ending

A sudden and unexpected turn in the action occurring at the end of a work, especially a *short story. Such a conclusion is a *trick ending if it has not been previously hinted at or prepared for. See FORESHADOWING.

surrealism

A *style in *literature and painting that stresses the subconscious or the nonrational aspects of man's existence. *Surrealism,* which means "above, beneath, or beyond reality," was first applied to a movement which sprang up in France at the end of World War I. Influenced by *Freudianism and horrified by the brutality of war, some painters and writers presented *imagery by stressing chance effects in disorderly array, much like the random sequence of events or recollections experienced in dreams. Surrealism, which has been largely confined to French writers and artists, was a development from dadaism. Much of the work of Salvador Dali, a Spanish painter, has been surrealistic; parts of Joyce's *Finnegans Wake* illustrate some qualities of surrealism.

suspense

A state of mental uncertainty, excitement, or indecision. *Suspense,* which involves awaiting an outcome or decision, is derived from Latin words meaning "hanging up" and therefore left undecided. In literature, *suspense* refers to the anticipation of readers (or of an audience) concerning the outcome of events in a *novel, *story, or *play. Suspense is a quality of *tension in a *plot which sustains interest and makes readers ask "what happens next?" Suspense may vary from the introduction of a clue in a *formula *detective story to that employed in Sophocles's *Oedipus Rex* (withholding of the knowledge that Oedipus has killed his real father). In this drama, the suspense involved is not a writer's trick: readers or spectators, fully aware that Oedipus will eventually understand, share his doubts, fears, and uncertainties throughout the play.

suspension of disbelief

Denial of doubt; withholding questions about truth and actuality. The phrase was first used by Coleridge in *Biographia Literaria:* "that willing suspension of disbelief for the moment, which constitutes poetic faith." Earlier, Ben Jonson had written, "To many things a man should owe but a temporary belief, and suspension of his own judgment." The willingness of readers to suspend doubt about the real truth or *verisimilitude of a *character or happening in literature makes possible the acceptance of imaginative creations in prose and verse. See BELIEF.

syllable

A segment of speech (that is, a word or part of a word) produced with a single pulse of air pressure (one vocal impulse) from the lungs: *boy, love, strength.* In writing, a syllable is a character or set of characters representing such an element of speech. As an *archaism, *syllable* also meant "to speak," as in Milton's line in *Comus:* "And airy tongues that syllable men's names." That *syllable* implies both sound and time is suggested by Shakespeare's phrase in *Macbeth:* "To the last syllable of recorded time."

syllepsis

The use of a word or expression to perform two grammatical functions. Syllepsis, a form of *zeugma, is illustrated under that entry.

syllogism

A *formula or pattern for the logical presentation of an argument. In a syllogism, an argument is presented in three divisions: a major *premise, a minor premise, and a conclusion. A typical syllogism is

Major premise: All men are mortal.
Minor premise: My friend is a man.
Conclusion: My friend is mortal.

or

All X is Y; all Y is Z; therefore, all X is Z.

See ARGUMENTATION, DEDUCTION, ENTHYMEME, INDUCTION, LOGIC.

symbol

Something used for, or regarded as, representing something else. More specifically, a symbol is a word, phrase, or other expression having a complex of associated meanings; in this sense, a symbol is viewed as having values different from those of whatever is being symbolized. Thus, a flag is a piece of cloth which stands for (is a symbol of) a nation; the cross is a symbol of Christianity; the swastika was a symbol of Nazi Germany; the hammer and sickle is a symbol of communism. Many poets have used the rose as a symbol of youth or beauty; the "hollow men" of T. S. Eliot are a symbol of *decadence; Moby Dick is a symbol of evil; the *allegory and the *parable make use of symbols. See GENERAL SEMANTICS, SEMANTICS, WORD.

symbolism

The practice of representing objects or ideas by *symbols or of giving things a symbolic (associated) character and meaning. John Bunyan built all of his *The Pilgrim's Progress* on symbolism: the story of man's progress through life to heaven or hell as told through the adventures of Christian, Faithful, Mr. Worldly Wiseman, and others who symbolize man in his various guises. Coleridge's *The Rime of the Ancient Mariner* is symbolism throughout: mankind's universal journey into despair and wickedness and then back to repentance, punishment, and stability and wholesomeness of spirit.

Symbolism is also applied to a nineteenth-century movement in the literature and art of France, a revolt against *realism. Symbolists of this era tried to suggest life through the use of symbols and *images. Among leaders of this movement were Baudelaire, Rimbaud, and Verlaine, who influenced the movements of *impressionism and *imagism.

sympathy

Fellow feeling, compassion. *Sympathy* applies to a feeling of harmony between persons of like opinions or tastes, persons who share a sense of congeniality. When a reader experiences concern, admiration, or pity for a literary character, he is feeling sympathy; if he actually feels with such a character on a personally and deeply involved basis, he is experiencing and expressing *empathy. An author's sympathetic (understanding, perceptive) treatment of a character induces in readers such feelings as sorrow, compassion, love, approval, and commiseration. See CATHARSIS.

synecdoche

A figure of speech in which a part is used for the whole or the whole for a part, the special for the general or the general for the special. Synecdoche, a kind of *metaphor, is illustrated by the use of *five sail* for *five ships;* "Give us this day our daily bread," with *bread* representing not only *food* but general sustenance; *motor* for *automobile; the fleet* for *a group of sailors; a Jezebel* for *a wicked woman,* etc. In a sonnet, Shakespeare uses the word *rhyme* to refer to the entire poem:

> Not marble, nor the gilded monuments
> Of princes, shall outlive this powerful rhyme.

synesthesia

The close association of an *image or sensation perceived by one of the senses with that received by another. In synesthesia a certain sound, for example, induces the sight of a certain color. *Blue note* (sight, sound) and *cool green* (touch, sight) are synesthetic expressions. The French poet Baudelaire described certain scents as being "soft as oboes, green as meadows" (smell, touch, sight, sound).

synonym

A word having the same, or nearly the same, meaning as another in the same language. Rarely are two words identical in meaning, but many do share a similar "denotative" sense. (See CONNOTATION, DENOTATION.) For example, synonyms for *sad* are *depressed, dejected, despondent, disconso-*

late, discouraged, downcast, downhearted, gloomy, melancholic, mournful, and *unhappy.* Synonyms for *glad* include *cheerful, cheery, elated, happy, joyous,* and *merry.* Words roughly synonymous with *habitation* or *dwelling* include *abode, domicile, home, house, residence.*

synopsis

A condensed statement providing a general view of a topic or subject. A synopsis is a form of *abridgment and is closely related in meaning to *compendium, *conspectus, *résumé, and *summary. The term is more often used with *fiction than with *nonfiction.

T

tale

A narrative relating the details of some real or imaginary event or *incident. From an *Old English word for *speech*, *tale* is often applied to simple, loosely plotted stories told in the first person. Examples of tales are those in Chaucer's *The Canterbury Tales*, Jonathan Swift's *A Tale of a Tub* (a comedy in verse), and Sir Walter Scott's *Wandering Willie's Tale* (from *Redgauntlet*). The term may also refer to a *novel: *A Tale of Two Cities* (Dickens), *The Old Wives' Tale* (Arnold Bennett). See FICTION, NARRATION, SHORT STORY.

tall tale

A narrative which relates bizarre, exaggerated, hard-to-believe events or occurrences. The exploits of Davy Crockett, Mike Fink, and Paul Bunyan are tall tales. Mark Twain's *The Celebrated Jumping Frog of Calaveras County* is an excellent example of the tall (exaggerated, incredible) tale.

tanka

A *form of Japanese poetry similar to the haiku. A tanka consists of thirty-one syllables arranged in five lines. See HAIKU, IMAGISM.

telestich

A poem in which the last letters of successive lines form a word, phrase, or consecutive letters of the alphabet. See ABECEDARIUS, ACROSTIC, MESOSTICH.

tenor

The course of thought and meaning that runs through a
*composition; the drift or purpose of anything written or
spoken. As a term in *rhetoric, *tenor* is referred to as the
subject of a *metaphor: in "She is an angel," *she* is the ten-
or of the *figure of speech. When Macbeth refers to life as
"a tale told by an idiot," *life* is the tenor of this figurative
phrase.

tension

In *New Criticism, tension is thought of as the quality that
provides *form and *unity for an artistic work. Presumably,
this concept has grown from the ancient Greek notion that
the universe is a conflict of opposites regulated by a Supreme Mind, or external justice. Certain critics maintain
that tension exists between the *literal and metaphorical
meanings of a work of art, between what is written and its
implications.

tercet

A *stanza of three lines rhyming together or connected by
*rhyme with an adjacent group of three lines, a *triplet.
(See TERZA RIMA.)

> When as in silks my Julia goes,
> Then, then, methinks, how sweetly flows
> That liquefaction of her clothes.
>
> Next, when I cast mine eyes, and see
> That brave vibration, each way free,
> O, how that glittering taketh me!
>
> Robert Herrick, *Upon Julia's Clothes*

terminal rhyme

Identity of sound occurring at the ends of lines of poetry. See
END RHYME.

terza rima

Originally, an Italian form of iambic verse consisting of eleven-
syllable lines arranged in *tercets, the middle line of each tercet
rhyming with the first and last lines of the following *stanza:
aba, bcb, cdc, ded, etc. (See RHYME SCHEME.) Terza rima,
meaning "third rhyme," is the metrical form of many of the
best-known poetic works in world literature, Dante's *The Divine Comedy* being the most famous of all. Here are two stanzas in terza rima from Shelley's *Ode to the West Wind:*

Make me thy lyre, even as the forest is:
What if my leaves are falling like its own!
The tumult of thy mighty harmonies

Will take from both a deep, autumnal tone,
Sweet though in sadness. Be thou, Spirit fierce,
My spirit! Be thou me, impetuous one!

testament

An agreement, or covenant. *Testament* is most often applied
to the two major portions of the *Bible, the Old and New Testaments, but the term also means "last will," "bequest," and "dispensation of property." A recent example of the use of
testament in the sense of "witness" and "affirmation" is Robert
Bridges's *The Testament of Beauty,* a compendium of the
experience and wisdom of an artistic spirit.

tetralogy

Four works which make up a set; a series of four related *novels,
*operas, or *plays. *Tetralogy,* from Latin terms meaning
"four" and "words," applies to two groupings of Shakespearean
history plays: (1) the three parts of *Henry VI* and *Richard
III;* (2) *Richard II,* the two parts of *Henry IV,* and *Henry V.*
A tetralogy in music is the four parts comprised in Wagner's
Ring of the Nibelungs. See TRILOGY.

tetrameter

A line of four metrical feet. See METER.

textual

An adjective applying to the text (actual wording) of anything
written or spoken. In literature, it is often used in the phrase
textual criticism, an activity which tries to reconstruct the
original *manuscript or authoritative text of a literary work. See
EXPLICATION.

texture

The interwoven or intertwined threads and strands which
make up a fabric. Thus, the phrase *fabric of fiction* refers to
the framework and *structure of *novels and *short stories. In
*New Criticism, however, *texture* is a term applied to all the
elements of a literary work, especially a poem, after its essential,
or basic, meaning has been abstracted or paraphrased. Such
elements include *meter, *imagery, *metaphor, *rhyme, and
*tone. By this criterion, *structure consists of the "statement"

or "argument" of a selection, and texture includes everything else: sequence of *images, connotative meanings of words, phonetic patterns, etc. Combined, texture and structure provide what some New Critics refer to as the ontology of a poem.

theater
(1) A building, part of a building, or outdoor area for the housing and staging of dramatic presentations; (2) dramatic works collectively, such as the theater of Ibsen or the theater of France; (3) the quality and effectiveness of dramatic presentation, as "good theater," "dull theater," etc. *Theater,* from Greek words meaning "seeing place," has been variously interpreted and applied since the expression was first used to refer to outdoor spaces such as the Theater of Dionysus on the sloped side of the Acropolis in Athens. But the term has been a living part of literature for thousands of years and still involves a basic meaning of the presentation in *dialogue or *pantomime of *action involving *conflict between *characters.

theater-in-the-round
A current *synonym for arena theater, a viewing place with seats surrounding, or nearly surrounding, a central platform. Entrances and exits are usually made through the aisles. See ARENA THEATER.

Theater of the Absurd
An *avant-garde style of playwriting and presentation in which *conventions of *structure, *plot, and *characterization are ignored or distorted. In this contemporary form of drama, an irrational quality of nature is stressed, and man's isolation and aloneness are made central elements of *conflict. In Theater of the Absurd (*absurd* means "senseless," "illogical," "contrary to common sense"), *characters may appear in different forms and identities and may change sex, age, and personality; the presentation may have no fixed or determinable *setting; the sequence of time is fluid and indefinite. (See SURREALISM.) Among playwrights of this *genre may be included Edward Albee, Samuel Beckett, Jean Genet, Eugène Ionesco, and Harold Pinter. See EXISTENTIALISM.

theme

(1) The central and dominating idea in a literary work; (2) a short *essay, such as a school or college *composition; (3) the message or moral implicit in any work of art. Thus, the theme (central idea) of Keats's *Ode on a Grecian Urn* is the permanence of art and the shortness of human life; the theme of Euripides's *The Trojan Women* is anguish over the seeming necessity for war. For further comment, see CARPE DIEM, UBI SUNT THEME.

thesis

A *proposition for consideration, especially one to be discussed and proved or disproved; a *dissertation involving research on a particular subject. Thesis, from a Greek term meaning both "a setting down" and "something set down," differs from *theme in that the former deals with specific subject matter, whereas the latter refers to a general, pervasive, and dominating idea.

A thesis novel (or play), sometimes referred to as a novel (or drama) of ideas, illustrates, develops, and reinforces an attitude or *point of view of its author. See PROBLEM NOVEL, PLAY; PROPAGANDA; ROMAN À THÈSE; SOCIOLOGICAL NOVEL, PLAY.

three unities

Classical principles of dramatic construction. See UNITIES, THREE; UNITY.

threnody

A *poem, *song, or speech of sorrow and lamentation. A threnody is a *dirge, a funeral song, a *lament. See MONODY.

tirade

An outburst of bitter words. *Tirade,* derived from Italian meaning "to shoot" or "a volley," may also refer to a long, uninterrupted speech on stage. (See CURSE, HARANGUE, INVECTIVE, MALEDICTION, SOLILOQUY.) The long speech in Dickens's *David Copperfield* in which Wilkins Micawber contemptuously unmasks Uriah Heep as a "transcendent and immortal hypocrite and perjurer" is a tirade.

tone

(1) An author's attitude or *point of view toward his subject; in this sense, the tone of Flaubert's *Madame Bovary* is realistic, somber, and depressing; the tone of *The Swiss Family*

Robinson is romantic and adventurous. (2) The devices used to create the *mood and *atmosphere of a literary work; in this sense, the tone of a poem consists of its *alliteration, *assonance, *consonance, *diction, *imagery, *meter, *rhyme, *symbolism, etc. (3) The musical quality in language. In *The Science of English Verse,* Sidney Lanier, an American poet and critic, suggested that the sounds of words exhibit the qualities of timbre in music. The coordination of a series of sounds (rhyme to rhyme, vowel to vowel, etc.) he called tone color.

tour de force

A French phrase meaning "feat of strength or skill." The phrase applies to an exceptional achievement by an author, a stroke of genius unlikely to be equaled. (See CHEF D'OEUVRE.) André Malraux's *Man's Fate* was a tour de force. The phrase also refers to an adroit maneuver or skillful *technique in handling a difficult *situation. In *The Glass Key,* a hard-boiled *detective story, Dashiell Hammett has his fictional sleuth not only track down a murderer but, by a tour de force, also break up a bootlegging gang. The technique by which the *meter mirrors and echoes the pounding of hoofbeats in Browning's *How They Brought the Good News from Ghent to Aix* is a tour de force.

tract

A pamphlet, leaflet, or brief treatise, usually dealing with a political or religious topic. *Tract* is derived from a Latin word meaning "to handle," "to treat."

tradition

A body of customs, beliefs, skills, or *sayings handed down from generation to generation or age to age. Thus, *popular ballads, *folktales, and *proverbs have been passed down through the centuries by oral tradition, or *oral transmission. Tradition, from Latin words meaning "given through," may be thought of as a body of literary *conventions inherited from the past: the tradition of *pastoral literature has lived for more than 2,000 years. Repairing stone walls was, and remains, a New England tradition, as is indicated in Robert Frost's *Mending Wall.* Nearly all the acts, customs, and beliefs of rustic natives in Hardy's *The Return of the Native* are traditional.

tragedy

A calamity, disaster, or fatal event. In literature, *tragedy* refers to any *composition with a somber *theme carried to a disastrous conclusion. From a Greek term meaning "goat song," tragedy involves death just as the sacrifice of goats, totems of primitive peoples, did in ancient rituals.

Specifically, *tragedy* is applied to a dramatic work, in prose or verse, that traces the career of a noble person whose character is flawed by some defect (jealousy, excessive ambition, pride, etc.) and whose actions cause him to break some moral precept or divine law, with ensuing downfall and destruction.

In the eighteenth century, writers of tragedy began to consider men and women of the middle classes as *protagonists. In today's theater, tragedy is often concerned with *proletarian themes; in such plays, the cause of downfall is the evils of society rather than flaws in character or the intervention of fate. See ACT, AGON, CATHARSIS, COMEDY, CONFLICT, DRAMA, HAMARTIA, HUBRIS.

tragic flaw

The principal defect (weakness in character) which leads to destruction. *Tragic flaw* and *hamartia are *synonyms.

tragicomedy

Any literary *composition, especially a *drama, combining elements of *tragedy and *comedy; an *incident or *episode of mixed tragic and comic action. *Tragicomedy* is usually applied to *plays in which events are apparently leading to a *catastrophe but in which happy endings are brought about by changes in circumstances or the intervention of a *deus ex machina. Shakespeare's *The Merchant of Venice* is a romantic comedy, but it is also a tragicomedy. Another example of the type is Corneille's *Le Cid.*

tranche de vie

A French term meaning "slice of life." See SLICE OF LIFE for discussion of this technique of presenting a segment of actual and direct human experience.

transcendentalism

A form of philosophical *romanticism which places reliance on man's intuition and conscience. From Latin words meaning "climbing beyond," transcendentalism held that man's inner consciousness is divine, that in nature is revealed the whole of God's moral law, and that ultimate truth can be discovered by man's inmost feelings and a morality guided by conscience.

Transcendentalism was based on doctrines of various European philosophers, especially the German Immanuel Kant (1724–1804), and was advanced by Goethe, Carlyle, and Coleridge. It took on special significance in New England, where Emerson and Thoreau were its chief sponsors. The two *documents that best express transcendentalism are Emerson's *Nature* and Thoreau's *Walden*. These two authors and other transcendentalists believed in living close to nature, accepted the dignity of manual labor, sought intellectual companionship, and revered self-reliance. In essence, transcendentalism was a religious movement, a branch of epistemology, a "way of knowing."

transitory

An adjective meaning "brief, short-lived, temporary." One of the enduring themes of literature, especially lyric *poetry, is the transitory nature of man's life, of love, of happiness. Thousands of writers have expressed in hundreds of ways the truth that nothing which is human is enduring, permanent, or eternal. See UBI SUNT THEME.

translation

(1) A change or conversion to another form or appearance, such as Dr. Jekyll's changing into Mr. Hyde in Stevenson's famous short story; (2) bearing, carrying, or moving from one place to another, such as the translation of an Old Testament prophet into Heaven; (3) the rendering of something written or spoken into another language. The best-known translation in English is the King James *Bible. (See AUTHORIZED.) Keats's sonnet *On First Looking into Chapman's Homer* was inspired by a translation from Greek by George Chapman (1559–1634), an English poet and translator.

travesty

A *burlesque of a serious literary work, marked by ludicrous, grotesque, and debased imitative style. Travesty, from a French word meaning "disguised" and Latin terms for "across" and "clothes," treats a dignified topic frivolously or absurdly, whereas a *mock epic treats an unimportant subject seriously. Cervantes' *Don Quixote* is a travesty on the medieval *romance.

trick ending

A *synonym for *surprise ending. A trick ending, also called a twist ending, occurs when a totally unexpected and unprepared-for turn of events alters the outcome of action in a narrative work. The use of a *deus ex machina device usually results in such a conclusion. Many of the short stories of O. Henry have been judged to have trick endings, but some of them develop outcomes that are as imaginative and ingenious as they are tricky.

trilogy

A series of three novels, plays, or operas that, although individually complete, are related in *theme or sequence. (See SEQUEL.) The three parts of Shakespeare's *Henry VI* form a trilogy; so do John Dos Passos' *The 42nd Parallel, Nineteen-Nineteen,* and *The Big Money* (combined in *U.S.A.*) and Arnold Bennett's *Clayhanger* sequence: *Clayhanger, Hilda Lessways,* and *These Twain.* The term *trilogy* was originally applied to a group of three tragedies performed in *Dionysia, such as the *Oresteia* of Aeschylus that dramatized the Agamemnon-Orestes story. See TETRALOGY.

trimeter

A verse (line) of three feet. For examples of trimeter, see METER.

triolet

An eight-line *stanza employing only two *rhymes. *Triolet* means "little trio," a sense explained by the fact that the first line is repeated three times. This triolet is by Thomas Hardy:

> How great my grief, my joys how few,
> Since first it was my fate to know thee!
> Have the slow years not brought to view
> How great my grief, my joys how few,
> Nor memory shaped old times anew,
> Nor loving-kindness helped to show thee
> How great my grief, my joys how few,
> Since first it was my fate to know thee?

triplet

Three successive lines or verses, especially when rhyming and of the same length; a *stanza of three lines. (See TER-

CET, TERZA RIMA, TRISTICH.) This is a triplet by Archibald MacLeish:

> Graves in the wild earth: in the Godless sand:
> None know the place of their bones: as for mine
> Strangers will dig my grave in a stony land.

tristich

A *strophe, *stanza, or *poem consisting of three lines. A tristich, from Greek words meaning "three rows" or "three lines," is a synonym for TERCET, which see.

tritagonist

The third actor in ancient Greek tragedy. *Tritagonist* should be compared with *antagonist and *protagonist. See AGON.

trivium

The three studies leading to a bachelor's degree in medieval universities: grammar, *logic, and *rhetoric. The trivium was the lower division of the *seven liberal arts. See QUADRIVIUM.

trochee

A *foot of two syllables: a long (stressed) syllable followed by a short (unstressed) one as in the word *lucky.* For an example of the trochee, or trochaic verse, see METER.

trope

Any literary or rhetorical device (such as *metaphor, *metonymy, *simile, etc.) which consists of the use of words in other than their *literal sense. *Trope,* from a Greek word meaning "turn" or "turning," involves a turn or change of sense and is a *synonym for *figure of speech. *Trope* also refers to an addition to medieval liturgical *drama or to the *liturgy of religious services. One such amplification, the *quem quaeritis trope, was an important part of liturgical plays and *pageants.

tropism

A term from biology, tropism is the orientation (adjustment) of an organism through growth, rather than movement, in response to an external stimulus. In literature, a tropism is a compulsive reaction from external stimuli, the ideas and emotions within characters that are not spoken in *interior monologue and are not transmitted by sensations. Tropisms may also be defined as the things which are not said, the movements which cross the consciousness of characters fleetingly and vaguely. A tropism in *avant-garde writing is a form of "subconversation." See STREAM OF CONSCIOUSNESS.

troubadour

A *medieval lyric poet who wrote and sang *songs, chiefly on the theme of *courtly love. Troubadours were noted for inventiveness and experimentation in metrical forms. Troubadours were also known as trouvères, although the latter wrote songs of adventurous deeds as well as of chivalric love. See GLEEMAN, JONGLEUR, MINNESINGER.

Tudor

A reference to the reigns of Tudor monarchs in England, 1485–1603. Tudor was the name of the fifteenth-century Welshman, Owen Tudor, whose line became the ruling dynasty of England with the coronation of Henry VII in 1485 and ended with the death of Elizabeth I in 1603.

type

(1) A block, usually of metal, having on its upper surface a letter or character in relief; (2) a literary *genre, a *form of writing such as the novel, the essay, etc.; (3) a person with specific characteristics and qualities. In that type of *composition called the novel, Sinclair Lewis depicted a type of American businessman whose name has entered the language as Babbittry. See PROTOTYPE.

u

ubi sunt theme

This name is derived from the Latin words meaning "where are?" that began numerous *medieval poems. The full phrase, *Ubi sunt qui ante nos fuerunt* ("Where are those who were before us?"), suggests the impermanence of youth, beauty, and life itself. The ubi sunt theme (also referred to as a *formula and *motif) is memorably illustrated in the entry for BALLADE. See TRANSITORY.

ultima Thule

The highest degree attainable; the farthest point; the limit of any journey. Ultima Thule, a legendary island in "the Northern Ocean," has come to signify the *epitome of remoteness or any unattainable ideal or goal. These lines appear in Poe's *Dream-Land:*

> I have reached these lands but newly
> From an ultimate dim Thule—
> From a wild, weird clime that lieth, sublime,
> Out of Space—out of Time.

understatement

A form of *humor or *irony in which something is intentionally represented less strongly or strikingly than facts would warrant. *Understatement,* remarks phrased in moderate, restrained terms, is an *antonym of *exaggeration and *hyperbole. See LITOTES, MEIOSIS.

unities, three

Principles of dramatic composition. According to *Aristotelian *aesthetics, a play was required to represent action as taking place in one day (unity of *time*), as occurring in one place (unity of *place*), and as having a single plot (unity of *action*). Plays in English have not usually observed these unities, which tend to restrict dramatic possibilities and limit *characterization. However, Shakespeare's *Comedy of Errors* and *The Tempest* do comply with these principles. A modern play which follows the unities of time, place, and action is Tennessee Williams's *Cat on a Hot Tin Roof.*

unity

Oneness; the state of being one. In literature, *unity* involves the concept that a work should exhibit some principle of *organization in which all parts are related in such a way that an organic whole is formed. Although a unified literary selection has a clear and logical relation of part to part, the source of unity varies from work to work. *Plot or *characterization or *mood or *theme may each be a unifying force. See CONTROLLING IMAGE, DOMINANT IMPRESSION, THESIS.

universality

The comprehensiveness of the universe; existence everywhere. Universality is a quality in literature which gives it a significance and appeal not limited to place or time. When writing presents emotions and actions common to all people of all civilizations in ways that remain meaningful indefinitely, that writing possesses universality. Longinus, a Greek philosopher of the third century, wrote, "We may regard those words as truly noble and sublime which please all and please always." For further comment on universality, see CLASSIC.

usage

Custom, practice. In literature, *usage* applies to the *form and *structure of *types (*genres), to *conventions, to such diverse matters as spelling, punctuation, *format, typography, sentence structure, and dozens of related matters. In speech, usage is the standard which decrees what is "right" and "wrong" in oral communication. In general, usage refers to the customary manner in which a language is written or spoken.

utilitarianism

An eighteenth-century doctrine of ethics teaching that virtue and goodness are based on utility (usefulness) and that conduct should attempt to promote the greatest happiness for the greatest number of persons. *Utilitarianism* was considered synonymous with *pleasure* by its founder (Jeremy Bentham), but later writers, including John Stuart Mill, considered pleasure and happiness to be qualitative (matters of degree) rather than quantitative. See HUMANISM.

utopian

Founded upon or involving ideal or imaginary perfection. *Utopian,* from a Greek word meaning "no place," "nowhere," is often applied to a *type of literature in which an ideal society is depicted. *Utopia,* which now means an ideal country or region, was a name (title) given in 1516 by Sir Thomas More to a book describing an imaginary island that enjoyed perfection in laws, politics, customs, etc. Among many earlier and later works dealing with a utopia as a visionary system of living are Plato's *Republic,* Francis Bacon's *New Atlantis,* Samuel Butler's *Erewhon,* Edward Bellamy's *Looking Backward,* H. G. Wells's *A Modern Utopia,* and Aldous Huxley's *Brave New World.* Numerous treatments of utopian subjects are obviously satiric. See SATIRE.

Utopian is also applied to persons considered idealistic and visionary and to ardent but impractical political or social reformers.

vade mecum

A Latin phrase meaning "go with me" and applied to any of several items a person might carry with him for frequent or regular use. *Vade mecum* is used most often for a manual, handbook, or other volume designed for ready reference and utilized as a "companion." The term is occasionally applied to one's controlling philosophy or fixed beliefs in life.

vapors

Now an archaic term, *vapors* was used constantly in the eighteenth century to explain the eccentric behavior of people. Persons who acted strangely—in a mental depression, with low spirits—were said to be suffering from exhalations given off by the stomach or other organs. Heroines in novels of the era were especially subject to "attacks of the vapors," as is suggested in these lines by Edward Young:

> Sometimes, thro pride, the sexes change their airs:
> My lord has vapours, and my lady swears.

variorum

An adjective meaning "containing different versions of the text by various editors." A variorum edition of an author's work contains notes and comments by a number of scholars and critics. The term is an abbreviation of a Latin phrase, *cum notis variorum* ("with notes of various people"). Possibly the best-known variorum edition in English is the New Variorum Shakespeare.

vaudeville

A variety show, theatrical entertainment consisting of individual performances, acts, dances, dramatic sketches, acrobatic feats, and other unrelated stunts. The term is derived from Vau-de-Vire, a valley in France noted for satirical songs. Vaudeville has declined in popularity since the advent of talking films and, later, television.

vehicle

A vehicle is a means of conveyance or transport. In literature, *vehicle* is extended to suggest the means by which one accomplishes his purpose. Thus it is said that an author used the vehicle of prose or poetry or that he chose the vehicle of *satire or *humor or whatnot. See GENRE.

verbatim

A term meaning "in exactly the same words," "corresponding word for word to the original source or text." During the *Middle Ages (before the advent of printing), copyists spent long hours making verbatim copies of *manuscripts. An *anthology contains verbatim copies of the literary works it includes.

verisimilitude

Likelihood, probability, the appearance or semblance of truth. A work in which action and characters seem to readers to be "acceptable" and to "make sense" as an adequate representation of reality is said to possess verisimilitude. This quality, whether the actuality and *realism of Steinbeck's *The Grapes of Wrath* or the imaginative power of Maugham's *Of Human Bondage,* is achieved by a skillful selection and presentation of what the reader is convinced is the stuff of life. The term can loosely be translated as "like truth."

vers de société

Humorous, light, and even sportive verse dealing with the follies and fashions of the era in which it is composed (see LIGHT VERSE). The term, French in origin and meaning "society verse," is applied to works that deal amusedly and amusingly with polite society and its often frivolous concerns. Vers de société is sometimes gently satiric and elaborately amorous, but it is always witty in intention if not in actuality. The Earl of

Rochester wrote vers de société in this proposed *epitaph for Charles II of England:
> Here lies our sovereign lord, the King,
> Whose word no man relies on.
> He never says a foolish thing,
> Nor ever does a wise one.

verse

A term of several meanings, only one of which is basic and fully accurate: one line of a poem. *Verse* comes from a Latin word meaning "a turning" and is properly applied to the method by which one metrical line "turns" into a new line. A verse is also mistakenly called a *stanza, which is actually a succession of lines (verses) bound together by some scheme (usually *rhyme) and forming one of a series of similar groups that make up a *poem. *Verse* is also a name given to metrical composition in general. For a distinction between verse and a poem, see POETRY.

versification

Metrical *structure, the art and practice of composing verse in terms of related mechanical elements. Versification involves *accent, *foot, *meter, *rhyme, *rhythm, and *stanza form. For further discussion of versification, see METRICS, PROSODY, SCANSION. For a working definition, consider versification as a matter of the structural form of a *verse or a *stanza.

vers libre

A French term for *free verse. Vers libre, also known as *polyphonic prose, is distinguished from conventional verse by its irregular metrical pattern. Vers libre relies more upon *cadence than uniform metrical *feet and does not always follow the usual *rhythm of poetry. Vers libre (free verse) is an ancient form; the Psalms and the Song of Solomon from the Bible are in free verse. Much of the poetry of Walt Whitman and Carl Sandburg is vers libre, a form of experimentation that has contributed to freeing poetry from formal conventions of *structure and subject matter. An example of vers libre and a statement of its purpose appear in these lines by Ezra Pound:
> Go, little naked and impudent songs.
> Go with a light foot!
> (Or with two light feet, if it please you.)
> Go and dance shamelessly!
> Go with impertinent frolic.

verso

A left-hand page of a manuscript or book. *Verso* is an abbreviation of Latin *verso folio* ("with the page turned"). See RECTO.

Victorian

An adjective applied to the reign of Queen Victoria (1837–1901) and to the characteristic attitudes and qualities of that era. Specifically, the term *Victorian* suggests complacency, hypocrisy, smugness, and moral earnestness. Features of the epoch were self-satisfaction caused by greatly increased national wealth and prosperity; scientific and industrial advances; and strengthened standards of decency and morality. As applied to literature, *Victorian* usually connotes humorlessness, unquestioning acceptance of orthodoxy and authority in religious and political matters, prudishness, and rigid adherence to moral and social *conventions. Actually, Victorian literature is complex and many-sided, but the word *Victorian* somewhat incorrectly carries labels of "empty respectability," "false modesty," and "callous unconcern."

vignette

A French term meaning "little vine" (from the vinelike decorations in early *manuscripts and books), *vignette* is now usually applied to a *sketch or other brief literary work notable for precision of phrasing and delicacy of feeling. It suggests "a pleasing picture" or "a brief impression" of a *scene, *character, or *situation.

villain

A character in a *play, *novel, *short story, or other work who constitutes an evil or unwholesome agency in the *plot. A villain acts in opposition to the *hero. (See AGON, ANTAGONIST.) In some works of literature, the villain is the center of interest: Satan in Milton's *Paradise Lost,* Macbeth in Shakespeare's *Macbeth,* Othello in Shakespeare's *Othello,* and Don Juan in works by Molière, Mozart, Dumas, Corneille, and Rostand.

villanelle

A short poem of fixed form, written in five three-line *stanzas (*tercets) and a concluding four-line stanza (*quatrain). Only two rhymes are employed in the entire length (nineteen lines) of a villanelle. Here are the first three stanzas of a villanelle by W. E. Henley:

A dainty thing's the Villanelle,
Sly, musical, a jewel in rhyme.
It serves its purpose passing well.

A double-clappered silver bell,
That must be made to clink in chime,
A dainty thing's the Villanelle.

And if you wish to flute a spell,
Or ask a meeting 'neath the lime,
It serves its purpose passing well.

virelay

An old French form for a short *poem. A virelay is composed of short lines using two *rhymes and having two opening lines recurring at intervals. Another form of virelay consists of *stanzas made up of shorter and longer lines, the lines of each kind rhyming within one stanza and with the rhymes of shorter lines within one stanza rhyming with longer lines in a succeeding stanza. Neither form appears in English literature of merit, possibly because of difficulties with the set rhyming of English words, to say nothing of monotony.

volta

An Italian word meaning "a turn," *volta* is used to refer to the change in thought and feeling which divides the *octave from the *sestet in some *sonnets. In many sonnets, the first eight lines (the octave) state a premise, ask a question, or suggest a theme; the concluding six lines (the sestet) resolve the problem suggested by providing a conclusion or giving some sort of answer. See ITALIAN SONNET.

Vulgate

The Latin version of the Bible, prepared in the fourth century A.D. and used as an *authorized version in *liturgical services by the Roman Catholic Church. *Vulgate* has been extended to apply to any commonly recognized version or text of a work and further extended to mean "common" and "generally accepted."

W

Walpurgisnacht
The eve of May Day, when, according to legend, the witch world was supposed to revel in certain places. (The term is German for Walpurgis Night; Walpurgis was an eighth-century English nun involved in introducing Christianity to the Germans.) The word is used to suggest evil or bedlam.

Wanderjahr
A German term meaning "a year of wandering." The word is applied to a period in a person's life during which he is absent from his normal place of work or study and is engaged in travel, thought, and a search for new experiences or insight.

weak ending
A verse ending in which metrical *stress falls on a syllable or word which would not normally be stressed. In this excerpt from Shakespeare's *The Tempest,* stress falls on *and* at the end of the first line:

> Thy mother was a piece of virtue, and
> She said thou wast my daughter.

Weltanschauung
A German term for "manner of looking at the world." The term is sometimes applied to the philosophy of an individual or a group, sometimes to one's conception of world civili-

zation and one's relation to it. A related word, also German, is *Weltansicht,* meaning "a world view," "an attitude toward life and reality."

Weltschmerz

This German word meaning "world pain" may be defined as "sentimental pessimism." It expresses the sorrow, disillusionment, and discontent that one feels and reluctantly accepts as a part of life. Many writers of the past and present have exhibited Weltschmerz in their writings, actions, and attitude toward society, especially *avant-garde and *existentialist authors.

Western story

The traditional Western pits bad guys against good guys, depicts a long and dramatic chase or pursuit, and ends with the good guys bloody but victorious. The usual setting is a short main street in a frontier village. In recent years, some accomplished writers such as Walter Van Tilburg Clark, Conrad Richter, A. B. Guthrie, and H. L. Davis have written Western stories that avoid hackneyed situations and stereotyped characters, that treat the West as a dramatic *symbol, and that stay closer to real history than pulp writers and film serials do.

whimsy

Fanciful, capricious, or playful *humor dealing with odd or bizarre situations. Whimsical writing, such as the essays of Charles Lamb or the plays of Sir James M. Barrie, is inspired by fanciful or fantastic moods. *Whimsy* is formed from *whim* (freakish fancy, sudden desire) and *fantasy* (unrestrained imagination). Both *whimsy* and *whim* suggest a quaint, humorous inclination; *whim* emphasizes the idea of capriciousness, *whimsy* that of fancifulness. Peter Pan, the boy who never grew up, is a thoroughly whimsical character.

wit

Acute perception and cleverly appropriate expression of ideas providing amusement and pleasure. *Wit* is derived from an Old English word (*witan*) meaning "to know"; hence comes the definition of *wit* as primarily a matter of sense and understanding. In comparison with *humor, wit is an intellectual display of cleverness and quickness of perception, whereas humor is less obviously mental in its approach to the weaknesses, foibles, and absurd ideas and actions of people generally. Wit is wholly dependent upon apt phrasing; humor rises from situations or incidents and does not rely on sharpness or felicity of expression. Humor involves a sympathetic recognition of humanity and its incongruities; wit plays with words, develops startling contrasts, and appears often in *epigrams and *paradoxes.

The ability to see, and to express recognition of, what is amusing and clever (the basic purpose of wit and humor) is clearly shown by that superb wit and humorist Falstaff in Shakespeare's *Henry IV,* Part 1. Falstaff's use of puns and his verbal fencing illustrate his wit. Falstaff's bluffing, his inward laughter at himself, and his and the reader's understanding of the ludicrousness of situations involved are elements of humor.

word

A unit of language, a particular kind of sign called a *symbol. A word has three relationships: with other words with which it is used; with persons who write, read, hear, or speak it; with the thing (object, idea) that it represents—its referent. The relation of words with each other is a matter of grammar. Relation between words and people is the concern of *general semantics. The relation of words to their referents is a matter of *semantics.

No word can ever really have a meaning as exact as, for instance, the measurements of a physical object. Words exist in people's minds and, since minds differ, no word can inevitably call up an identical meaning for everyone who uses or hears it. When Humpty Dumpty told Alice, "When I use a word, it means just what I choose it to mean—neither more nor less," he was far from speaking nonsense. Words are symbols whose arbitrary relation to what they represent must always be kept in mind.

X

xenophobia

Unreasonable fear or hatred of foreigners or strangers or of customs and attitudes that appear foreign or strange. The attitude of Antonio and other characters to Shylock in Shakespeare's *Merchant of Venice* has been termed an example of xenophobia. The Moorish ancestry and background of Iago in *Othello* are considered by some readers an example of xenophobia as displayed in a *characterization containing elements of Satan, vice, malcontent, and envy.

xerography

A process for making copies of printed, pictorial, or written material from paper or film. Areas on a sheet of plain paper corresponding to areas on the original to be reproduced are sensitized with static electricity. The term derives its name from *xero,* a Greek combining element meaning "dry," and *graphy* ("drawing, writing").

Y

yahoo
A coarse, rough, uncouth person. The term was coined by Jonathan Swift, who applied it in *Gulliver's Travels* to a race of manlike brutes. Mark Twain and other writers have used *yahoo* to refer to yokels or louts (rustics, bumpkins).

Yahweh
A name for God that is commonly rendered as Jehovah. It is also spelled *Yahwe, Yahveh,* and *Yahve.*

yarn
An informal name for a *tale, especially a long, rambling story of adventure or bizarre events.

yearbook
A book published annually that contains information and statistics about the year just ended. College yearbooks and encyclopedia yearbooks are illustrative. See ALMANAC, ANNALS, ANNUALS.

Zeitgeist

A phrase from German meaning "the spirit of the time." It refers to the general trend of thought or feeling characteristic of a particular period of time. For example, during the era immediately following World War I, many writers felt that, as a result of social upheaval, the world was in a Zeitgeist of cultural, political, and emotional instability. See LOST GENERATION.

zeugma

The use of a verb with two subjects or two objects or of an adjective with two nouns, although the verb or adjective is appropriate to only one noun: "to wage war and peace." This joining, or yoking, is called *syllepsis if the construction is grammatically correct. Strictly speaking, "with tearful eyes and hearts" is zeugma (an incorrect construction), and so is Dickens's statement in *The Pickwick Papers:* "Miss Bolo...went straight home, in a flood of tears, and a sedan chair." "Neither John nor we are willing" is an example of syllepsis (the construction is correct, although the verb *are* does not agree in number with one of its subjects). See ENALLAGE.

Catalog

If you are interested in a list of fine Paperback
books, covering a wide range of subjects
and interests, send your name and address,
requesting your free catalog, to:

McGraw-Hill Paperbacks
1221 Avenue of Americas
New York, N.Y. 10020